THEORY OF MONEY AND FIDUCIARY MEDIA

THEORY OF MONEY
and
FIDUCIARY MEDIA

ESSAYS IN CELEBRATION OF THE CENTENNIAL

Edited by

Jörg Guido Hülsmann

MISES
INSTITUTE

AUBURN, ALABAMA

Ludwig von Mises Institute
518 West Magnolia Avenue
Auburn, Alabama 36832
mises.org

ISBN: 978-1-61016-258-6

Contents

Introduction

IN DECEMBER OF 1911, Ludwig von Mises finished revising the proof pages of his *Theorie des Geldes und der Umlaufsmittel*. He had worked on the book for most of the previous six years, and he had also submitted the manuscript to the University of Vienna as a habilitation thesis in order to obtain the much-coveted license to lecture on the university level (*venia legendi*). A few months later, he would hold the first copies in his hands. At the mere age of 30, he had published a great treatise, the first out of four such works that he would publish in his life-time, in addition to a plethora of smaller books, pamphlets, and articles.[1]

His book was a magnificent synthesis of six strands of literature that hitherto had only been very loosely connected: (1) the classical theory of money, most notably in its Ricardian coloration; (2) the mid-nineteeth century debate revolving around currency and banking principles; (3) the standard German textbooks on money and banking, including works by Adolf Wagner, Carl Knies, and Wilhelm Lexis; (4) the works of the Austrian School pertaining to subjective value, prices, capital, and money; and (5) the recent literature on money and banking at the onset of the twentieth century, including the writings of Knut Wicksell, Irving Fisher, and Carl

---

1   The other three treatises are *Socialism* (Indianapolis: Liberty Fund, 1981), *Human Action* (Auburn, Ala.: Mises Institute, 1998), and *Theory and History* (Auburn, Ala.: Mises Institute, 1985). See the complete Mises bibliography at http://mises.org/misesbib.asp. For general biographical information on Mises see Murray Rothbard, *Ludwig von Mises: Scholar, Creator, Hero* (Auburn, Ala.: Mises Institute, 1988), Israel Kirzner, *Ludwig von Mises: The Man and His Economics* (Wilmington, Del.: ISI Books, 2001), and J.G. Hülsmann, *Mises: The Last Knight of Liberalism* (Auburn, Ala.: Mises Institute, 2007).

Helfferich. Mises also paid due attention to (6) the publications of the most important money cranks (*Geldreformer*)—authors such as Pierre-Joseph Proudhon, Silvio Gesell, and Ernest Solvay—who proposed to heal all sorts of economic ills through policies designed to increase aggregate monetary spending. At the time their ideas had been rejected out of hand by academic economists. Nevertheless they continued to have a significant impact on the larger public, not least of all because nobody bothered to refute them by following their arguments to their ultimate conclusion.

The visible ambition behind the *Theorie des Geldes und der Umlaufsmittel* was to integrate all the valid elements in the previous literature into one coherent and systematic whole, to build this theory up from first principles—that is, from Carl Menger's theory of value—and to root out the most important errors about money and banking in the light of the new synthesis. Mises's treatise closed a century of monetary thought. In the same breath, it opened up new areas for the future development of economic theory, most notably in the fields of economic calculation, business accounting, expectations, business cycles, currency competition, monetary interventionism, and monetary reform.

One of the great misfortunes of the twentieth century was that Mises's book was not published some thirty or forty years earlier. Fundamentally new ideas need at least a generation or two to become the majority opinion among the experts, and thus to have any practical impact. The *Wealth of Nations* (1776) had such an impact only as from the 1840s, after many years of vociferous and strong support from outstanding economists such as David Ricardo, James Mill, and Jean-Baptiste Say. Mises did not have such support. The wrong ideas that he had very effectively refuted—most notably, the ideas of the Banking School—enjoyed the support of John Stuart Mill and other respected economists. They had already begun to work their way through the minds of academia and politics. By the time Mises published his treatise, this ill-fated movement was in full swing and had conquered the hearts and minds of the new generation. John Maynard Keynes read and even appreciated Mises's book, but all in all he considered it to be old-fashioned. However, he later confessed that his German language skills were superficial.[2] Irving Fisher had worked for many years

---

2   Keynes had written a book review of Mises's treatise, stating it "is the work of an acute and cultivated mind. But it is critical rather than constructive, dialectical and not original. The author avoids all the usual pitfalls, but he avoids them by pointing them out and turning back rather than by surmounting them." (*Economic Journal*, September 1914,

on turning economics into a quantitative discipline, and many others had joined their forces. They would not be deterred because of some difficulties on the level of basic theory, such as the ones Mises had highlighted in his treatise.

As a consequence, for many years, the *Theorie des Geldes und der Umlaufsmittel* has been read, studied, criticized, and developed mainly by Mises's own students. F.A. Hayek and Fritz Machlup in the interwar period, and Hans Sennholz, Murray Rothbard, and George Reisman after WWII were first in line. They preserved the Misesian approach throughout the dark ages of socialism and rampant interventionism.

But even the most ardent love for their teacher could not have kept the flame alive. The growth of attention to Mises's monetary treatise—slow for many years, almost explosive within the past two decades—has been spurred by two other forces.

The first one is the power of truth. Mises's book is not just a very solid piece of scholarship, both in its factual foundation and in its argument. It is also original, written with a philosophical bent and with an astounding knowledge of the history of money and banking. Its judgements are amazingly mature for an author of barely thirty years of age. These qualities give it unequalled depth, width, and balance. They have attracted readers all throughout the past century, and even in its darkest hours. The book has been in print almost without interruption and was translated into six languages. Of particular interest is the English translation by Harold E. Batson, first published in 1934 in London by Jonathan Cape and republished in all subsequent American editions.[3] The book was also translated into Spanish,[4]

---

p. 417). Sixteen years later he stated that "in German, I can only clearly understand what I know already!—so that new ideas are apt to be veiled from me by the difficulties of language." Keynes, *A Treatise on Money* (London: Macmillan, 1930), vol. I, p. 199, note 2.

3   The 1953 edition (New Haven, Conn.: Yale University Press) included an additional fourth part on "monetary reconstruction" that Mises had written for this new edition. In that form the book was published again three more times: 1971 (Irvington-on-Hudson, N.Y.: Foundation for Economic Education; second print in 1978), 1981 (Indianapolis: Liberty Fund), and 2009 (Auburn, Ala.: Mises Institute).

4   Several Spanish translations (*La Teoría del Dinero y Del Crédito*) have been made: one by Antonio Riaño, published in 1936 (Madrid: M. Aguilar), one by José Ma. Claramunda Bes (Barcelona: Ediciones Zeus, 1961), and one by Juan Marcos (Madrid: Union Editorial, 1997).

Japanese,[5] Chinese,[6] Russian,[7] and French.[8] Even the second German edition of 1924 (without the fourth part of the American editions) has recently been reprinted by the original publisher (Berlin: Duncker & Humblot, 2005).

The second force sustaining interest in Mises's book is, ironically, the almost complete neglect of its content in mainstream thought. In the post-WWII era, academic monetary economists have turned themselves into handmaidens of central banks and other monetary authorities. In their quest to be "practical" and "relevant" they have neglected to study, and to question, the theoretical foundations of the "conventional" approach that they had inherited from the Banking School. As a consequence, they have eventually adopted a great number of the inflationist ideas of the nineteenth century. Some of those who a century ago would have been considered to be cranks are today respected academic experts on money and banking.

Unsurprisingly, we have trodden down the expansionary-monetary-policy-road all the way to its logical dead end. One hundred years of monetary experiments and manipulations have *not* ushered into a brave new world of growth, stability, and liberty. Rather, in all countries they have produced rampant cronyism, uncontrolled growth of the state, economic and political dependence of the great mass of the population, comparatively sluggish growth even in the midst of enormous technological progress, and never-ending sequences of booms and busts.

This sorry state of affairs invariably raises questions about the state of economic knowledge. Those who ask such questions are likely to end up reading Mises. Whoever is earnest enough to enquire into the shortcomings of contemporary mainstream economics, and to look for alternatives,

---

5   The Japanese translation was made from the second German edition by Yoneo Azuma: *Kahei oyobi Ryūtüjshudan no Riron* (Tokyo: Jitsugyo no Nipponsha, 1949) and republished in 1980 (Tokyo: Nihon Hyöron-Sha).

6   Translated by H.P. Yang (Taiwan: Taiwan Bank, Economic Research Department, 1969).

7   The Russian translation, along with annotations, was made by G. Sapov who used both the American edition and the second German edition: Теория денег и кредита (Chelyabinsk: Sotsium, 2012).

8   The French edition (*La Théorie de la monnaie et du crédit*) is incomplete and only available on the Internet (http://herve.dequengo.free.fr/Mises/Tmc/TMC_1_1.htm). A print edition is forthcoming along with a preface from Antoine Gentier (Paris: Editions de l'Institut Charles Coquelin).

is likely to encounter the *Theorie des Geldes und der Umlaufsmittel* or some of the works it has inspired.

In a word, Mises's book is a classic, but it is more than a classic. It is of current interest, and will remain so, as long as the majority of the economists rely in their monetary thought precisely on those wrong foundations that Mises demolished once and for all in 1912. Its current interest will actually grow if professors of economics think they can go on writing, teaching, and counselling without doing their homework. It will grow unless they start reading Mises, and the literature he quotes, and the literature he has inspired.

Unfortunately, such a change of heart is nowhere near in sight. At the very moment of this writing, two eminent academic economists in the United States have gone to some length trying to discredit Mises's monetary thought—which they believe to be the intellectual backbone of a political campaign that they despise—yet without making the slightest effort to acquaint themselves with the views they are attacking. One of them even surmises that Mises's opposition to fraction-reserve banking "springs out of Medieval Christian (and earlier) condemnations of usury as unjust enrichment." He then goes on to speculate on "where von Mises is coming from," again, without taking the time to actually read and study any of Mises's writings, except for short paragraphs quoted seemingly at random. Unsurprisingly, he ends up imputing all kinds of views to Mises that the latter did not endorse at all, for example, the view that fractional-reserve bankers are inherently fraudulent: "These people, Ludwig von Mises says, are thieves: thieves pure and simple." Or, another half-baked characterization, this time of Mises's business-cycle theory: "And, Ludwig von Mises would say, the larger the unbacked circulating medium the bigger the lie and the theft. It is all guaranteed to end in tears. Whenever society thinks that it is richer than it is, plans will be inconsistent and unattainable. When that unattainability becomes manifest, that will trigger the crash and the depression. That is, I think, where von Mises is coming from."[9]

Admittedly, these statements were made in a journalistic publication. But even so they do betray a sorry lack of erudition and integrity. It can

9   Brad Delong, "Paul Krugman Asks a Question: On the 'Austrian' Hatred of Fractional Reserve Banking, Paper Money, etc. Weblogging" (http://delong.typepad.com/sdj/2012/09/paul-krugman-asks-a-question-on-the-austrian-hatred-of-fractional-reserve-banking-paper-money-etc-weblogging.html#more; accessed on 3 October 2012, at 9h32 CET)

only be hoped that the rising generation of academic economists will not follow this example.

Fortunately, Mises's monetary thought is being carefully studied by a growing number of scholars—many at the beginning of their career—from all over the world. The following pages feature thirteen essays written in celebration of the centennial of the first publication of the *Theorie des Geldes und der Umlaufsmittel*. Accordingly, the title of the present volume—*Theory of Money and Fiduciary Media*—is the literal translation of that original German title, which unfortunately had not been used for the English edition of 1934, and for all subsequent American editions.[10]

Most of the following papers (chapters 1, 2, 5, 6, 7, 9, 12, and 13) were presented at a symposium within the Austrian Scholars Conference in Auburn, Alabama on March 8-10, 2012. Chapters 4 and 11 were prepared for that symposium, but could not eventually be presented there for technical reasons. And chapters 3, 8, and 10 were solicited from their authors after the symposium as a complement for the present volume.

Our opening chapter outlines the logical structure of Mises's book and highlights the evolution of his monetary thought, with special emphasis on the changes between the two German editions of his treatise, and on its English translation. One main finding is that Mises's arguments initially revolved around the so-called inner exchange value of money, whereas in later works he criticized the pertinence of that perspective and focused more on the question of how money is being produced (competitively or monopolistically).

In the second chapter, Amadeus Gabriel studies the continuities and differences between Mises's treatise and the standard German-language textbooks on money and banking in the late nineteenth and early twentieth century. He highlights several intriguing facts, most notably, that these forerunners were well acquainted with the existence and relevance of Cantillon effects, and with the idea that the use-value of money was a function of its previous purchasing power. However, they did not endorse the monetary axiom of Hume, Ricardo, and the Currency School according to which the size of the money stock was essentially unrelated to the production of wealth.

Malavika Nair stresses the importance of Mises's subjectivist typology of money for current historical research and she traces the basic distinction

---

10   On the shortcomings of the Batson translation, see chap. 1, below.

between money and money substitutes back to Eugen von Böhm-Bawerk's economic analysis of legal rights and legal obligations (chapter 3). She points out that Böhm-Bawerk had elaborated his own theory starting from a critical discussion of the monetary theories of John Law and Henry D. Macleod.

In the subsequent chapter 4, Mateusz Machaj revisits one of Mises's neglected achievements in the *Theorie des Geldes und der Umlaufsmittel*, namely, the transformation of Carl Menger's theory of value. Mises based the theory of subjective value squarely on the phenomenon of choice. At his hands it became so-to-say a decisional theory of value. Machaj compares this approach to the present-day neoclassical approach. He stresses the fact that, in the Misesian framework, subjective value is context-dependent, whereas in the neoclassical framework it is an ultimate given. He highlights the implications for the debate on economic calculation in socialist economies.

Joseph T. Salerno revisits the on-going debate on free banking and examines the question whether Mises's monetary thought stands in the tradition of the Currency School (chapter 5). He emphatically answers this question affirmatively. However, he underscores that Mises, at least in the more mature exposition of his theory of money in *Human Action*, did not endorse the typical policy stance of the Currency School. Rather, he became a champion of free banking precisely because he expected free banking to limit the money supply much more effectively than any government intervention.

In chapter 6, Matthew McCaffrey sets forth an in-depth study of three young Viennese authors who in the early twentieth century became famous for their treatises on money and banking: Schumpeter, Hilferding, and Mises. Most notably he examines the question to which extent these writers worked in the continuity of the nineteenth century debate between the Currency School and the Banking School. He finds that Mises was essentially a representative of the Currency School, Hilferding a champion of the Banking School, whereas Schumpeter occupied some intermediate position. Intriguingly, all three authors tried to complement the earlier theories by focusing on the dynamic transformation of the economy resulting from changes in monetary conditions.

Switching from the history of thought to philosophy, Gary North takes issue with the epistemological status of one of Mises's most famous monetary theorems, namely, the regression theorem (chapter 7). He argues that this theorem cannot be deduced from the logical structure of human action. It is not part of praxeology. Rather, it is more akin to some sort of conjectural history, or to "developmentalism" as understood by Robert Nisbet.

The next paper (chapter 8) stresses the relevance of Mises's theory of international monetary relations for the present-day debate on international competitiveness. David Howden argues that Mises anticipated most of the later literature in focusing his analysis on individual prices, expectations, and exchange rates. Mises's argument that expansionary monetary policy was not likely to increase a country's competitiveness was reinforced through later refinements of his business cycle theory. Still, Howden states that Mises never got to integrating these two elements cohesively and completely.

The next three chapters revolve around one of the most important achievements of Mises's treatise, namely, his theory of economic crises. In chapter 9, Eduard Braun argues that the presentation of this theory in *Human Action* (1949) does not rely on the core concept of the subsistence fund, used by previous authors such as the classical economists and also by Böhm-Bawerk. As a consequence, the explanation of the turning point of the business cycle becomes unconvincing. The original exposition of the theory in the *Theorie des Geldes und der Umlaufsmittel* did not suffer from this shortcoming and must therefore be considered to be superior to his later work, at least in that regard. It was also the starting point for refinements of Mises's theory by F.A. Hayek and Richard von Strigl.

Nikolay Gertchev extends Mises's theory of banking by considering the impact of the inter-bank market on fractional-reserve banking (chapter 10). He argues that inter-bank loans are foundational for the latter, that is, fractional-reserve banking could not get off the ground without relying on an inter-bank loan market. Moreover, Gertchev points out that the very existence of an inter-bank market tends to destroy any limitations on the overall issue of fiduciary media within a fractional-reserve banking system. Despite Mises's and Rothbard's contentions to the contrary, free banking would therefore not be a suitable institutional arrangement to limit the expansion of the money supply.

In chapter 11, Philipp Bagus compares Mises's business cycle theory with the prevailing conceptions of booms and busts in our day. He considers Friedman's plucking model, equilibrium business cycle theory, real business cycle theory, new Keynesian business cycle theory, and Minsky's financial instability hypothesis. Bagus comes to the stern conclusion that what is valid in the present-day theories has been stated more pertinently in Mises's framework, whereas the genuinely new elements in contemporary business-cycle theory are unacceptable, lacking as they are in coherence and realism. According to Bagus, this explains the current popularity of the Austrian approach among market analysts.

The next paper sets out for a similar comparison, but from a more fundamental point of view. Examining present-day textbooks on money, Renaud Fillieule raises the question whether and to which extent these works come to grips with a number of basic insights that can be found in Mises's one-hundred-year-old treatise (chapter 12). He focuses on the functions of money, the typology of money, the determination of the purchasing power of money, the demand for money, and the neutrality of money. Fillieule comes to the startling conclusion that there is an inverse relationship between the sophistication of a present-day text and its pertinence on those issues. The more "advanced" texts tend to be more deficient than the more elementary ones.

In the final chapter of the present volume (chapter 13), Thorsten Polleit reviews Mises's arguments against central banking, as exposed in his monetary treatise, and compares them with present-day mainstream theoretical arguments in favor of central banking, both on economic and ethical grounds. He focuses in particular on price-level stabilization policies, on the destabilizing effects of central banking, and on the regression theorem. Polleit concludes that on each account, Mises's case is stronger than the case for central banking.

Current research in Austrian economics is still very much indebted to, and inspired by, Ludwig von Mises's foundational works, most notably his theory of money and fiduciary media. Looking back at this masterful treatise, reviewing it with a critical eye, informed by the experience of the past century, is like a journey back to one's roots. It is patent that these roots still nourish, and will continue to feed, the theory of money and banking in the twenty-first century. It is therefore our hope that the works contained in the present book will provide useful starting points for future research and the further growth of the Austrian School.

JÖRG GUIDO HÜLSMANN
Angers, 10 October 2012

1

JÖRG GUIDO HÜLSMANN

The Early Evolution of Mises's Monetary Theory

THE PUBLICATION OF LUDWIG VON MISES's *Theorie des Geldes und der Umlaufsmittel* in 1912 marks a turning point in the history of economics, and of the Austrian School in particular. Mises integrated the theory of money within the framework of the theory of subjective value pioneered by Carl Menger. Based on this foundation he revisited all the great monetary debates of his time and of the preceding century, and weighed in these debates with original and penetrating arguments, each of which he articulated at its proper place within the edifice of an encompassing monetary treatise.

He also made an astounding number of other major contributions, so-to-say in passing. Most notably he developed the general theory of subjective value itself by stressing that value was rooted in choice. He developed a subjectivist typology of money starting from which he delivered a systematic theory of the causes and consequences of money prices. He applied that theory to international relations, thus becoming a pioneer of international monetary economics. He analyzed the pricing process in unorganized markets. He delivered in-depth refutations of the mechanical quantity theory of money, of mechanical price theories,

---

JÖRG GUIDO HÜLSMANN is professor of economics at the University of Angers in France.

of the index-number method, of Currency School theory, and of Banking School theory. Last but not least, he developed a theory of economic crises, stressing that monetary expansion is likely to entail inter-temporal disequilibria of the structure of production. Side by side with these major contributions, Mises fleshed out various other noteworthy themes. For example, he highlighted particular features of economics as compared to neighboring disciplines such as law or history; and he made several important observations on monopoly theory, on economic calculation, and on the consequences and limitations of government interventionism.

Mises's monetary thought would remain the backbone of his entire economic theory. Eventually he would articulate it within the larger context of a general theory of human action, but the main theses remained unaltered.[1] The first publication of his treatise in 1912 presented more than a full-fledged theory of money prices. It opened virtually all other major threads of his later work as well, with the notable exception of epistemology.[2] While Mises changed his mind on a certain number of issues (see Gertchev 2004) his theory of money features a remarkable continuity throughout the four decades stretching from the first to the last edition of his treatise.[3] The purpose of the following pages is to highlight the logical structure of his treatise and its chief contributions, as well as the most notable changes made to the second German edition of 1924 and the English edition of 1934.[4]

---

1   "Writing my *Nationalökonomie* afforded me the opportunity to think through my theory of money and credit yet again and present it in a new form. . . . Thus did I carry out the plan I had conceived thirty-five years earlier; I combined the theory of indirect exchange with the theory of direct exchange into a unified system of human action." Mises (2009, pp. 94f.)

2   However, the most important facts which eventually would become the starting points for his methodological and epistemological reflections were already highlighted in the *Theorie des Geldes und der Umlaufsmittel* in 1912. See below, pp. 4f.

3   To our knowledge, no scholar has so far traced the evolution of Mises's economic thought back to the first edition, which was never translated into English. This also concerns most notably Pallas (2005) and Hülsmann (2007).

4   All references to page numbers of the first edition of 1912 are preceded by the letter "A". Similarly, references to page numbers of the second edition of 1924 are preceded by the letter "B" and the letter "C" refers to the widely used American edition of 1981, which is identical with the English edition of 1934, except for the spelling and the additional fourth part added to the 1953 American edition.

THE LOGICAL STRUCTURE OF HIS TREATISE

In *Theorie des Geldes und der Umlaufsmittel*, Mises extended and developed Carl Menger's (1871, 1892) general approach to economic analysis and the theory of money in particular. Menger had shown that the market prices of economic goods were caused by the subjective marginal value of these goods. However, he had neglected the special case of monetary prices, and well-known critics such as Carl Helfferich and Knut Wicksell had argued that it was impossible indeed to apply the new subjective-value theory to the monetary economy. Mises stepped in to fill this gap with the publication of his *Habilitation* thesis.

Following in Menger's footsteps, he set out to explain the causes and consequences of money prices. But he did not simply apply the Mengerian concepts to a special case that hitherto had been neglected. In the first part of the book, he completely revised Menger's framework itself to lay the foundations for a new theory of money. Most notably, Mises revised the general theory of subjective value and developed a new typology of monetary objects in line with the subjectivist approach. He also stressed the methodological importance of that approach. All economic phenomena had to be traced back to individual decision-making, lest the analysis be vitiated and lead to wrong conclusions. Let us highlight these contributions in some more detail.

New Foundations for the Theory of Money and Banking

Mises stressed that a correct causal analysis of market prices requires tracing the explanation back to individual human behavior. Again and again, at crucial junctures of his argument, he emphasized that aggregate considerations lead into error, and that a correct causal analysis of the pricing process must start from individual choices. For example, discussing one of Helfferich's contentions, Mises stated:

> The error in this argument is to be found in its regarding the utility of money from the point of view of the community instead of from that of the individual. . . . All consideration of the value of money must obviously presuppose a state of society in which exchange takes place and must take as its starting point individuals

acting as independent economic agents within such a society, that is to say, individuals engaged in valuing things.[5]

Mises did not just apply the theory of subjective value that he had received from Menger and Böhm-Bawerk. Rather, he purged that theory from all elements of cardinal value, respectively cardinal utility, and stressed the ordinal nature of subjective value, which springs from human choices.[6]

Moreover, right from the first edition of his book, Mises repeatedly emphasizes that human action takes place in a context of uncertainty (see for example, A6, A117, A162, A182) and points out that the very existence of money is premised on this fact. Indeed, people want "to hold a sum of money in reserve against unforeseen and indefinite expenditure. (A349, C338). Most importantly, human choice respectively, subjective value is itself one source of uncertainty. The relative impact of any cause of an exchange ratio is mediated through the individual value judgements. Quantitative factors therefore never have a constant impact on market prices. For example, the apple price might remain constant even in the presence of changes in the apple stock and the money stock, if the value judgements of buyers and sellers offset these changes. Similarly, the apple price might change even though both the apple stock and the money stock remain constant. In Mises's words:

> . . . in monetary theory, as in every other branch of economic investigation, it will never be possible to determine the quantitative importance of the separate factors. Examination of the influence exerted by the separate determinants of prices will never reach the stage of being able to undertake numerical imputation among the different factors. All determinants of prices have their effect only through the medium of the subjective estimates of individuals; and the extent to which any given factor influences these subjective estimates can never be predicted.[7]

---

5   A130f., C144. See also A6, A142, A155, A159.

6   "Every economic transaction presupposes a comparison of values. But the necessity for such a comparison, as well as the possibility of it, is due only to the circumstance that the person concerned has to choose between several commodities" (A15, C51f.). See also A119, A130, A178, A234, A354, A373. We have discussed Mises's contribution to the theory of value in some detail in Hülsmann (2003) and Hülsmann (2007).

7   C218. The original text: "Wie in jedem anderen Zweige der nationalökonomischen Forschung wird es nämlich auch auf dem Gebiet der Geldtheorie niemals möglich sein, zur Bestimmung der quantitativen Bedeutung der einzelnen Faktoren zu gelangen. Die Prüfung der Einwirkung der einzelnen Preisbestimmungsgründe wird niemals dahin

In short, there are no constant relationships between market prices (A216, A471). This entails the related impossibility to measure any variations of the purchasing power of money (PPM). The causal analysis of economic theory traces the change in the exchange ratio between any two goods—money included—back to the demand for and supply of the two goods, and from there to their subjective values. But this theoretical analysis can never establish *how much* of the observed change was due to which cause. It can never make a quantitative determination. Hence, the demand for money and the impossibility to measure the purchasing power of money both have their origin in the pervasive fact of uncertainty.

Mises therefore questioned the usefulness of quantitative methods in economic analysis. He eventually acknowledged that index numbers can "perform useful workaday services for the politician" if they are based on "points of time that lie close to one another."[8] But he always rejected outright the possibility to demonstrate any contention about causes and consequences with statistical or other quantitative methods.[9]

The subjectivist approach which Mises had adopted from Menger led him straight to a new classification of monetary goods. In order to explain money prices as resulting from individual choices, it is necessary to consider how individuals evaluate the different monetary economic goods when they exchange them against non-monetary economic goods. Mises stressed that, while this evaluation process has certain general features, there are also categorical differences in the evaluation of different types of money. These differences do not stem from the *physical characteristics* of the goods, but from *man-made differences* rooted in legislation, contracts, and business practice.[10]

Mises's classification of money relies on the fundamental distinction between money—respectively money proper[11]—and money substitutes.

---

kommen, die zahlenmäßige Zurechnung an die verschiedenen Faktoren vorzunehmen. Alle Preisbestimmungsgründe wirken nur durch das Medium der subjektiven Wertschätzungen der Individuen; wie stark ein bestimmtes Moment die subjektiven Werturteile beeinflußt, kann aber niemals vorausgesagt werden" (A217, B173).

8   C222, B177. The section where he makes this concession to the practical utility of index numbers has been added to the second edition of the book.

9   See A171, A216, A276, A405, A474.

10   Thus Mises deals with one of the major shortcomings of the conceptions of the Currency School. See below.

11   He calls money also "money in the narrow sense." Most economists today call it

This *economic* distinction must not be confused with the *physical* characteristics of the respective monetary objects. A paper note can be a money substitute, but it can also be fiat money, depending on whether it is redeemable into some other economic good that serves as money. Gold coins or silver coins are not per se money proper, but can also be money substitutes if redeemable into some other economic good that serves as money. Token coins are not a separate form of money, but are a metallic form of money substitutes.[12]

As far as money proper is concerned, Mises distinguished three forms: commodity money (including precious metals), fiat money, and credit money (see A43–48). In all three cases, the monetary object is evaluated in its own right. It is wrong, therefore, to interpret money in general as a claim or as an "assignment" to some other good.[13] While some monetary goods are indeed claims, money itself is not by its very nature a claim. It can *be used to bid for* other goods in market exchanges. But, unlike a claim, money proper cannot be *redeemed* into other goods.[14]

Yet there are monetary objects that are truly claims on something else—namely, on money proper respectively money in the narrow sense—and which can therefore be evaluated *as though* they were money. They are "money substitutes." Regarding such money substitutes, he stressed the difference between fully covered substitutes, which he called "money certificates," and substitutes without any coverage, which he called "fiduciary media."

"base money." Notice that Mises argued that the essential function of money is to serve as a generally accepted medium of exchange. All other functions are consecutive functions. They are derived from this primary one (A10–12). Mises endorsed Knies classification of money as a good *sui generis*, that is, as distinct from consumers' goods and from capital goods. The reason is, again, that these three types of goods are subject to different laws of valuation and pricing (A79).

12   Mises argued most notably that the fatal error of the Currency School, which otherwise had sound conceptions that he endorsed in his book, was to regard banknotes as some form of money, whereas it considered demand deposits as pure credit instruments and not as a form of money. This was in Mises's eyes a distinction without a difference and it led to the practical failure of Peel's Act. We will deal with this issue in more detail below.

13   During WWI, Mises refuted the assignment theory in a 1916 journal article "on the classification of monetary theories." This paper would then be incorporated into the 1924 edition of his *Theorie des Geldes und der Umlaufsmittel* (chapter 9 of the second part; see B242–63) and remained as an appendix in the 1953 edition (see C503–24).

14   See North (1993, p. 159).

The upshot of these distinctions is that fiduciary media feature a number of very particular causes and consequences.[15] Most notably, while the production of money proper or of money certificates is costly and therefore constrained within fairly narrow limits, fiduciary media are essentially costless to produce and can therefore in principle be produced in unlimited amounts. Their production is constrained in practice only because of accidental circumstances such as a lacking coordination among banks or legal interference. Most importantly, the creation of fiduciary media tends to bring about economic crises, whereas no such consequence results from an increase of the supply of money proper or of money certificates. To highlight these very particular features of fiduciary media was a central achievement of Mises's book. This was also reflected in its title, which in a literal translation reads *Theory of Money and Fiduciary Media*.[16]

In the second part of his book, Mises set out to analyze the causes and consequences of the "value of money" in general. He did so by presupposing hypothetically that all money substitutes were fully covered by money. In other words, he assumed there would be no fiduciary media at all. In the third part, he would drop this assumption and turn to study the particular features of "fiduciary media and their relationship to money." He pointed out (A145, A206, B407) that this procedure had already been the methodological approach of the Currency School, which based its reasoning on the hypothesis of a "purely metallic currency" in comparison to which it had analyzed the impact of banknotes.

The Value of Money

The second part of the *Theorie des Geldes und der Umlaufsmittel* deals with the "value of money" (Geldwert). This expression is shorthand for the cumbersome Mengerian concept of the "inner exchange value of money."[17]

---

15   They are not different in all respects. For example, increasing the supply of fiduciary tends to entail an increase of the price level, just as it would be in the case of an increased supply of money proper or of money certificates.

16   Unfortunately, the English rendering as *Theory of Money and Credit* obscured this central theme. We will address the problems of this translation below.

17   See Menger (1968 [1909], pp. 73–75, 80–91. In the English edition the distinction between inner and outer exchange value was completely dropped. In a footnote (on p. C146) Batson explains: "Since this distinction has not been usual in English terminology, it has been omitted from the present version; and, in what follows, wherever 'the objective exchange value of money' is referred to, it is the *innere* exchange value that is meant unless the contrary is explicitly stated."

Following the classical economists and Thomas Malthus in particular, Menger developed his monetary analysis starting from the concrete phenomenon of money prices.[18] He contended that the latter were directly determined by four factors: the demand for and supply of the non-monetary goods that were being traded for money; and the demand for and supply of money itself. All four factors colluded to entail the concrete purchasing power of money (PPM), which Menger called the "outer exchange value" (äusserer Tauschwert) of money. But from an analytical point it was possible to single out the monetary conditions (demand for and supply of money) and call their impact on the PPM the "inner exchange value" (innerer Tauschwert). Conceptually, according to Menger, it was even possible to stabilize the latter, whereas the stabilization of the PPM presupposed comprehensive government price controls.[19]

Somewhat reluctantly, Mises endorsed this terminology.[20] It was a fateful choice. With it came the heavy baggage of the analytical focus on the exchange value of money. With it too came the unfortunate focus on the possible stability of monetary conditions. And last but not least, it risked entailing utter confusion in Mises readers, especially in those who became acquainted with his thought only through the English edition, for the nuance of the distinction between the exchange value of money and the "inner" exchange value of money was dropped in that edition. As a consequence, the Mengerian-Misesian vocabulary—especially "inflationism," "monetary policy," "inflation," and "deflation"—was inaccurately translated.

Thus, Mises defines inflation as "an increase in the quantity of money (in the broader sense of the term, so as to include fiduciary media as well), that is not offset by a corresponding increase in the need for money (again in the broader sense of the term), so that a fall in the *inner* objective exchange

---

18   He repeatedly referred to Mathus's *Principles of Political Economy*. See especially Menger (1968 [1909], p. 82).

19   See Menger (1968 [1909], p. 75).

20   In a passage where he explained that distinction (not translated into English), he stated (A132f., B104): "Both expressions are somewhat odd. But they have become accepted in science ever since Menger used them. Therefore they shall be used where appropriate in the following investigations." (Beide Ausdrücke sind nicht gerade glücklich gewählt. Aber sie haben einmal in der Wissenschaft das Bürgerrecht erlangt, seit Menger sie verwendet hat; darum sollen sie auch in den folgenden Untersuchungen dort gebraucht werden, wo dies mit Nutzen geschehen kann.)

value of money must occur."[21] The same problem pertains to the entire final chapter of the second part of his book—the one dealing with "monetary policy"—in which Mises studies government interventions designed to influence the *inner* exchange value of money. Indeed, the original German title of that chapter is *Geldwertpolitik* (Policy designed to influence the value of money), and Mises defines it as follows: "Questions of currency policy are questions of the inner objective exchange value of money."[22]

Causes and Consequences of the Value of Money

Mises found that the traditional literature on the purchasing power of money (PPM) had entirely focused on analyzing the impact of *changes* in the supply of and demand for money. But before even getting to this question it was necessary to explain the *level* of PPM in the first place. Only in a second step could one set out to explain the transition from one level to another. Mises provided this missing foundational analysis, highlighting the central role of the subjective value of money and formulating what he would later call the "regression theorem." He argued that the PPM is directly determined by the subjective value of money—that is, the relative importance of money as compared to the non-monetary goods for which it is being exchanged, in the eyes of all the partners to these exchanges. Thus the subjective value of money explains the equilibrium level of the PPM.

Mises refuted the objections formulated by Wicksell and Helffering against the very possibility of this approach, stressing that they had analyzed the PPM from an overall point of view, whereas the pricing process could only be adequately understood by adopting the subjective point of view of the exchange partners. The subjectivist approach was not unproblematic.

---

21   B200, my emphasis JGH. The word "inner" lacks in the English edition, see C272. Similarly, see the definition of the term "inflationism" on A265 (deleted from the second edition). Mises was reluctant to use the term inflation at all, referring to the reservations expressed by Pigou. He thought scientific analysis could do without them. For a penetrating history of the common definitions of the terms inflation and deflation see Bryan (1997).

22   A246, B200. Again, the English edition lacks the words "inner" (see C248). The translator, Batson, also tried to make a distinction between *Geldwertpolitik*, *Geldpolitik*, and *Währungspolitik* (see C247, footnote), whereas Mises used all three terms synonymously, as is common in the German-language literature. Similarly, Mises stated that monetary policy in that sense is the "complement" or "corollary" (Gegenstück) of policies designed to influence the prices of single commodities or groups of commodities. Batson translates *Gegenstück* out of context as "antithesis."

The central difficulty was the interdependence between the subjective value of money (SVM) and the PPM. Money was valuable because it had purchasing power, but the purchasing power resulted from the SVM. This seemed to be an instance of circular reasoning, not of causal analysis. But Mises could solve this problem by developing an explanation which he found in Wieser: SVM and PPM did not determine one another *simultaneously*—which would have precluded causal analysis—but *diachronically*. Today's SVM determined today's PPM, which in turn determines tomorrow's SVM, which determines tomorrows PPM, etc.[23]

Mises then proceeded to analyze the consequences of *changes* in the demand for and supply of money. He first dealt with their impact on money prices, especially the price level, and then with their impact on the production and distribution wealth and income. He concluded this part of the book by discussing the policy implications of his findings. Let us highlight his chief contributions in turn.

Concerning the impact of changes in the demand for and supply of money on the price level, Mises made three contributions. First he delivered a subjectivist interpretation of the quantity theory of money, arguing that the money supply and the price level were positively correlated, but stressing at the same time that this relationship was not mechanical. There was no fixed quantitative relationship between an X% variation of the money supply and some Y% variation of the price level.

Second, then, Mises delivered an in-depth critique of the most important variants of the traditional rigid quantity theory, refuting the conceptions of Hume, Mill, and Fisher. Most notably, he argued that, even if one fictitiously assumed that increases in the money stock had no impact on the distribution of wealth and income, such increases would still modify individual value scales and therefore entail a different price structure than the one that had existed before. While the marginal value of money would diminish for each individual, it would not diminish in exactly the same proportion.[24] Again, the mechanical quantity theory does not apply. In the 1924 edition (C168, B126f.), Mises added an additional paragraph to clarify this argument:

---

23   Amadeus Gabriel highlights the interesting fact that the core idea of the regression theorem can be traced back to the contemporary German literature. See Gabriel (2012) in the present volume, chapter 2.

24   See A154f., B122f., C164.

If we compare two static economic systems, which differ in no way from one another except that in one there is twice as much money as in the other, it appears that the purchasing power of the monetary unit in the one system must be equal to half that of the monetary unit in the other. Nevertheless, we may not conclude from this that a doubling of the quantity of money must lead to a halving of the purchasing power of the monetary unit; for every variation in the quantity of money introduces a dynamic factor into the static economic system. The new position of static equilibrium that is established when the effects of the fluctuations thus set in motion are completed cannot be the same as that which existed before the introduction of the additional quantity of money. Consequently in the new state of equilibrium the conditions of demand for money, given a certain exchange value of the monetary unit, will also be different. If the purchasing power of each unit of the doubled quantity of money were halved, the unit would not have the same significance for each individual under the new conditions as it had in the static system before the increase in the quantity of money. All those who ascribe to variations in the quantity of money an inverse proportionate effect on the value of the monetary unit are applying to dynamic conditions a method of analysis that is only suitable for static conditions.

Third, he discussed various complications, considering most notably the impact of changes in the demand for money on the PPM (neglected in the traditional theory), as well as inter-local price differences (he denied that they could exist in equilibrium) and the theory of exchange rates (he resuscitated Ricardo's purchasing-power-parity theorem).

Mises here also briefly touches upon the impact of changes in the demand for and the supply of money on interest rates, but does not yet present his views on the matter, which would have led him to discuss his business cycle theory already in this second part of the book (where it in fact belonged from a systematic point of view). He merely points out that, traditionally, the problem of the purchasing power of money had been completely neglected in inter-temporal exchanges, both by theoreticians and by investors and other practitioners.[25]

---

25   In a passage deleted as from the second edition (see A244f.), Mises discusses Irving Fisher's attempt to empirically validate his contention about the relationship between real and nominal interest rates. Mises points out that Fisher succeeded only in those cases in which the inter-temporal exchange (the credit) involved several currencies; but not in those cases in which the credit was given and returned in terms of a commodity money.

Mises proceeded to study the impact of changes in the demand for and supply of money on the *production and distribution of wealth and income.* Here he emphasizes right from the outset, and then repeatedly throughout the remainder of the book, that there is no relationship between the money supply and aggregate output. Increases of the money supply do not spur, and decreases of the money supply do not hamper the production of wealth. The first time he brings up this point is in the context of his discussion of the general differences between money and all other goods. Here he states:

> Both changes in the available quantity of production goods or consumption goods and changes in the available quantity of money involve changes in values; but whereas the changes in the value of the production goods and consumption goods do not mitigate the loss or reduce the gain of satisfaction resulting from the changes in their quantity, the changes in the value of money are accommodated in such a way to the demand for it that, despite increases or decreases in its quantity, the economic position of mankind remains the same. An increase in the quantity of money can no more increase the welfare of the members of a community, than a diminution of it can decrease their welfare.[26]

Thus right from the outset he makes three fundamental points. One, the real money supply (the aggregate purchasing power of all cash balances) tends to adjust to the real demand for cash balances. Two, as a consequence, the nominal money supply is irrelevant for the services provided by money. Three, as a further consequence, *changes* in the nominal money supply are equally irrelevant for those services. Only under exceptional circumstances could an increase of the nominal money supply, directly or indirectly, bring about advantages from the overall point of view. Increases of the money supply usually did not tend to increase the supply of consumers' goods (see A227, A335). They had just an impact on the distribution of those goods. Mises reiterated this point again and again as the starting point for all reflection on the social effects of money.[27]

However, Mises stressed almost in the same breath that any change in monetary conditions (demand for and supply of money) affects the

---

26   A78, C101f. See also A263, A402f.

27   At one point he almost justified his repetitiveness, stating: "This was not recognized for a long time and to a large extent it is not recognized even nowadays" (A403, C379).

distribution of income and wealth. In other words, although there is no causal relationship between the money supply *level* on the one hand and aggregate production on the other hand, any *change* in that level, and any change in the demand for money, entails a redistribution of real incomes and therefore also a redistribution of wealth. The reason is that any such change does not affect all prices at the same time and to the same extent. For example, the first users of newly produced money units tend to gain real revenue at the expense of later users, because they can spend these new units right away, while their purchasing power is still relatively high; whereas the later users have to spend them when their purchasing power has already somewhat decreased. These causal relations also play out in the international sphere and affect trade patterns and capital flows.

Based on these elements, Mises concludes the second part of his *Theorie des Geldes und der Umlaufsmittel* with an in-depth discussion of the nature and scope of monetary policy. He starts off by distinguishing between traditional and modern monetary policy (A246, B200). Traditional interventionism, which involved most notably the depreciation of silver and gold coins, had a purely fiscal motivation. By contrast, modern monetary policy does not necessarily have such a motivation. Rather, its characteristic feature is the hypothesis that changes in the "inner objective exchange value of money" (IOEVM)—especially a decreasing IOEVM—are beneficial. The explanation why they are beneficial varies from one author to another, but the common conviction is that such benefits exist.[28] Thus modern monetary policy is from the outset at crossroads with classical economics à la Ricardo, which rejected the notion that the value of money had anything to do with the wealth of nations. Modern monetary policy seeks to pursue its objectives by modifying the money supply. This presupposes that the modification of the money supply is technically feasible in the first place. It follows, therefore, that the most important tool of modern monetary policy is the choice of the kind of money to be used within the country. In Mises's words:

> The principal instrument of monetary policy at the disposal of
> the state is the exploitation of its influence on the choice of the
> *kind* of money. It has been shown above that the position of the

---

28   The monetary interventionism recommended by mercantilist authors such as John Law was therefore not modern monetary policy in Mises's sense. The mercantilists wished to increase the money stock, but they did not wish to diminish the PPM (even though they might have accepted this consequence as a collateral effect of their policies). See A263f.

state as controller of the mint and as issuer of money substitutes
has allowed it in modern times to exert a decisive influence over
individuals in their choice of the common medium of exchange.
If the state uses this power systematically in order to force the
community to accept a particular sort of money whose employment it desires for reasons of monetary policy, then it is actually
carrying through a measure of monetary policy. . . . If a country has a metallic standard, then the *only* measure of currency
policy that it can carry out by itself is to go over to another kind
of money. It is otherwise with credit money and fiat money.[29]

The remainder of the chapter on monetary policy has undergone the
most momentous changes in the second edition. We will highlight these
changes in a subsequent section. In what follows we shall take a closer look
at the flow of his initial argument, as presented in the first edition.

Policy Designed to Influence the Value of Money

In the first edition, Mises had approached the actual practice of monetary policy in a very peculiar manner. His discussion is very largely carried on from a historical point of view, and the policy conclusions almost
appear as generalizations from the empirical record. This approach was
probably motivated by the fact that the book was supposed to earn him a
Habilitation degree. Mises had to demonstrate thorough acquaintance with
the historical aspects of his field. But he also had to avoid antagonizing
his examiners. A straightforward theoretical approach—in line with the
previous chapters, as well as with the later ones—would have put his libertarian policy conclusions in stark relief and thus might have compromised
his success. As a consequence, the thirteenth chapter of the first edition
clashes in style and content with the rest of the book. On these pages Mises
writes more like Adam Smith, rather than like Ricardo. The result is pleas-
ant to read and contains many intellectual gems. In what follows we will
largely focus on the elements pertaining to causal analysis.

In sections 3 and 4 of chapter 13 (§§3 and 4 of part two, chapter seven
in the German editions) Mises presented a very detailed analysis of the history of deflationary ("restrictionist") and inflationary policies. He especially
focused on the nineteenth century, as well as on the history of thought relating to these policies. Mises first deals with the deflationary policies of
Austria-Hungary (section 3, A251–58) and then delivers a theoretical ex-

---

29   C250, A250, B203.

planation of the unpopularity of such policies in general.[30] He argued that the lacking popularity of such policies was essentially due to two factors. One, deflationist policies are usually applied only in a part of the world economy, but this implies that the exports of this country will diminish, while its imports increase—a highly unpopular result. Two, such policies are not advantageous for the ruling classes. Rather, they benefit creditors and "policies favoring creditors at the expense of debtors have never been popular. Lenders of money have been held in odium, at all times and among all people."[31]

Next (section 4) he turns to the history of inflationary policies, first dealing with the case of England (A264–68), then with the British colonies in North America and with the United States (A268–76), and finally with continental Europe (A276–79). Remarkably, Mises barely mentions the motivations for these policies, deeming them unworthy of discussion. By contrast, he stresses that the actual driving force of such policies was in fact not to be found in theoretical arguments, but rather in the observed stimulation of the economy that had resulted from them (A267).

He goes on (section 5) to discuss the case for inflationism and starts off with the observation that such a policy does not work one time for all, because its effects are only temporary (A279f.). It is therefore necessary to constantly reduce the IOEVM in order to realize the desired objectives. But this is not possible in practice, for three reasons (A280–86). One, the necessary knowledge about quantitative causal relations does not exist. Two, an inflationary policy would invariably wet the appetites of special-interest groups and thus be pushed to exaggerated levels. Three, such a policy would entail disadvantages in respect to international economic relations.

This result seems to suggest that the ideal monetary policy should seek to *stabilize* the IOEVM.[32] But Mises refutes this conclusion with four related arguments (A287f.). One, such a policy could only be carried out with the help of fiat money and it would require permanent interventions. Two, the quantitative knowledge necessary to carry it out does not exist. Three, special-interest groups would constantly try to exploit this lack of knowledge to their advantage. Four, inflationary policy invites abuse by the state.

---

30   He points out that the monetary history of Austria-Hungary in the nineteenth century was one of the most important cases of deflationist policies (A257).

31   C264, A261, B217. At this point he quotes Bentham's *In Defence of Usury* (1790).

32   In the second edition, too, he characterizes a stable inner objective exchange value of money as a—yet unattainable—ideal of monetary policy (see B401).

What is, then, the best monetary policy? Mises presents a surprising solution—surprising because nothing in his previous argument had prepared it. He argues that in light of his previous considerations "the state should at least refrain from exerting any sort of influence on the value of money. A metallic money, the augmentation or diminution of the quantity of metal available for which is independent of deliberate human intervention, is becoming the modern monetary ideal."[33] He adds: "The significance of adherence to a metallic-money system lies in the freedom of the value of money from state influence that such a system guarantees."[34]

Causes and Consequences of Fiduciary Media

Mises's discussion of monetary policy concludes the second part of his book, which deals with the causes and consequences of the inner exchange value of money *in general*. In the subsequent third part, he turns to the *particular* characteristics of the demand for and supply of fiduciary media.

The entire third part can be read as one long, systematic, and exhaustive commentary on the great nineteenth century debate between the Currency School and the Banking School. It has not the form of a commentary, though, but of a treatise. Mises walks his readers through the six great questions under contention: (1) the nature of fiduciary credit, respectively the difference between genuine (commodity) credit and (false) fiduciary credit; (2) the question whether the production of fiduciary media has any limits, and which; (3) the crucial question whether the production of fiduciary media tends to be elastic in the sense that it would accommodate changes in the demand for money; (4) the role of bank reserves for maintaining the redemption of fiduciary media into species; (5) the disequilibrating nature of fiduciary media; (6) the appropriate policy to deal with them.

Mises had announced this discussion right from the preface to the first edition (not translated into English). There he wrote that the theory of banking was in a less satisfactory state than the theory of money (which could rely on the works of Menger and Wieser), even though the writings of the classical economists had provided remarkable elements, which in turn had been elaborated by the Currency School. The basic shortcoming

---

33   C269f., B222, A288. Notice that the English text falsely translates *Sachgeld* (commodity money) as metallic money.

34   C270, B222, A290.

of that school was that it lacked a solid foundation; it lacked the modern theory of value. Mises went on to declare:

> Some of its errors have been rightly criticised by Tooke and Fullarton. But what the latter two have put at the place of the currency theory is not a useful theory at all. The banking theory does not just contain errors, it goes wrong in the very way it states the problem.[35]

In the second part of the book, Mises had criticized one important element of the Banking School doctrine, namely, its contention that changes in money hoarding tended to neutralize the impact of changes in the money supply on the price level, and that therefore the quantity theory did not hold (see A160–65). Now he brought his critique full circle, refuting Fullarton's and J.S. Mill's contention that owning a banknote means granting credit to the bank (A311, C304f.), as well as the "law of reflux" (A355, C342) and other elements of the doctrine pioneered by Tooke and Fullarton. He concluded (A408f., C383f.):

> The fatal error of Fullarton and his disciples was to have overlooked the fact that even convertible banknotes remain permanently in circulation and can then bring about a glut of fiduciary media the consequences of which resemble those of an increase in the quantity of money in circulation. Even if it is true, as Fullarton insists, that banknotes issued as loans automatically flow back to the bank after the term of the loan has passed, still this does not tell us anything about the question whether the bank is able to maintain them in circulation by repeated prolongation of the loan. The assertion that lies at the heart of the position taken up by the Banking School, namely, that it is impossible to set and permanently maintain in circulation more notes than will meet the public demand, is untenable; for the demand for credit is not a fixed quantity; it expands as the rate of interest falls, and contracts as the rate of interest rises. But since the rate of interest that is charged for loans made in fiduciary media created expressly for that purpose can be reduced by the banks in the first instance down to the limit set by the marginal utility of

---

35   AIV. The original text: "Manche ihrer Fehler sind von Tooke und Fullarton mit Recht getadelt worden. Aber das, was diese beiden an die Stelle der Currency-Theorie gesetzt haben, ist mit nichten eine brauchbare Theorie. Die Banking-Theorie enthält nicht nur Irrtümer, sie fehlt schon in ihrer Problemstellung."

the capital used in the banking business, that is, practically to zero, the whole edifice built up by Tooke's school collapses.

Mises went on to state that, in distinct contrast to the overrated Banking School, "the works of the much abused Currency School contain far more in the way of useful ideas and fruitful thoughts than is usually assumed . . ." (A409, C384).

He himself had highlighted the shortcomings of the Currency School in due detail. Its champions had based their reasoning about money prices on a mechanical interpretation of the quantity theory. In analyzing the production of fiduciary media, they had considered only the problems for independent groups of banks increasing its issues while some other banks did not follow suit, thus neglecting the fundamental theoretical question whether those problems could be overcome by a generalized expansion of the money supply through all banks at the same time (see A421, C393). Thus they were unable to come to grips with the question whether credit could be costless—which in his eyes was "the chief problem in the theory of banking.[36]

Most importantly, however, the Currency School had failed to recognize that demand deposits and banknotes shared the same economic nature (see A438f., C407). In other words, it had remained stuck at the surface of visible phenomena, whereas the relevant essential differences were those between covered and uncovered money substitutes, irrespective of the physical embodiment.

But even this central shortcoming "is of small significance in comparison with that made by the banking principle" (A439, C408). Right from the first edition of his book, therefore, Mises endorsed both the basic methodological approach of the Currency School (comparative analysis of a purely metallic currency relative to a currency consisting of fiduciary media) as well as its central policy prescription (stopping the further creation of fiduciary media). He himself developed the theory of the Currency School and integrated it into the Mengerian approach. In 1912 as in his later publications on money and banking, he would highlight the central importance of the Currency School as a forerunner of his own thought.

---

36   A417, C390. Mises mentions the circumstance that explains this neglect: Currency School and Banking School agreed amongst themselves that there could be no such thing as costless credit. See A406f., C381.

The most famous element that Mises added to the theoretical edifice of the Currency School was his business cycle theory, presented in a chapter on "Geld, Umlaufsmittel und Zins" (Money, Fiduciary Media, and Interest). This theory was Mises's answer to the fundamental question whether credit could be gratuitous. It was the crowning achievement of the third part of his book.

Mises begins with a discussion of the causes of monetary interest, continuing the analysis begun in the second part. His analysis starts most notably from Böhm-Bawerk's conception, according to which inter-temporal subjective values determine the size of the subsistence fund, which in turn determines the interest rate.[37] Another starting point is Wicksell's distinction between natural interest and monetary interest.[38] Mises first focuses on the impact of money in the narrow sense on interest rates, making three related claims: (1) There is no constant *direct* relationship between the supply of and demand for money on the one hand, and the interest rate on the other hand. (2) Neither is there any direct relationship between *changes* in monetary conditions and *changes* in the interest rate.[39] (3) However, monetary conditions and the interest rate are *indirectly* related, because changes in the demand for and supply of money affect the distribution of incomes and wealth, and thereby also affect the interest rate. Thus Mises concludes the analysis of the social consequences of a changing value of money, which he had begun in chapter 12 (chapter 6 of the second part).

After these preliminary clarifications, he turns to analyzing fiduciary media. Here he raises the same basic question as before, namely, whether there is any relationship between the supply of and demand for fiduciary media on the one hand, and the interest rate on the other hand. Most

---

37   See A410, A412, A415–17, A428–30.

38   This distinction is one of the central concepts to which Mises refers constantly through the entire book. See pp. A80, A145, A353, A358, A358, A419, A422, A429, A430f., A432, A435f., A445, A452.

39   The only exception concerns commodity money. Here an increase in the demand for money tends to entail increases of the interest rate; but Mises contends that this fact is without practical significance. For a more recent re-interpretation of the significance of this fact see J.G. Hülsmann, "The Demand for Money and the Time Structure of Production," Hülsmann and Kinsella, eds., *Property, Freedom, and Society: Festschrift for Hans-Hermann Hoppe* (Auburn, Ala.: Mises Institute, 2009); Dan Mahoney, "Free Banking and the Structure of Production: A Contrast of Competing Banking Systems," *Libertarian Papers* 3, no. 14 (2011).

importantly, was it possible, by increasing the supply of fiduciary media, to bring the interest rate down to zero? In Mises words (A417, B360, C390):

> It is indisputable that the banks are able to reduce the rate of interest on the credit they grant down to any level above their working expenses (for example, the cost of manufacturing the notes, the salaries of their staffs, etc.). If they do this, the force of competition obliges other lenders to follow their example. Accordingly, it would be entirely within the power of the banks to reduce the rate of interest down to this limit, provided that in so doing they did not set other forces in motion which would automatically re-establish the rate of interest at the level determined by the circumstances of the capital market, that is, the market in which present goods and future goods are exchanged for one another. The problem that is before us is usually referred to by the catch-phrase "gratuitous nature of credit." It is the chief problem in the theory of banking.

He went on to discuss the three principal answers to this question that could be found in the literature (see A418–24). The first answer was the one of the money cranks, which asserted that, indeed, credit could be gratuitous if only the money supply was sufficiently increased. The second answer was the one of the Banking School. Its answer was to say that the problem did not exist. It was impossible to increase the money supply beyond the needs of trade. Therefore, the interest rate could not fall to zero. The third answer came from Knut Wicksell. He argued (a) that commercial banks would sooner or later be concerned about the redemption of their issues, and (b) that as a consequence of the increase of the overall money supply, the price level would increase, and therefore also the price of gold. Thus sooner or later people would start redeeming their fiduciary media into gold and the banks then had to stop issuing them. Mises replied that argument (b) only concerned commodity-money systems, but not fiat-money systems, and that argument (a) contradicted Wicksell's own assumption, namely, that money had been entirely replaced by fiduciary media.

Mises answer was different. He argued that the increase of the supply of fiduciary media entailed an inter-temporal disequilibrium that put the entire economy on an unsustainable path. In his words:

> Now if the rate of interest on loans is artificially reduced below the natural rate as established by the free play of the forces operating

in the market, then entrepreneurs are enabled and obliged to enter upon longer processes of production.[40]

... The situation is as follows: despite the fact that there has been no increase of intermediate products and there is no possibility of lengthening the average period of production, a rate of interest is established in the loan market which corresponds to a longer period of production; and so, although it is inadmissible and impracticable from an overall point of view, a lengthening of the period of production becomes at first profitable. But there cannot be the slightest doubt as to where this will lead. A time must necessarily come when the means of subsistence available for consumption are all used up although the capital goods employed in production have not yet been transformed into consumption goods. This time must come all the more quickly inasmuch as the fall in the rate of interest weakens the motive for saving and so slows up the rate of accumulation of capital. The means of subsistence will prove insufficient to maintain the laborers during the whole period of the process of production that has been entered upon.[41]

Sooner or later, therefore, it will be impossible to continue the investment projects that have been begun under the impact of the initial expansion of the

---

40   A428f., B369f., C399.

41   A430f. In the second edition, he modified the argument concerning the nature of the impossibility of artificially lengthening the period of production. He stated "and so, although it is *in the last resort* inadmissible and impracticable, a lengthening of the period of production *promises for the time* to be profitable" (C399; emphasis JGH). The original text of the second edition: "damit wird die Verlängerung der Produktionsperiode, obwohl in letzter Linie unzulässig und undurchführbar, zunächst scheinbar rentabel" (B371). The original text of the first edition reads: "damit wird die Verlängerung der Produktionsperiode, obwohl volkswirtschaftlich unzulässig und undurchführbar, privatwirtschaftlich zunächst rentabel" (A430). Thus whereas Mises argued at first that the artificial expansion of the money supply entailed a contradiction between overall possibilities and the individual assessment of those possibilities, he later argued that it temporarily entailed illusory profits. Clearly this new argument is problematic, because not all profits in the boom phase are illusory. The main motivation behind the change of argument seems to be Mises's general quest, in the second edition, to get rid of all references to an overall or macroeconomic (volkswirtschaftlich) point of view, to emphasize methodological individualism, and to deny the existence of possible contradictions between individual interests and the common good. Thus we find in the new chapter on "the monetary policy of étatism" the following statement: "In this case, as in all others in which similar assertions are made, it is not true that there exists an opposition between the interests of the individual and the interests of the community" (B240, C290).

money supply. Further expansions, even if pursued with utmost determination, can only delay, but not prevent the eventual outbreak of the crisis (see A436, B375, C404).

In the light of these considerations, Mises comes to endorse his policy conclusions in the last chapter of the third part of his book, dealing with the "Legal limitation of the issue of fiduciary media and discount policy," as well as in the final fourth part giving an "Outlook into the future of money and fiduciary media."[42] The central point of his position is the recommendation to outlaw the issue of any further fiduciary media.

Mises does not recommend outlawing any and all fiduciary media, but only *further* issues. The reason is that the disappearance from one day to another of *all* fiduciary media would have a very strong deflationary impact on the price level and thus on distribution of income and wealth (see A376–79).

Mises opposes further issues of fiduciary media, first because they lead to price inflation and thus also to a redistribution of incomes and wealth; second, and most importantly, because they inevitably lead to wasteful boom-bust cycles and, in fact, to the ultimate destruction of the monetary and banking system.[43] He recommends *outlawing* any such further issues because he does not think that competition between fractional-reserve banks is a sufficient bulwark against the virtually unlimited expansion of fiduciary media. He acknowledges that competition slows down this expansion:

> So long as the banks do not come to an agreement among themselves concerning the extension of credit, the circulation of fiduciary media can indeed be increased slowly, but it cannot be increased in a sweeping fashion. Each individual bank can only make a small step forward and must then wait until the others

---

42   The chapter title has subsequently been changed into "Pre-war policy problems relating to fiduciary media" (Probleme der Umlaufsmittelpolitik in der Zeit vor dem Kriege; English translation: "Problems of credit policy before the war"). The concluding fourth part of the first edition (A467–76) has subsequently been deleted respectively integrated into the final pages of the last chapter of part three.

43   "It would be a mistake to assume that the modern organization of exchange is bound to continue to exist. It carries within itself the germ of its own destruction; the development of the fiduciary medium must necessarily lead to its breakdown" (A472, B419, C448).

have followed its example. Every bank is obliged to regulate its
interest policy in accordance with that of the others.[44]

However, the banks have a very strong self-interest in coming to an
agreement. In practice the coordination between commercial banks has
been promoted by governments and central banks. But even without such
political support, the banks would eventually work out an agreement
anyway.[45] The long-run implication is patent: "The quantity of fiduciary
media in circulation has no natural limits. If for any reason it is desired
that it should be limited, then it must be limited by some sort of deliberate human intervention—that is by banking policy" (A360, C346). Mises
therefore recommends a monetary reform in the spirit of Peel's Act, with
the explicit objective of suppressing "all further issues of fiduciary media."
In his words: "The basic conception of Peel's Act ought to be restated and
more completely implemented than it was in the England of his time by
including the issue of credit in the form of bank balances within the legislative prohibition" (A473, B418, C447). This was his bottom-line and
conclusion from the first German edition of 1912 to the last American
edition of 1953.

IMPORTANT CHANGES IN THE SECOND EDITION

While the essence of Mises's argument, as outlined above, remained unchanged between the first (1912) and the second edition (1924), he made a
certain number of substantial changes to various elements of his treatise.[46]

---

44   A444, C411. See also A360, A420, and A425.

45   "We know . . . that all credit-issuing banks endeavor to extend their circulation of
fiduciary media as much as possible, and that the only obstacles in their way nowadays are
legal prescriptions and business customs concerning the covering of notes and deposits, not
any resistance on the part of the public" (A426, C397).

46   A noteworthy *minor* change, for example, is Mises's acknowledgement that index
numbers can "perform useful workaday services for the politician" if they are based on
"points of time that lie close to one another" (C222, B177). The section where he makes this
concession to the practical utility of index numbers has been added to the second edition
of the book. Another intriguing minor change is the footnote on B347 (C378), in which
Mises for the first time expresses his reservations about Böhm-Bawerk's theory of interest.
He also presents his theory of the business cycle as a full theory in its own right, not just one
possible explanation of economic crises to be used in conjunction with other explanations
(compare A433–36 with B374, C403f.; see also Hülsmann 2007, p. 506). Finally, we also
consider the already-mentioned addition of the chapter on the classification of monetary
theories, first published as a journal article in 1916, to be a minor addition.

While some of these changes are of a purely theoretical nature and unrelated to personal experience, most of them do reflect the progression of his thought resulting from personal confrontation with the disastrous events of the war economy, of the Austrian (1922) and German (1923) hyperinflations, as well as of communal and national experiments with socialist policies, both abroad and in his hometown of Vienna. In what follows we shall highlight four major areas of changes.

Value Theory

The 1912 edition contained a mixed value theory including both praxeological and psychological elements. Following the psychological conception of value as it was prominent at the time in the writings of Jevons, Wieser, and Böhm-Bawerk, Mises declared that the ultimate foundation of market prices was in human psychology (see A118), that demand and supply sprang from the pleasure and pain associated with owning those goods (A301f.). Subjective value itself was characterized as a "feeling" (A16). Human action sprang from "economic motives" on the one hand, but also from other, non-economic motives; and accordingly there were also economic and non-economic prices.[47]

However, on the other hand, right from that first edition he also emphasized the strictly praxeological dimension of value, which sprang from acts of judgement and choice.[48] By the time of preparing the second edition, he must have come to realize that these two conceptions were unhappy bedfellows and he purged his argument from the psychologizing elements (see Hülsmann 2007, pp. 591f.).

Business Accounting and Anticipations

One of the topics that Mises dealt with in more detail as from the second edition is the significance of variations in the PPM for business accounting. In particular, such variations would have to be considered in evaluating non-monetary assets (Sachgüter) and in write-downs, as well as in the profit-and-loss-statement, lest capital would be consumed.[49] Mises was possibly the first economist to draw attention to this completely ne-

---

47   See A107, A110, A157, A181, A181f., A192, A383, A411

48   See A15, A16, A119, A130, A178, A234.

49   See B187–89, C235f.

glected problem in the aftermath of WWI.[50] By 1924, hyperinflations had ravaged both Austria and Germany, and in both cases had dramatically reinforced capital consumption. Switching to gold prices as the basis for business accounting could provide an antidote. However, this presupposed that the gold standard had not itself been depreciated.[51]

Already in the first edition, Mises had pointed out that inflation was bound to induce capital consumption because it compromised the accuracy of business accounting. Now he added that capital consumption was likely to result, too, when creditors *anticipated* the decline of the value of money. Mises stated:

> Depreciation of money can benefit debtors only when it is unforeseen. If inflationary measures and a reduction of the value of money are expected, then those who lend money will demand higher interest in order to compensate their probable loss of capital, and those who seek loans will be prepared to pay the higher interest because they have a prospect of gaining on capital account. . . . And if those who were seeking credit were inclined to refuse to pay this additional compensation, the diminution of supply in the loan market would force them to it. . . . [T]he more the development of capitalism has made money loans (bank and savings-bank deposits and bonds, especially bearer bonds and mortgage bonds) the most important instruments of saving, the more has depreciation necessarily imperiled the accumulation of capital, by decreasing the motive for saving.[52]

A few pages later, Mises explained that such anticipations might completely offset any and all economic policy. Fifty years before Friedman and Lucas, Ludwig von Mises articulated the essential conclusions of the so-called rational-expectations theory, yet without falling into the exaggeration of that later theory. He wrote that individuals had the power to "eliminate" the consequences of policy-induced changes in the value of money if they "clearly recognize that the purchasing power of money is constantly sinking and act accordingly" (B210, C257f.). He went on:

> If in all business transactions they allow for what the objective exchange value of money will probably be in the future, then all the effects on credit and commerce are finished with. In proportion

---

50   See Mises (1919a, pp. 129ff.).

51   See B190, C236f.

52   C252f., B204f. See also C255, B208.

as the Germans began to reckon in terms of gold, so was further depreciation rendered incapable of altering the relationship between creditor and debtor or even of influencing trade. By going over to reckoning in terms of gold, the community freed itself from the inflationary policy, and eventually even the government was obliged to acknowledge gold as a basis of reckoning.

Right from the first edition of his treatise, Mises had realized that anticipations were an essential element in all pricing processes. He had occasionally highlighted this fact, yet without giving it any systematic consideration. For example, we find the following intriguing statement in the chapter dealing with the social consequences of changes in the exchange value of money:

> He who makes long-run contracts without including provisions against falling or rising prices, and without hedging himself on the financial-futures market, will be significantly hurt by any ex-post change in price which he did not anticipate and reckon for.[53]

This sentence was deleted in the 1924 edition, probably because Mises then set out for a more in-depth discussion in chapter 12. There we find the following passage, added to the 1924 edition:

> . . . so long as continued depreciation is to be reckoned with, those who lend money demand higher rates of interest and those who borrow money are willing to pay the higher rates. If, on the other hand, it is expected that the value of money will increase, then the rate of interest will be lower than it would otherwise have been.[54]

Referring to J.B. Clark, Mises drew the conclusions:

> Thus if the direction and extent of variations in the exchange value of money could be foreseen, they would not be able to affect the relations between debtor and creditor; the coming

---

53   A224. The original text: "Wer lange laufende Abschlüsse ohne Baisse- und Hausseklausel und ohne die Sicherung der entsprechenden Deckungsgeschäfte auf dem Terminmarkt getätigt hat, wird durch jede nachträglich eintretende Preisverschiebung, die er nicht vorausgesehen und mitkalkuliert hat, wesentlich betroffen."

54   B184, C231. Mises adds a footnote referring to Knies and Fisher. In the subsequent chapter presenting his business cycle theory, Mises also modifies his argument accordingly, stressing that as a consequence of the anticipation of a quickly rising price level, interest rates are likely to explode in a panic-driven movement. See B373, C402.

> alterations in purchasing power could be sufficiently allowed for
> in the original terms of the credit transaction.[55]

These thoughts imply, ultimately, that the analytical focus on the exchange value of money and on the stability of that exchange value—a focus inherited from classical economics—was an intellectual dead end. It did not matter whether the price level increased or decreased. The problems of price-inflation and price-deflation—respectively of increases and decreases of the "inner" exchange value of money—were secondary both in practice and for economic theory. The true problems pertained to the creation of money. Who should be authorized to produce money? Which limitations came into play? Which consequences followed from excessive money production?

Starting in the 1920s, Mises slowly made that shift in analytical focus. The second edition of his monetary treatise was an important milestone, followed by *Geldwertstabilisierung und Konjunkturpolitik* (1928), then by his great treatises *Nationalökonomie* (1940) and *Human Action* (1949), and finally by the fourth part that he added to the 1953 first American edition of *Theorie des Geldes und der Umlaufsmittel*. Here Mises makes a case for "monetary reconstruction" aiming at the re-establishment of an effective gold coin circulation, just as he had already done in 1924. But the argument he presents does no longer revolve around the inner or outer exchange value of money. His emancipation from the value theory of the classical economists was finally complete. And thus he reinforced the classical case for sound money.

Monetary Policy

In the second edition, Mises deleted more than 20 pages dealing with deflation and inflation from a historical point of view, and added some 10–15 pages full of new considerations. He now approached his subject from a theoretical point of view and presented a series of hard-hitting arguments and conclusions. Meanwhile he had lived through WWI and through a hyperinflation in Austria. He had witnessed the even more catastrophic hyperinflation in Germany. He had refined his thoughts on a good number of

---

55   Ibid. He added right away that the premise is never actually given. He went on to discuss the merits of a tabular standard or commodity standard, pointing out that the latter might actually increase the uncertainty of future payments. This was also the bottom-line of his discussion in the first edition. However, there he had not acknowledged the theoretical possibility of anticipating the future evolution of the PPM.

elements of economic analysis[56] as well as his social philosophy in general. He had published *Nation, State, and Economy* (1919a) as well as his magnificent treatise *Socialism* (1922). All of these elements came to be reflected in the new edition. He completely rewrote the monetary policy chapter[57] and he added a new chapter on the monetary policy of statism.

Mises devoted particular attention to the argument of those who held that inflation had to be accepted as the collateral effect of the fiscal use of the printing press; it was the lesser of two evils. This argument had been at the heart of monetary policy in Germany and Austria during and after WWI. The governments of the two countries did not have enough tax revenues to cover their expenditure. Neither could they obtain new credits at interest rates that were affordable to them. Therefore, they used the printing press to cover the public deficit.[58] Rebutting this argument, Mises raised the question why it would be the case that government could not obtain revenue through taxation or credit. This is his answer:

> A government always finds itself obliged to resort to inflationary measures when it cannot negotiate loans and dare not levy taxes, because it has reason to fear that it will forfeit approval of the policy it is following if it reveals too soon the financial and general economic consequences of that policy. Thus inflation becomes the most important psychological resource of any economic policy whose consequences have to be concealed; and so in this sense it can be called an instrument of *unpopular,* that is, of antidemocratic, policy, since by misleading public opinion it makes possible the continued existence of a system of government that would have no hope of the consent of the people if the circumstances were clearly laid before them. That is the political function of inflation. It explains why inflation has always been an important resource of policies of war and revolution and why we also find it in the service of socialism. When governments do not think it necessary to accommodate their expenditure to their revenue and arrogate to themselves the right of making up

---

56   This concerned most notably the classification of monetary theories, international trade, socialism, government interventionism, hyperinflation, and currency competition.

57   See especially the section on "inflationism," pages B203–15 (C251–61). Here he brings into play the experiences from the war and from hyperinflation.

58   Mises stressed (B207) that inflationary war finance was an important factor in prolonging the war.

the deficit by issuing notes, their ideology is merely a disguised absolutism.[59]

Mises also analyzed in great detail the adjustment of market participants to a strongly inflationary environment, emphasizing the inner dynamics of this process which ultimately destroyed the monetary system or, more precisely, the replacement of the inflationary fiat money with commodity money.[60] Indeed, permanent inflation was not likely to merely entail an increase of the price level. It would also motivate the market participants to abandon the inflationary money and turn to using other monies—natural monies such as gold and silver coins, or foreign fiat money that was not plagued by inflation. The final station in this process was currency reform through the market:

> The collapse of an inflation policy carried to its extreme—as in the United States in 1781 and in France in 1796—does not destroy the monetary system, but only the credit money or fiat money of the state that has overestimated the effectiveness of its own policy. The collapse emancipates commerce from etatism and establishes metallic money again.[61]

Banking Policy

Apart from the chapters dealing with monetary policy, the most visible addition to the second edition concerned the last chapter of part three. Here Mises added a lengthy section on "problems of post-war policies related to fiduciary media" (Probleme der Umlaufsmittelpolitik in der Zeit nach dem Kriege). His argument revolves around three related claims.

One, the ever-expanding production of fiduciary media under the gold-exchange standard undermines the principal advantage of the gold standard, namely, independence from politics.[62] The gold price is no longer

---

59   C255, B208.

60   See C258–61, B211–14.

61   C261, B214. His analysis of currency competition in an inflationary environment was first presented in two lengthier articles published in the aftermath of WWI (see Mises 1919b, 1923). In some of his work he underlined that these mechanisms could be relied on for free-market monetary reforms that drove inflation-bent governments out of the production of money (see Hülsmann 2008).

62   "Those protagonists of the gold-exchange standard who have recommended it as a general monetary system and not merely as an expedient for poor countries, have overlooked this fact. They have not observed that the gold-exchange standard must at last mean

effectively independent of government policies, most notably of the policy of the U.S. government. Thus banking policy is at a crossroads. It is senseless to incur the costs of the gold-exchange standard without enjoying the benefits for which it seemed to be desirable. Therefore, either one has to return to the effective use of gold—to a monetary system based on the circulation of gold coins—or one should go the full way of monetary expansion, abandon any ties to gold whatsoever, and base the banking system on fiat monies. Mises underlines that the return to an effective gold circulation would have certain undesirable consequences (price deflation). "But all its disadvantages must be accepted as part of the bargain if other services are demanded of the monetary system than that of preparing for war, revolution, and destruction" (B405, C434).

Two, he discusses and refutes the Fisher Plan to introduce fiat money and stabilize its PPM based on an index-number method (see B411–17, C438–45). Mises starts off underscoring that the popularity of Irving Fisher's proposal stems from the fact that a return to an effective gold coin circulation was likely to produce a very strong price deflation. Then he argues that the plan was impossible to apply in the case of long-term credits, and superfluous to provide protection in short-term contracts. Most importantly, the plan did not provide any protection at all against the redistribution of incomes and wealth resulting from Cantillon effects, and it was completely unsuited to make the value of money independent of political inference.

Three, Mises now makes a conditional case for free banking (see B407–09). He argues:

> Unfortunate experiences with banknotes that had become valueless because they were no longer actually redeemable led once to the restriction of the right of note issue to a few privileged institutions. Yet experience of state regulation of banks-of-issue has been incomparably more unfavorable than experience of uncontrolled private enterprise. What do all the failures of banks-of-issue and clearing banks known to history matter in comparison with the complete collapse of the banking system in Germany? Everything that has been said in favor of control of the banking system pales into insignificance beside the objections that can

---

depriving gold of that characteristic which is the most important from the point of view of monetary policy—its independence of government influence upon fluctuations in its value" (B403, C431f.).

nowadays be advanced against state regulation of the issue of notes. The etatistic arguments, that were once brought forward against the freedom of the note issue, no longer carry conviction; in the sphere of banking, as everywhere else, etatism has been a failure.[63]

We have already shown that the dangers envisaged by the currency principle exist only when there is uniform procedure on the part of all the credit-issuing banks, not merely within a given country, but throughout the world. Now the monopolization of the banks-of issue in each separate country does not merely fail to oppose any hindrance to this uniformity of procedure; it materially facilitates it.[64]

But his endorsement of free banking was far from being unreserved and unconditional. Taking exception to the freedom of fractional-reserve banks, he recommended outlawing small-denomination banknotes (B405f., B408). He also stressed that no institutional arrangement in banking can provide sufficient safeguards against government encroachment if the statist ideology is not abandoned. For example, a competitive banking system would not have been a bulwark against inflationary war finance in WWI:

The governments of the belligerent-and neutral-states overthrew the whole system of bank legislation with a stroke of the pen, and they could have done just the same if the banks had been uncontrolled. There would have been no necessity at all for them to proceed to issue Treasury notes. They could simply have imposed on the banks the obligation to grant loans to the state and enabled them to fulfill this obligation by suspending their obligation to redeem their notes and making the notes legal tender. The solution of a few minor technical problems would have been different, but the effect would have been the same. For what enabled the governments to destroy the banking system was not any technical, juristic, or economic shortcoming of the banking organization, but the power conferred on them by the general sentiment in favor of etatism and war.[65]

---

63   B406, C434f.

64   B408f., C437.

65   B407, C436.

Mises admitted that "in recent times" competitive banking had provided effective protection against excessive issues of fiduciary credit. But things might change in the years to come. Then it would become necessary to impose legal limitations.[66] Therefore, in spite of his favorable reconsideration of free banking, Mises still maintained the general conclusion from the first edition, in which he advocated the legal interdiction of any further issues of fiduciary media.

LOST IN TRANSLATION

The first English edition of Mises monetary treatise was translated from the second German edition and published in 1934. American editions followed in 1953, 1971, 1981, and 2009. The latter were identical to the English edition except for the spelling.

On the foregoing pages, we have occasionally pointed out misleading or erroneous translations in that text. However, there is one mistranslation that is systematic and concerns fiduciary media. As the original German title *Theorie des Geldes und der Umlaufsmittel* suggests, the core subject matter of Mises's book was the comparative analysis of fiduciary media. This concern is also reflected in the very structure of the three parts: nature of money—value of money—fiduciary media and their relationship to money. This gets lost in all the translations of titles and chapter headings including the word *Umlaufsmittel*. The English version always renders this as "credit." Thus the title of the book becomes *Theory of Money and Credit*; *Umlaufsmittelzirkulation* (circulation of fiduciary media) is translated as "credit circulation," *Zirkulationskredit* as "bank credit," *Umlaufsmittelbanken* as "credit-issuing banks," *Umlaufsmittelzirkulation und Wirtschaftskrisen* as "credit and economic crises," *Umlaufsmittelpolitik* as "credit policy," etc.

This might be explicable by the translator's concern to avoid unusual terminology, especially since the term *Umlaufsmittel* was—and still is—unusual even in the German scientific literature. But the plain fact is that Mises chose this terminology for the one perfectly good reason that justifies terminological innovation, namely, that there was no other terminology available at all to describe the phenomenon that was at centre stage in his

---

66   "In this respect, we cannot yet know how circumstances will shape. If it should prove easier now for the credit-issuing banks to extend their circulation, then failure to adopt measures for limiting the issue of fiduciary media will involve the greatest danger to the stability of economic life" (B410, C439).

analysis. The translator completely missed the point that there was no inherent link between fiduciary media and credit at all. In modern banking, it is true, fiduciary media are virtually always issued in credit contracts. But this is not necessarily so, and historically it has not always been so. This was the reason why Mises stressed the difference between the *bankmäßige* issue of fiduciary media (that is, in the form of bank loans) and the *nicht bankmäßige* issue, in which fiduciary media are created, not to earn revenue, but for other reasons. (The translation renders this as "two ways of issuing fiduciary media"—that is, it sidesteps the challenge to find adequate English terms.)

To top it all, the English edition contains a diagram to illustrate Mises's typology of money which demonstrates a complete lack of understanding for its subject.

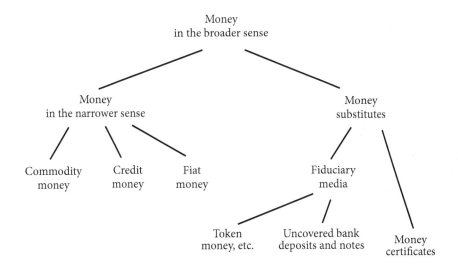

Figure 1

DIAGRAM ADDED TO THE 1934 EDITION OF THE
THEORY OF MONEY AND CREDIT

The diagram reflects precisely that sort of thinking about money that Mises wished to overcome. It clings to the physical surface of things. Token coins seem to be always fiduciary media, and money certificates seem to have nothing to do with deposits or tokens or banknotes, etc. The very point of Mises's theory was that these physical manifestations could be very different economic goods, depending on the legal and contractual context.[67] A more appropriate graphical representation of his typology of money would look like this:

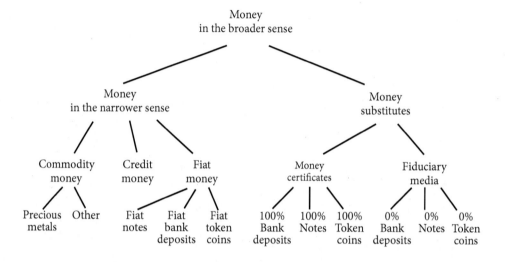

Figure 2

<small>CLASSIFICATION OF MONETARY GOODS ACCORDING TO MISES
(ELABORATED FROM HÜLSMANN 2007, P. 216)</small>

CONCLUSION

Ludwig von Mises's *Theorie des Geldes und der Umlaufsmittel* is a masterpiece and a milestone in the history of economic thought. On the foregoing pages we have tried to trace back the evolution of his early monetary thought, covering in particular the first two German editions and the first English-language edition. Two findings stand out.

---

67   He was perfectly familiar with the problem. In private correspondence he once wrote: "I am outright horrified about the sense-distorting errors that I have found in French and German translations of my English publications, and in English and French translations of my German books." (Ludwig von Mises to Rudolf Berthold, letter dated November 4, 1959; *Grove City Archive*: Berthold file) It is a mystery why he condoned these known practices.

First, Mises slowly shifted his analytical focus, ever more away from the exchange value of money (which he inherited from classical economics through Carl Menger), and ever more toward the political economy of the production of money. This transition was completed in the 1953 first American edition of his monetary treatise.

Second, the English edition of his book is plagued by numerous inaccuracies and outright wrong renditions. Hopefully his students will not have wait for the next centenary to obtain a better translation.

Bibliography

Bryan, Michael F. 1997. "On the Origin and Evolution of the Word Inflation." *Federal Reserve Bank of Cleveland Economic Commentary* (October 15).

Gabriel, Amadeus. 2012. "Why was the Reception of the First Edition of Mises's *Theory of Money and Credit* so Lukewarm?" In *The Theory of Money and Fiduciary Media: Essays in Celebration of the Centennial.* J.G. Hülsmann, ed. Auburn, Ala.: Ludwig von Mises Institute.

Gertchev, Nikolay. 2004. "Dehomogenizing Mises's Monetary Thought." *Journal of Libertarian Studies* 18, no. 3: 57–90.

Hülsmann, Jörg Guido. 2003. "Introduction to the Third Edition: From Value Theory to Praxeology." Ludwig von Mises, *Epistemological Problems of Econoimcs.* 3rd ed. Auburn, Ala.: Ludwig von Mises Institute.

——. 2007. *Mises: The Last Knight of Liberalism.* Auburn, Ala.: Mises Institute.

——. 2008. "Mises on Monetary Reform: the Private Alternative." *Quarterly Journal of Austrian Economics* 11, no. 3: 208–18.

——. 2009. "The Demand for Money and the Time Structure of Production." In *Property, Freedom, and Society: Festschrift for Hans-Hermann Hoppe.* J.G. Hülsmann and S. Kinsella, eds. Auburn, Ala.: Mises Institute.

Mahoney, Dan. 2011. "Free Banking and the Structure of Production: A Contrast of Competing Banking Systems." *Libertarian Papers* 3, no. 14.

Menger, Carl. 1871. *Grundsätze der Volkswirtschaftslehre.* Vienna: Braumüller.

——. 1909. "Geld" *Handwörterbuch der Staatswissenschaften*, 3rd ed. Reprinted in *Gesammelte Werke.* F.A. Hayek, ed. Tübingen: Mohr, 1968. Vol. IV, pp. 1–124.

Mises, Ludwig von. 1912. *Theorie des Geldes und der Umlaufsmittel.* 1ˢᵗ ed. Munich: Duncker & Humblot.

——. 1919a. *Nation, Staat und Wirtschaft.* Vienna: Manz.

——. 1919b. "Der Wiedereintritt Deutsch-Österreichs in das Deutsche Reich und die Währungsfrage." *Schriften des Vereins für Sozialpolitik* 158.

——. 1923. "Die geldtheoretische Seite des Stabilisierungsproblems." *Schriften des Vereins für Sozialpolitik* 164.

——. 1924. *Theorie des Geldes und der Umlaufsmittel.* 2nd ed. Munich: Duncker & Humblot.

——. 1928. *Geldwertstabilisierung und Konjunkturpolitik.* Jena: Fischer.

——. 1981. *Theory of Money and Credit.* Indianapolis, Ind.: Liberty Fund.

——. 1949. *Human Action.* New Haven, Conn.: Yale University Press.

——. 2009. *Memoirs.* Auburn, Ala.: Ludwig von Mises Institute.

North, Gary. 1993. *Salvation through Inflation: The Economics of Social Credit.* Tyler, Texas: Institute for Christian Economics.

Pallas, Carsten. 2005. *Ludwig von Mises als Pionier der Geld- und Konjunkturlehre.* Marburg: Metropolis.

Selgin, G., and L. H. White. 1999. "A fiscal theory of government's role in money." *Economic Inquiry* 37.

2

Amadeus Gabriel

Why was the Reception of the First Edition of Mises's *Theory of Money and Credit* so Lukewarm?

1. Introduction

THE GERMAN MONETARY THEORISTS OF the nineteenth century are virtually unknown in English-speaking countries. And yet, their influence on the work of great economists like Carl Menger, Joseph Schumpeter, or Alfred Marshall cannot be denied.[1] This is also true of their influence on Ludwig von Mises. This paper addresses the question if—and in what way—the German monetary theorists were the forerunners of Mises's first edition of *Theory of Money and Credit*. Likewise, this paper will not only focus on their influence, but also on the similarities and differences of their theoretical approaches regarding monetary theory. This evaluation will shed

---

AMADEUS GABRIEL is a Ph.D. candidate at the University of Angers in France.

1   On this, the author recommends the outstanding paper "The Influence of German Economics on the Work of Menger and Marshall" by Erich W. Streissler (1989). In this essay, Streissler shows in what way and to what extent the concepts of marginal utility, opportunity cost, Marshall's demand curve and others can already be found in the writings of German economists. In addition, Streissler comes to the conclusion that "the real revolutionary was Schmoller, not Menger" (Streissler 1989, p. 44).

light on why the response to his treatise was so lukewarm in the German-speaking world. In the late 1920s, looking back on the reactions to the first edition of 1912, Mises wrote:

> Sixteen years ago when I presented the circulation credit theory of the crisis in the first German edition of my book on *The Theory of Money and Credit* (1912), I encountered ignorance and stubborn rejection everywhere, especially in Germany. (Mises 2006, p. 54)

In his memoirs (1978), Mises dedicates a whole chapter to *Theory of Money and Credit* and states that "as could be expected, my book was rejected summarily by the journals of the German social sciences" (Mises 1978, p. 61). In his book, he had bluntly stated that he did not appreciate the work of most of his German colleagues. That was certainly not conducive to a warm reception by German academia at the time.[2]

Neither the lukewarm reception of *Theory of Money and Credit* nor Mises's view of the value of German monetary theory are justified. The leading German monetary theorists of the nineteenth century were Carl Knies, Karl Heinrich Rau, Wilhem Roscher, and Adolph Wagner,[3] and all made significant contributions to monetary theory. The works of the economists who came next, Menger, Schumpeter, and Marshall, were heavily influenced by these earlier theorists,[4] as was Mises himself (Mises 1912, p. 441). So to say that Menger single-handedly revolutionized the way in which monetary theory is examined, as Mises does, may not be appropriate (Mises 1912, p. 408).

---

2   For instance, Mises states that "It is undeniable that there are some excellent works of a descriptive nature to be found among the huge piles of valueless publications on banking policy of recent years, but it is equally undeniable that with a few honorable exceptions their contribution to theory cannot compare with the literary memorials left by the great controversy of the Currency and Banking Schools" (Mises 1981, p. 381). Later on, he stated with some satisfaction, that "Men such as Knapp, Bendixen, Liefmann, Diehl, Adolf Wagner and Bortkiewicz who then were celebrated in Germany as 'monetary theorists' are no longer considered authorities" (Mises 1978, p. 61) .

3   Mises quotes Knies no less than ten times, Wagner five times, Helfferich four times, Roscher twice, and Rau only once. The high number of references to the work of Knies confirms (even in the case in which the quotations serve as a form of criticism) of his influence in the writings of Mises. All things considered, it is without a doubt evidence that Mises was familiar with the writings of the German economists.

4   On this, cf. for example Otto Hübner, Johann Louis Tellkampf, Adolf Wagner, and so forth.

In this paper, I analyze the theoretical similarities and differences in Mises's work concerning such topics as the nature of money, the value of money, the quantity of money, the redistribution effects of money productions, banks of issue and the consequences of uncovered paper money, and the necessity for a central bank. The similarities help us to understand why Mises's assessment of German banking theories is partly unjust.[5] The differences shed light on the question as to why the first edition of his treatise on monetary theory was rejected by German academia. Many of these ideas were welcomed, when they were first put forward by older German economists of the nineteenth century.

Most German economists of the older generation did not explain the nature of money by the existence of conventional agreements. They were aware of the establishment of money as a natural fruit of indirect exchange and its role as a common medium of exchange. Likewise, Mises's famous regression theorem can be found similarly expressed in the writings of these economists. The dynamics of fiduciary media and its dangers were not unfamiliar to the older German theorists either. Mises's approach to state intervention in the banking system and his skepticism about its effectiveness were totally shared by the younger Adolph Wagner.[6]

The main theoretical difference between Mises and the older generation of German economists is the treatment of the socially optimum amount of money. Whereas German economists propose an approach, where the velocity is the main explanatory variable, Mises claims that every amount of money is optimal for the needs of society. When the *Theory of Money and Credit* was first published most German economists were in favor of central banking. Mises was skeptical about central banking and its function, only becoming a full-fledged advocate of free banking with the publication of the second edition. Considering the favorable light in which central banking was esteemed by the political environment and advocated in policy, the rejection of the first edition can be understood and maybe expected. Things

---

5   I do not want to imply that the German economists were the originators of these ideas. Many of these concepts had appeared earlier. For instance, Monroe (2001); Schumpeter (1994) treat in much detail the theoretical developments in monetary analysis by authors such as Bodin, Cantillon, Law, and others. This paper focuses on the German economists as I attempt to understand the rebuttal of Mises's first edition by the German academia. Yet, in some places, I point out the original authors to avoid any confusion.

6   Wagner was one of the major figures, together with Knies, in the discussion about free banking versus central banking (Smith 1990, p. 79).

changed after World War I. The former scientific authorities in monetary theory rapidly lost their reputation when the implementation of their policies led to disastrous developments in Germany. Not surprisingly, the second edition had a more favorable reception.

The paper is structured as follows. We first analyze the literature pertaining to the nature of money (Section 2), and then deal accordingly with the determination of the value of money (Section 3); the optimal quantity of money (Section 4); the redistributive effects of money production (Section 5); the consequences of uncovered paper money (Section 6); as well as the necessity of a central bank (Section 7). We present our conclusions in the final Section 8.

2. THE NATURE OF MONEY

One of the great insights of Austrian monetary theory is that money had to be a commodity in the first place and not just some sort of numeric value. Mises points out in several places that a commodity can never become money just because the state decides to attribute a value to it. Money is the fruit of indirect exchange (Mises 1912, p. 45). The spontaneous emergence of money becomes necessary as the division of labor increases and wants become more refined (Mises 1912, p. 5). Individuals only choose indirect exchange when the goods they can acquire are more marketable than those which they surrender.

The most marketable commodities will become common media of exchange and their position is strengthened as their relative marketability increases in comparison to other commodities (Mises 1912, p. 6). The main function of money is its universal use as a general medium of exchange (Mises 1912, p. 7). The secondary functions of money can mostly be neglected and deduced from its function as medium of exchange. As Mises says:

> The simple statement, that money is a commodity whose economic function is to facilitate the interchange of goods and services, does not satisfy those writers who are interested rather in the accumulation of material than in the increase of knowledge. (Mises 1981, p. 46f.) [7]

---

7   In German: "Die einfache Umschreibung der volkswirtschaftlichen Funktion des Geldes, dass es ein den Austausch von Gütern und Dienstleistungen vermittelndes Verkehrsgut sei, konnte alle jene nicht befriedigen, welche in der Wissenschaft nicht so sehr die Tiefe der Erkenntnis als die Fülle von Material suchen" (Mises 1912, p. 10).

As mentioned earlier, goods can only become a common media of exchange through their use by those who take part in commercial transactions (Mises 1912, p. 59). For this purpose, it would not be appropriate to attribute the function of money—money being always an economic good—to a certificate which constitutes only a claim.

One might say that Mises's statements on the nature of money are simply the integration of Menger's ideas formulated in his famous essay on the origins of money, thereby reflecting Menger's influence on Mises. Menger's paper was written in 1892. In his treatise, Menger denounces Roscher as being among the economists who believe that the medium of exchange has been established by general convention or law and points out, referring to the convention claim, that "even the more modern developments in the theory of money have not in substance got beyond this standpoint." (Menger 1892, sec. II) I will show that not all German economists of this time can be put into this category and the statement is an oversimplification. Many arguments of nineteenth-century German monetary theorists can be found within Menger's work on money.

As a consequence, Mises was perhaps not influenced directly by these German economists, but rather indirectly by Menger's work. German theorists before him had also recognized the spontaneous emergence of money. Knies points out that money is the natural fruit of indirect exchange, but at the same time refuses to recognize the need of conventions in order to establish money.

As Knies puts it:

> The use of money is not the result of one special agreement between human beings and not the consequence of a law by the state. It actually originates everywhere as a natural fruit of exchange. (Knies 1873, p. 107)[8]

Hence, if an object has been chosen as the new general medium of exchange, it is not due to some arbitrary judgment. Rather, it is the flexible and durable commodity which is highly demanded for its properties. It naturally becomes the most marketable commodity and serves to set the

---

8   In German: "Der Gebrauch des Geldes ist nicht das Ergebnis einer besondern Uebereinkunft der Menschen und nicht Folge einer gesetzlichen Vorschrift des Staates. Er wächst vielmehr überall als eine natürliche Frucht des Tauschverkehres an sich" (Knies 1873, p. 107). All translations are by the author of the essay.

standard of value of the other commodities (Knies 1873, p. 108). Money, in the sense that some "economic" value is estimated or measured, has to be a commodity of great value (Knies 1873, p. 114). Knies's stance on the concept of objective exchange value does not really differ from Mises's,[9] but this aspect will be analyzed more precisely in the next section. But how did the other German economists define money?

Roscher's definition of money differs from that of Knies. Roscher believed that money needs the approval of the state, as a medium of payment, in order to bring a commodity as money to perfection (Roscher 1854, p. 222).[10] The development of money circulation goes hand in hand with that of personal freedom (Roscher 1854, p. 227). Only commodities with a generally accepted value have become money (Roscher 1854, p. 229).

Rau assumes that direct exchange is rare and after the introduction of money, indirect exchange divides a single transaction into two separate parts. These two parts consist of acquiring a desired good through the use of a more marketable good, in other words, by purchasing and selling the more marketable good (Rau 1868, p. 317). He describes the spontaneous emergence of money by the following procedure:

> One must therefore assume that a generally popular and sought after commodity was even more frequently accepted by persons who did not want to use it themselves; in this way it obtained gradually the nature of money and the utility emanating stepwise from this kind of use was recognized more clearly. (Rau 1868, p. 317)[11]

Knies emphasizes that money by itself is not one function. Rather, it is the function of an economic commodity that is used for some special purpose (Knies 1873, p. 163). Claims cannot be qualified as money (Knies

---

9   As Knies, Mises points out that "If in this sense we wish to attribute to money the function of being a measure of prices, there is no reason why I should not do so" (Mises 1981, p. 62).

10   Actually, this differs only slightly from what Menger said: "On the other hand, however, by state recognition and state regulation, this social institution of money has been perfected and adjusted to the manifold and varying needs of an evolving commerce, just as customary rights have been perfected and adjusted to statute law" (Menger 1892, sec. IX).

11   In German: "Man muss daher vermuten, dass eine allgemein beliebte und gesuchte Waare allmälig immer häufiger auch von solchen Personen im Verkehre angenommen wurde, die sie nicht selbst gebrauchen wollten, dass sie auf diese Weise nach und nach die Natur des Geldes erhielt und hiebei auch stufenweise der hieraus entspringende Nutzen deutlicher erkannt wurde" (Rau 1868, p. 317).

1873, p. 164). Money must be a real commodity and not only a numeric value (Knies 1873, p. 182).

Furthermore, Knies attributes to money the role of a local transmitter of value through time and space (Knies 1873, p. 223). Mises criticizes this approach and claims that this function can also be traced back to its very existence as a common media of exchange (Mises 1912, p. 11).

The concept of hoarding can also be found in the work of Knies.[12] Hoarding is an artificial problem (Knies 1873, p. 211) because money can never lie idle. Mises and Knies share this viewpoint and emphasize that all money addresses itself to the service of a monetary function (Knies 1876, p. 284; Mises 1912, p. 61).

The famous threefold division into means of production, objects of consumption, and media of exchange by Mises has actually its origins in Knies's writings (Knies 1873, p. 20). Mises regrets that Knies's arguments on this were sloppy and thus attracted hardly any attention (Mises 1912, p. 70). Mises develops this point and the threefold division becomes part of his monetary analysis.

3. VALUE OF MONEY

German economists of the nineteenth century generally do not believe that conventions or the like are necessary for the establishment of money. The similarities in the approaches of Mises and the these German economists go even further.

Roscher and Rau derive the exchange value of commodity money from its natural scarcity and aesthetic properties (Rau 1868, p. 340; Roscher 1854, p. 235). The use value of the employed commodity determines its exchange value. The original use value of the non-monetary employment gets less important as the commodity becomes the common media of exchange (Roscher 1854, p. 239). Roscher uses the concept of supply and demand for money to determine its value (Roscher 1854, p. 241). Rau emphasizes that the good, which is now used as money, had to have a generally accepted value in the past, a value derived from its market value when it was still a commodity (Rau 1868, p. 317).

---

12   Mises elaborates on this point more thoroughly and more precisely in his later works (cf. Mises 1966).

Similarly, Knies argues that the objective exchange value of money, which already existed due to its past use as a precious metal, obviously determines its objective exchange value as a medium of exchange (Knies 1873, p. 141). Wagner concurs (Wagner 1857, p. 37).

These observations by Knies, Wagner, and Rau are especially interesting in light of Mises's explanation for the value of money, also known as the regression theorem. The regression theorem states that one traces back the objective exchange value of money only to that point where it ceases to be the value of money and becomes merely the value of a commodity (Mises 1912, p. 128). Mises's approach was an extension of Wieser's (1903) who argued that one has to go back in time to when money was still a commodity in order to understand the circularity problem of the value of money, which had been pointed out by Helfferich.

Most of the components of the regression theorem[13] can be found in the writings of Knies and Rau and are simply a refinement of existing ideas.

Knies and Wagner assert that a new demand for the service of precious metals is added to its previous demand for its services as jewelry, etc., as soon as it becomes the common medium of exchange. The two demands together determine the price for its use as money, as well as its use for other services (Knies 1873, p. 141; Wagner 1857, p. 38).

Mises points out that the value of money is determined by both its industrial employment and its monetary employment. However, it is impossible to say to which extent the value of money is influenced by one or the other (Mises 1912, p. 105).[14]

The notion of subjective valuations is not explicitly used by Knies, but he observes that the objective exchange value is determined by individuals who take part in commercial transactions. As a consequence, a governmental decree as such is insufficient to ascribe an objective exchange value to a commodity. As Knies puts it:

> Can a governmental authority, even if it were the most violent and the most persistent, attribute an exchange value to an object, which has no exchange value at all for the human beings that take part in the commercial life? (Knies 1873, p. 189)[15]

---

13   This term only appeared in Mises (1966).

14   This approach can be found in earlier writings by authors like John Law (cf. for example Law 1720).

15   In German: "Wir müssen vielmehr vor Allem grade fragen: Kann denn eine

Knies adds the following remark a little further on in his text:

> The government authority could declare just as well that a
> mountain is twice as high as it is in reality or that two pounds
> are actually six pounds. (Knies 1873, p. 189)[16]

Knies denounces that the law considers the value of money as being invariable and constant, whereas in fact no economic good has a stable value
(Knies 1873, p. 318).[17] Mises clearly sympathizes with this point of view
and insists that money can never be stable but "for the law, invariability of
the value of money is not a fiction, but a fact" (Mises 1981, p. 227).[18] This
is an important insight.

4. QUANTITY OF MONEY

German monetary theorists agree that velocity is the most important
explanatory variable for determining the money supply.[19] Roscher asserts
that the optimal quantity of money cannot be determined either as a function of the population figures or as one of the national income (Roscher
1854, p. 242). The transition from a medieval barter economy to the commercial monetary system necessarily implies a need for a higher quantity
of money. One taler that circulates ten times performs the same services as
ten talers that circulate just once (Roscher 1854, p. 242).

Rau takes a similar stance. The more a piece of money circulates between participants in commercial transactions, the more goods and services can be bought and a smaller quantity of money is needed in order to

---

Staatsgewalt, und wäre sie die gewaltsamste und hartnäckigste, einem Gegenstand, der
als solcher für das Wirthschaftsleben der Menschen keinen Tauschwerth hat, mittels einer
Vorschrift Tauschwerth schaffen?" (Knies 1873, p. 189).

16   In German: "Die Staatsgewalt könnte grade so gut erklären, ein Berg sei doppelt
so hoch, als er in Wirklichkeit ist, oder zwei Pfund seien sechs Pfund" (Knies 1873, p. 189).

17   Menger (1892) endorses the stabilization of the inner objective exchange value of
money, which corresponds, to a great extent, to the views of Knies.

18   Mises talks about this point in the first edition (Mises 1912, pp. 222–25), but it is
only in the second edition that he makes such a clear-cut statement.

19   As Monroe (2001, pp. 56, 58) points out, although there are some vague allusions
in the Spanish Scholastics, Bodin (1581) is still the father of quantity theorizing. However,
Cantillon (1755) is one of the first economists (together with John Locke or Bernardo Da-
vanzati), to treat the topic of velocity in more detail. Rau cites him for this reason (Rau
1868, p. 245).

fuel commerce (Rau 1868, p. 323). Rau actually formulates in a footnote an equation which corresponds to Irving Fisher's identity of exchange which shows the concept of velocity and the quantity of money. [20]

Knies is less clear about the optimal quantity of money. He agrees with Rau and Roscher that a unit of money can render more services if its circulation increases. For example, a coin that changes hands three times does the same service as three coins that circulate just once (Knies 1873, p. 180). The general opinion is that the more the money circulates the less quantity is required and vice versa.

Wagner, as a follower of Tooke, describes the money supply as the effect of money demand and not as the cause of it (Wagner 1857, p. 122). If the money supply increases, it is a *result* of more commercial activity causing prices to rise and not the *cause* as is put forth by the Currency School (Wagner 1857, p. 127). For instance, if the price of wheat increases due to a bad harvest, then the money supply has to increase (Wagner 1857, p. 128).

The scenario portraying the German theorists as being the predecessors of the quantity theory is not very enlightening with regard to how the socially optimal quantity of money is determined. Generally speaking, concepts of the social need of money are pretty imprecise and elusive. None of these German economists is capable of expressing a clear opinion about the social demand of money within the framework of a national economy. Actually, they seem to avoid direct consideration of this, referring to "the demand of the medium of payment for the commerce" without specifying anything in a precise manner. One desperately seeks a definitive predication, such as can be found in the works of the early Austrian economists. [21]

These points of view can clearly be distinguished from those of Mises. Mises's criticism of the quantity theory and, in particular, its concept of velocity is well known (Mises 1912, p. 142). The arguments of the quantity

---

20   Rau establishes the following equation: $u \cdot g = w \cdot p$, where u is the average velocity of the money (mittlere Umlaufszahl des Geldes); g is the quantity of money (Geldmenge); w is the turned over quantity of goods and services (umgesetzte Menge von Gütern und Leistungen) and p is the price level (Preisniveau). Hence, this example shows clearly to what extent the ignorance of German Economics is prevalent in the Anglo-Saxon perception of the history of economic thought. This finding has already been pointed out in the writings of other economists (ia. Streissler). For a more detailed analysis of the influence of German Economics on Marshall (in particular his demand curve), refer to Streissler (1989).

21   Böhm-Bawerk (1998, p. 217) writes for example: "Every quantity of money has the capacity to meet the national demand for money *fully* in the same way." (Jede Quantität von Geld ist dem Geldbedarf eines Volkes in *völlig* gleicher Weise zu genügen im Stande.)

theorists are too mechanical and their assumption that modifications in the value of money must be proportionate to changes in the quantity of money is not in accordance with empirical facts (Mises 1912, p. 139).

Rather, Mises derives the basis of the demand for and stock of money in the whole community by observing that as long as there are no money substitutes in use, the social demand for money and the social stock of money are merely the respective sums of the individual demands and stocks (Mises 1912, p. 145). Later in his text he further specifies the case when money substitutes are issued:

> It is thus obvious that a community's demand for money in the broader sense cannot be the sum of the demands of individuals of money and money substitutes, because the money that serves as a cover for them as the banks and elsewhere is to count the same amount twice over. (Mises 1981, p. 156) [22]

With regard to the socially optimal quantity of the money, Mises's statements are articulated in a forthright way. As Mises writes:

> In the first place, it must be pointed out that the levels of the total stock of money and of the value of the money unit are matters of complete indifference as far as the utility obtained from the use of the money is concerned. Society is in enjoyment of the maximum utility obtainable from the use of money. Half of the money at disposal of the community would yield the same utility as the whole stock, even if the variation in the value of the monetary unit was not proportioned to the variation in the stock of money. (Mises 1981, p. 165)[23]

---

22   "Es leuchtet somit ohne weiteres ein, dass der Geldbedarf einer Volkswirtschaft im weiteren Sinne nicht als die Summe des Bedarfes der Einzelwirtschaften an Geld und Geldsurrogaten erscheinen kann, weil durch die Zahlung des Bedarfes sowohl an Geldzertifikaten als auch an jenem Gelde, das als Deckung dieser bei den Banken usw. dienen soll, eine zweimalige Einstellung eines und desselben Postens erfolgen würde" (Mises 1912, pp. 144–45).

23   In German: "Zunächst muss festgestellt werden, dass die Grösse des Geldvorrates und des Wertes der Geldeinheit für die Grösse der vom Geldgebrauche ausgehenden Nutzwirkung überhaupt gleichgültig ist. Die Volkswirtschaft steht stets im Genusse der grössten durch das Geld erreichbaren Nutzwirkung. Die Hälfte des der Volkswirtschaft zur Verfügung stehenden Geldvorrates wurde auch dann die gleiche Nutzwirkung vollbringen wie der ganze Vorrat, wenn die Veränderung des Wertes der Geldeinheit nicht proportional zu der Veränderung der Grösse des Vorrates eintritt" (Mises 1912, p. 156).

This clear opinion, however, was put forward with some reservations.[24] For instance, he states that the need of money depends on the degree of modernization of a society, the season, and other magnitudes (Mises 1912, pp. 341–70). Similarly, he claims that there can be a lack of fiduciary media (Mises 1912, e.g., pp. 345, 350) which suggests that not every quantity of money is sufficient for the economy. This sort of explanation can already be found in the works of Roscher and Rau as I mentioned before.

5. REDISTRIBUTION EFFECTS OF THE PRODUCTION OF MONEY

It may be appropriate here to briefly outline the principle of money redistribution: The new money that enters the market affects the dynamic adjustment process. Richard Cantillon[25] recognized that the demand schedules of those initially affected by the monetary disturbance change before the demands of those who receive additional money balances only as the effects of the monetary change spread through the economy. This phenomenon results in a redistribution of income and wealth in favor of those who are close to the source of money production and at the expense of those who are among the final links of the redistribution chain.

Actually, one of the most important points of Mises's critique of the production of credit money is the redistribution effect of this procedure. He states that the new money always increases the quantity of money as it is disposed of by individual agents (Mises 1912, p. 150) and the increase in the quantity of money does not mean an increase of income for all individuals (Mises 1912, p. 152). Even if the increase of money was the same for every person, this would not necessarily mean a uniform price increase since the structure of demand is affected during every process of money production (Mises 1912, pp. 153–54).

Knies points out that the economy is dynamic and the prediction of the modifications of economic situations is generally impossible (Knies 1876, p. 135). He contradicts himself when he emphasizes that changes in

---

24   These reservations already diminished in the second edition of his *Theory of Money and Credit* are almost completely gone in his *magnum opus Human Action* (Mises 1966).

25   Roscher is the only author who mentions Richard Cantillon (cf. Cantillon 1755) in his work (Roscher 1854, p. 245).

prices due to the modifications of the quantity of money are only tempo-rary and are likely to be adjusted by those who are involved in the com-mercial transactions (Knies 1876, pp. 321, 326).

Rau shows that entrepreneurial profits increase as a result of the in-crease in the money supply. Consequently, there are incentives to expand production, and this in turn dampens the price increase. Rau observes that those higher entrepreneurial profits go in hand with "the affliction of other social classes" (Rau 1868, p. 330). The higher commercial activity (due to the new money) is only for the public good as long as it provides the ba-sis for an increase in production. Otherwise, those who sell goods receive advantages as a result of the additional expenditure of other citizens (Rau 1868, p. 375).

Mises's approach is similar. Money production per se cannot improve the welfare of the people except for the case of a production increase (Mis-es 1912, p. 235). Rau is less restrictive and states that an increase of the quantity of money always has a positive impact in the beginning of the pro-cess. Nevertheless, Rau clearly observes the redistribution effects of money production:

> ... [C]onsequently the price of the different goods in commerce cannot increase in the same proportion, some earlier and stron-ger, others later and weaker; many maladjustments arise, several win, others namely the holders of big sums of money, the credi-tors, the employees lose considerably. (Rau 1868, p. 378)[26]

As does Mises, Knies denounces governmental measures which aim at improving the situation of debtors at the expense of the creditors (Knies 1873, p. 250). He points out the absurdity that we are still surrounded by "the delusion as if the creditor were a rich, otiose senior citizen and that it would be necessary to relieve the burden of the poor, living in bitter mis-ery, by hook or by crook" (Knies 1873, p. 250). Wagner, too, was perfectly aware of the redistribution effects of fiat money. He observes that unre-deemable bank notes are a means for first receivers to enrich themselves at the cost of the last receivers (Wagner 1857, p. 83).

---

26   In German: ". . . folglich der Preis der verschiedenen im Verkehre befindlichen Gegenstände kann nicht in gleichem Verhältnis steigen, einige werden früher und stärker, andere später und schwächer vertheuert, es entstehen daher viele Missverhältnisse, wobei Einzelne gewinnen, anderen namentlich die Besitzer grosser Geldsummen, die Gläubiger, die Angestellten, ansehnlich verlieren" (Rau 1868, p. 378).

Similar to Mises, Rau observes that an increase in the quantity of money by 1 or 2 percent can actually be a large sum, but the consequences would not be remarkable since the ones who take part in the commercial transactions do not perceive it to the same extent (Rau 1868, p. 329). This explains the unjust enrichment of those in charge of the issue of money at the expense of the people who don't notice a modification of the quantity of money in the first place.

Knies explicitly mentions creditors as being the undeserved losers of "legal tender unredeemable paper money"[27] and that this should be emphatically denounced (Knies 1873, p. 285).[28] It is the creditor and not the debtor who bears the risk. Knies and Mises agree that this is also true in the case of bank notes where the holders, i.e., creditors of the bank, bear the risk of their credit. In this case the debtor, i.e., the bank, makes its profits by receiving the bank notes without paying interest (Knies 1873, p. 306; Mises 1912, p. 312). Without a doubt, these banks of issue benefit from the issue of notes (Knies 1876, p. 319).

Knies provides an explanation for the favoritism of the debtor at the expense of the creditor. Debtors benefit from better treatment since they are represented by the government (Knies 1873, p. 207); the largest debtor, though, is the state itself via the issue of governmental bonds that offer very favorable conditions to the creditors (Knies 1873, p. 143). If they ever get paid back, it is a long time coming (Knies 1876, p. 144).

6. Banks of Issue and the Consequences of Uncovered Paper Money

Knies is mistrustful of the banks of issue. The issuance of paper money must be legally restricted to guarantee the money at par. Compliance with regulations cannot be assured if it depends solely on individual attitudes and the short-sighted will of statesmen (Knies 1873, p. 279).

Similarly, Rau thinks that confidence in the government is an essential factor. Government attempts to avoid depreciation and to limit the losses for the receivers of money (Rau 1868, p. 379). He prefers redeemable paper money to unredeemable paper money since the issuance of an enormous

---

27   In German: "uneinlösliches Papiergeld mit Zwangscurs gegen Jedermann."

28   As shown in Monroe (2001, p. 78), Bodin already pointed out that creditors especially suffer when prices rises, but this insight only spread in later times.

quantity of fiat money is highly probable. Experience shows that the issuance of fiat money was always tempting and the consequences were always confusing for commerce (Rau 1868, p. 381). The lower the proportion of paper money is in comparison to the total quantity, the smaller is the danger of abuse (Rau 1868, p. 381).

As does Rau, Knies points out that it is much easier to refrain from a substantial issuance of paper money than to recover from it. The population always fears that the state benefits from its position and procures financial aid in the case of an emergency through the issue of notes (Knies 1873, p. 279). "The money supply is determined by the financial requirements of the government, rather than by the needs of the national economy" (Knies 1873, p. 208).

Knies cites a French incident from the first quarter of the eighteenth century to make his point. In this case, the "infinite fruitfulness of a paper press" (he uses this expression in an ironic way) and its consequences were clear, but in spite of everything, masses of supporters for this sort of procedure could still be found throughout that century (Knies 1876, p. 66). Knies describes the perpetual circulation of "depreciated paper money" as one of the worst plagues that could infest a national economy (Knies 1873, p. 281). The issuance of paper money is especially handy for the "weak, restricted, selfish and frivolous statesman" (Knies 1873, p. 274). He even develops a sort of business cycle[29] which is likely to be caused by the issue of unredeemable paper money. As Knies puts it:

> Suddenly one is exposed to the demoniacal rule of insuperable accidents, which one had once learned to perceive as a characteristic feature of "barbaric" economic conditions. Property and commerce become uncertain, even though the police and the courts continue their work as usual. Efforts made along time-tested paths, intense work in the pursuit of well-known objectives are paralyzed, and the floodgates are widely opened to the "adventurers." Even the profits that result from calculated

---

29   Phillipp Geyer, a German banking theorist who published his "Banken und Krisen" in 1865, actually formulated a theory which resembled, to some exten, the circulation credit theory of Ludwig von Mises. As Smith (1990, p. 78) observes, Geyer identified two major drawbacks of the banking system. "First, that it provides the material for trade crises and production cycles by producing 'artificial capital' up to a point where there is an excessive amount of capital in existence, and, secondly, that having produced the crisis, it intensifies it by contracting credit and causing forced sales." However, this theory was not fully developed and the explanation had its roots in underconsumption.

foresight are acquired only at the expense of others. No-one is grateful to the government for his undeserved profit, and everybody accuses it for his undeserved losses. Was it not one of the government's most important missions to vouch for the soundness of money? But how often has this already been said! How much to the point, how congruently have the consequences of depreciated paper money been perceived! (Knies 1873, p. 282)[30]

Similarly, Knies analyzes the consequences of the overissue for the value of paper money:

The paper money that has become subject to price fluctuations has become a medium of exchange whose market value should be established anew by every acceptor, whereas the great bulk of the population is unable to carry out such examinations. (Knies 1873, p. 284)[31]

The existing problems of price fluctuations are augmented with the uncertainty about the value of future payments. This is not brought about by fluctuations of value and price measures, but by the value fluctuations of the imposed media of exchange whose amount is also measured in money (Knies 1873, p. 284). Thus, there is a tendency toward the reduction of objective exchange value as has been pointed out by Mises (Mises 1981, p. 331). As Mises writes:

If the fiduciary media are perfect substitutes for money and do all that money could do, if they add to the social stock of money

---

30   In German: "Man findet sich plötzlich der dämonischen Herrschaft unbekämpfbarer Zufälle preisgegeben, die man als ein bezeichnendes Merkmal 'barbarischer' Zustände für wirthschaftlichen Verkehr anzusehen gelernt hatte. Unsicherheit des Vermögens und des Erwerbs greift Platz, trotzdem dass Policei und Gerichte nach wie vor ihres Amtes warten. Der auf erprobten Wegen wandelnde Fleiss, die angestrengte Arbeit auf wohlbekannte Ziele hin sind gelähmt, den 'Abenteuern' weit und breit Thor und.Thür geöffnet. Auch derjenige Gewinn, welcher Ergebniss vorschauender Berechnung ist, wird nur durch den Verlust Anderer erworben. Niemand ist der Staatsregierung dankbar für seinen unverdienten Gewinn und Jeder klagt sie an ob seines unverdienten Verlustes. War es nicht eine ihrer wichtigsten Aufgaben, für die Richtigkeit des Geldes einzustehen? Aber wie oft, wie zutreffend, wie übereinstimmend sind solche Wahrnehmungen über die Folgen eines entwertheten Papiergeldes ausgesprochen worden! (1873, pp. 282).

31   In German: "Das in Preisschwankung gerathene Papiergeld ist ein Tauschmittel geworden, dessen Verkehrswerth von jedem Abnehmer neu festgestellt werden sollte, während die grosse Masse der Verkehrenden gar nicht in der Lage ist, diese Prüfung vornehmen zu können" (1873, p. 284).

in the broader sense, their issue must be accompanied by appropriate effects on the exchange ratio between money and other
economic goods. (Mises 1981, p. 349)[32]

The effects of the uncovered notes also reach those who can deny the
acceptance of all notes (Knies 1873, p. 311). Similarly, Mises describes it in
the following way:

> The fact that is peculiar to money alone is not that mature and
> secure claims to money are as highly valued in commerce as the
> sums of money to which they refer, but rather that such claims
> are complete substitutes for money, and, as such, are able to ful-
> fill all the functions of money in those markets in which their
> essential characteristics of maturity and security are recognized.
> It is this circumstance that makes it possible to issue more of
> this sort of substitute than the issuer is always in a position to
> convert. And so the fiduciary medium comes into being in ad-
> dition to the money. (Mises 1981, p. 300) [33]

In addition, Knies points out that by the use of claims, people forget
about their real nature, i.e., claims for money which can be redeemed at the
bank (Knies 1873, p. 304). Similar, Mises declares:

> The immediately convertible note of a solvent bank is employable
> everywhere as fiduciary medium instead of money in commercial
> transactions, and nobody draws a distinction between the money
> and the notes which he holds as cash. (Mises 1981, p. 305) [34]

---

32   In German "Wenn die Umlaufsmittel als Geldsurrogate alle Dienste des Geldes
leisten, wenn sie den Geldvorrat der Menschen im weiteren Sinne vermehren, dann muss
ihre Ausgabe von entsprechenden Einwirkungen auf die Gestaltung des zwischen dem Gelde und den übrigen wirtschaftlichen Gütern bestehenden Austauschverhältnisses begleitet
sein" (1912, p. 363).

33   In German: "Nicht das ist dem Gelde allein eigentümlich, dass fällige sichere
Geldforderungen im Verkehre gerade so hoch geschätzt werden wie die Geldbeträge, auf
die sie lauten, vielmehr das, dass solche Forderungen als vollkommene Surrogate des Geldes alien Dienst des Geldes in jenen Marktgebieten, in denen ihre wesentlichen Eigen-
schaften: Fälligkeit und Sicherheit, erkannt sind, ohne vorherige Realisierung ver- sehen
konnen. Auf diesem Umstande erst beruht die Möglichkeit, mehr derartige Surrogate aus-
zugeben, als der Emittent jederzeit einzulosen in der Lage ist. Neben das Geldzertifikat tritt
das Umlaufsmittel" (Mises 1912, p. 306).

34   In German: "Die jederzeit einlösliche Note einer solventen Bank ist als Umlaufsmittel im Verkehre überall an Stelle des Geldes verwendbar, und niemand macht daher
einen Unterschied, ob er in seiner Kasse Geld oder Noten liegen hat. Die Note ist gerade so
ein gegenwärtiges Gut wie etwa das Geld" (Mises 1912, p. 311).

Governmental authorities have always used deposits to secure credits. Moreover, they accept the losses of the note holders if it helps to avoid the bankruptcy of the debtor (i.e., the national banks) (Knies 1873, p. 309). Knies denounces several times the idea of an interest free loan through the issuance of bank notes. This is a complete "abnormality" in the private loan sector (Knies 1873, p. 310). However, the bank of issue engages into this sort of business (Knies 1873, p. 311). That's why Knies prefers the constrained note issuance to one without limits even if it is not the perfect solution (Knies 1873, p. 312).

Likewise, Knies is opposed to the issuance of unredeemable paper money in combination with credits. Any deals that involve sums of money whose value equivalence cannot be guaranteed are likely to entail arbitrary gambling and betting about losses and profits determine the outcome (Knies 1876, p. 142).

Wagner is of the opinion that credits cannot create money. Banks should always have enough reserves to redeem the notes (Wagner 1857, p. 73). The devaluation of money is made possible by the introduction of fiat money (Wagner 1857, p. 96) and that is why bank notes must be redeemable at any time (Wagner 1857, p. 97). However, the same applies for deposits as they feature the same characteristics as bank notes (Wagner 1857, pp. 163, 214). Under the banking system with voluntary reserve ratios, there are no problems for the banks to fulfill the redemption demands of their clients. Under the new system with required reserve ratios, banks go bankrupt (Wagner 1857, p. 220).

Wagner already anticipated to some extent Mises's critique of the Currency School which failed to treat bank notes and deposits as a form of money (Mises 1912, pp. 43–48). Like Mises, Wagner claims that the physical characteristics of money is not important. Metallic and paper money are not really different in his opinion (Wagner 1857, p. 99).

Mises's insight, that banks of issue can diminish the interest of the loan market, in the short run, via the issue of new money (Mises 1912, p. 358) had been observed by Rau in a similar manner:

> Given that the supply of goods cannot be increased quickly
> enough during a substantial increase in the quantity of money,
> the prices must increase as a consequence and this is perceived
> as a difficulty to invest the new money in an advantageous way

that arranges for the rate of interest to decrease during a certain period. (Rau 1868, p. 375)[35]

Rau believes that banks of issue should have the freedom to issue three to four times more notes than they keep as a reserve in order to increase the profits of the banks (Rau 1868, p. 384). However, he perceives the danger for banks if they grant loans in a less cautious manner than capitalists normally do, thus giving incentives to undertake risky projects.

I have demonstrated that the viewpoint of German economists about the banks of issue and the consequences of issuing uncovered paper money are similar to those of Mises. However, they do not necessarily share the same opinion about the necessity of a central bank.

7. The Necessity for a Central Bank

As one would expect, Knies asserts that the minting and issuing of money is the vocation of the state, i.e., its right and its duty (Knies 1873, p. 293). It is now even more important than in the past that the state guarantees the soundness of the national money, even if it is necessary to collect taxes to cover the expenditures (Knies 1873, p. 292). Knies is totally opposed to the idea of competing banks and compares it to the establishment of weights and measures. Knies writes:

> Everybody concedes right away that it is unacceptable for sellers to enjoy the "liberty" of using different weights and measures, and that no buyer of a commodity should suffer harm due to the unreliability of weights and measures. Indeed, not everybody has the right to provide the weights and measures that shall be used in general commerce. Neither may private persons be entitled to provide those "weights and measures" of value, which shall be used in all spheres of the economic and legal life of a nation, in competition with the government. (Knies 1873, p. 294)[36]

---

35   In German: "Da jedoch das Angebot dieser Gegenstände bei einer beträchtlichen Geldvermehrung nicht schnell genug vergrössert werden kann, so muss der Preis derselben steigen, und es wird daher als eine Schwierigkeit empfunden, die neuen Geldsummen vortheilhaft anzulegen, auch sinkt im Anfange der Geldvermehrung der Zinsfuss auf einige Zeit" (Rau 1868, p. 375).

36   In German: "Jedermann gesteht sofort zu, dass es unzulässig ist, den Verkäufern, "der Freiheit wegen," den Gebrauch verschiedenster Maasse und Gewichte zu gestatten, und dass keinem Empfänger einer gekauften Waare ein Nachtheil aus einer Unzuverlässigkeit der Maasse und Gewichte erwachsen soll. In der That, es giebt kein Recht aller zur

Knies is a supporter of the Peel system and condemns the principle of free banking. However, Knies has a nuanced point of view. On the one hand, he is convinced that the state's issue of uncovered paper money is unjust. On the other hand, the legal authorization for private banks to engage in this business is inappropriate and must be condemned (Knies 1873, p. 297). Similarly, the practically costless issuance of bank notes makes free banking impossible (Knies 1873, p. 313).

The common man does not distinguish between private paper money and state paper money. Private banks can issue (quasi-) legal tender notes with the aid of the state and everybody must accept them whether they want to or not (Knies 1873, p. 305). Moreover, Knies thinks that money is of public utility. He points out that "the issue of the notes which have actually come into use as money is not the task of the private industry that aims at entrepreneurial profits" (Knies 1873, p. 306).[37]

Knies's feelings about currency competition in a bank note system are rather negative as well. He was in favor of uniform circulating notes that were used in the single states of Germany at the time when he wrote his book. His comment is quite harsh:

> One cannot alter the diastrous heritage of the last years and decades, that is, the conduct of "banking policy" on the level of the individual states; the existing presumptuous note-proletariat has regular certificates of origin and of residence. (Knies 1873, p. 312)[38]

The most important opponent of Knies was Adolph Wagner. According to Wagner, the freedom of banks is the best guarantee for the good management of banks (Wagner 1857, p. 15). He underscores his argument by including statistics of the Scottish and English banking system. The issue

---

Beschaffung von Maassen und Gewichten, welche als solche im allgemeinen Verkehr gebraucht werden sollen. Ebensowenig dürfen die Privatpersonen für berechtigt gelten, die in dem gesammten Wirthschafts- und Rechtsleben eines Volkes ununterbrochen zu handhabenden Werth- "Maasse und Gewichte" in Concurrenz mit der Staatsgewalt darzubieten (Knies 1873, p. 294).

37   In German: "die Ausgabe von Scheinen, welche thatsächlich wie Geld in der ganzen Masse des Volkes in Gebrauch gekommen sind, ist keine Aufgabe privatgeschäftlicher Industrie zur Erzielung von Unternehmeinkommen" (Knies 1873, p. 306).

38   In German: "Die unselige Erbschaft aus den letzten Jahren und Jahrzehnten der einzelstaatlichen Behandlung der "Bankpolitik" ist einmal da; das vorhandene aufdringliche Notenproletariat hat regelrechte Ursprungszeugnisse und Heimathschein (Knies 1873, p. 312).

of money was less reckless in Scotland,[39] where competition of banks was allowed (Wagner 1857, pp. 21, 59, 60). As long as bank notes are redeemable, it is impossible to have an "inundation" of notes under a system of free banking (Wagner 1857, p. 144). Wagner denounces the required reserve ratio of one third, which entailed the unintended consequence that deposits were backed less than before[40] (Wagner 1857, p. 172). Banks relied on the state to help out in the case of urgency. But "how can the state even know how many reserves a bank needs?" (Wagner 1857, p. 173). It is impossible to know a priori how many cash reserves are required and the competition among banks will sort it out (Wagner 1857, p. 214).

The legal imposition of a reserve rate is one of the worst state interventions, according to Wagner, as new banks are founded with lower reserves than required. This necessarily leads to a weaker banking system. In a framework of free banking, a bank would have to gain some reputation in order to hold lower reserves. Banks would only be founded where there is an actual need (Wagner 1857, p. 218). However, as pointed out by Smith (1990, p. 80), Wagner eventually became more and more prone to the influence of the German Historical School and ultimately stated that "all systems can be justified in the appropriate circumstances"[41] (Smith 1990, p. 80). This "partial recantation" of free banking by one of its most strident supporters, Adolph Wagner, represented the end of opposition to the idea of central banking in Germany[42] (Smith 1990, p. 81).

Mises's view on free banking evolved and this evolution and development can be seen in the different editions of *Theory of Money and Credit*. Hülsmann gives a full account of these differences (Hülsmann 2012). In the first edition, he found several justifications for the existence of central banks. He favored a system of redeemable paper money as it allows to save on metal for other uses (Mises 1912, p. 150). As stated in the previous section, Mises believed in the increase of production through forced saving and the promotion of commercial banking. He also considered the

---

39   A topic which eventually was treated in detail by Selgin (1988).

40   However, Wagner would still prefer such a system to that proposed by Peel. Even though the one-third ratio was arbitrary, it was still less constraining for banks.

41   Wagner still favored the free banking system to a larger extent.

42   The newer generation of the German Historical School, represented by Knapp, Somary, and Lotz were all in favor of central banking and criticized *Theory of Money and Credit* in their reviews (see Greaves 1993).

possibility of a potential lack of fiduciary media. This implied more or less the need for a central bank.

He only evolves into a complete free banker in the second edition. In his opinion, etatism has been a failure (Mises 1981, p. 435) and the current arguments for central banking are unsound (Mises 1981, p. 437). He fears the establishment of uniform procedures on the part of all the credit-issuing banks throughout the world. Furthermore, monopolization of the banks-of-issue in the separate countries would facilitate the uniformity of the procedures. As the banks proceed uniformly, there tends to be a permanent increase of the circulation of fiduciary media, and consequently a fall of the objective exchange value of money (Mises 1981, p. 347). But are the problems of uniformity the only reasons for his support of free banking? Actually, Selgin provides a complementary explanation by pointing out that Mises's support for free banking is based in part on his agreement with Cernuschi, who (along with Modeste) believed that freedom of note issue would automatically lead 100-percent reserve banking (which is contrary to what Knies advocated). In addition, Mises "believed that free banking will somehow lead to the suppression of fractionally-based inside monies" (Selgin 1988, pp. 62, 164).

8. Conclusion

This paper has compared Mises's monetary treatise with those of the major German monetary theorists of the nineteenth century, namely Knies, Rau, Roscher, and Wagner. Essential points of Mises's monetary theory can also be found in the writings of the German economists, in particular in that of Karl Knies.[43] Even if direct influence cannot be proven in all of the cases, it seems plausible that many German ideas found their way into Mises's work through Menger and Böhm-Bawerk.[44]

However, another purpose of this paper was to show the similarities and differences of the monetary theories of the leading German monetary economists of the nineteenth century compared to Mises's *Theory of Money and Credit* in order to understand the lukewarm reception of his first edition.[45]

---

43   The author would like to point out that Knies has been quoted ten times after all.

44   On the influence of Menger and Böhm-Bawerk on Mises, cf. Hülsmann 2007.

45   Again, it is not my claim that the German economists were the orginators of all these theories.

Thus, contrary to what is often supposed with regard to the tradition of the German economists, the nature of money is not explained by the existence of conventional agreements. German monetary theorists were aware of the establishment of money as a natural fruit of indirect exchange and its role as a common medium of exchange. Likewise, Mises's regression theorem can be found similarly expressed in the writings of these economists. The dynamics of fiduciary media and its dangers were not unfamiliar to the German theorists either. Adolph Wagner was a champion of "Bankfreiheit" and promoted the idea of free banking which is similar to Mises's approach to state intervention in the banking system, put forth in the second edition of *Theory of Money and Credit.*

What were the main differences? Mises claimed that any amount of money can serve the needs of society, thereby making a strong argument against state intervention. Free banking disappeared from the German academic scene with the gradual conversion of Adolph Wagner into a full historicist. However, Mises was not in favor of a full free banking system at that time in any case and was only partly skeptical of central banks. The rebuttal of the first edition has to be put into the context of the political environment which was supporting a strong central bank to control the economy, eventually leading to the German hyperinflation in 1923. Not surprisingly, the second edition which was published in 1924, had a much better reception. The German monetary theorists who rejected the first edition so thoroughly eventually disappeared from the forefront of monetary theory and Mises's treatise of money lived to see a revival in his second edition.

References

Bodin, Jean. 1581. *Les six livres de la République.* Paris: Chez Jacques du Puys.

Böhm-Bawerk, Eugen von. 1998. *Innsbrucker Vorlesungen über Nationalökonomie: Wiedergabe aufgrund zweier Mitschriften / Eugen von Böhm-Bawerk. Hrsg. von Shigeki Tomo.* Marburg: Metropolis-Verl.

Cantillon, Richard. 1755. *Essai sur le commerce.* London: Chez Fletcher Gyles.

Greaves, Bettina. 1993. *Mises: An Annotated Bibliography: A Comprehensive Listing of Books and Articles by and About Ludwig von Mises.* Irvington-on-Hudson, N.Y.: Foundation for Economic Education.

Helfferich, Karl. 1903. *Das Geld.* 1st ed. Leipzig: C.L. Hirschfeld.

Hülsmann, Jörg Guido. 2007. *Mises: The Last Knight of Liberalism*. Auburn, Ala.: Ludwig von Mises Institute.

———. 2012. "The Early Evolution of Mises's Monetary Thought." In *The Theory of Money and Fiduciary Media: Essays in Celebration of the Centennial*. J.G. Hülsmann, ed. Auburn, Ala.: Ludwig von Mises Institute.

Knies, Carl. 1873. *Geld und Credit. Darlegungen der Grundlehren von dem Gelde und des Credites. 1. Band. Das Geld*. Berlin: Weidmannsche Buchhandlung.

———. 1876. *Geld und Credit. Darlegungen der Grundlehren von dem Gelde und des Credites. 2. Band. Der Credit*. Berlin: Weidmannsche Buchhandlung.

Law, John. 1720. *Considérations sur le numéraire et le commerce*. La Haye: Chez Jean Neaulme.

Menger, Carl. 1892. "On the Origins of Money." *Economic Journal* 2: 239–55.

Mises, Ludwig. [1912] 2007. *Theorie des Geldes und der Umlaufsmittel*. 1st ed. Auburn, Ala.: Ludwig von Mises Institute.

———. 1966. *Human Action: A Treatise on Economics*. 3rd rev. ed. New York: Contemporary Books.

———. 1978. *Notes and Reollections*. Spring Mills, Penn.: Libertarian Press.

———. 1981. *The Theory of Money and Credit*. 5th ed. Indianapolis: Liberty Fund.

———. 2006. *The Causes of the Economic Crisis: And Other Essays Before and After the Great Depression*. Auburn, Ala.: Ludwig von Mises Institute.

Monroe, Arthur. [1923] 2001. *Monetary Theory before Adam Smith*. Ontario: Batoche Books.

Rau, Karl Heinrich. 1868. *Lehrbuch der politischen Ökonomie. Grundsätze der Volkswirthschaftslehre*. 8th ed. Leipzig and Heidelberg: Winter'sche Verlagshandlung.

Roscher, Wilhelm. 1854. *Die Grundlagen der Nationalökonomie: ein Hand- und Lesebuch für Geschäftsmänner und Studierende*. 6th ed. Stuttgart: Verlag der J. G. Cotta'schen Buchhandlung.

Schumpeter, Joseph. 1994. *History of Economic Analysis*. 12th ed. New York: Routledge.

Selgin, George. 1988. *The Theory of Free Banking*. Lanham, Maryland: Rowman & Littlefield Publishers.

Smith, Vera. 1990. *The Rationale of Central Banking and the Free Banking Alternative.* 2nd ed. Indianapolis: Liberty Press.

Streissler, Erich. 1989. *The Influence of German Economics on the Work of Menger and Marshall.* Duke University Program in Political Economy.

Wagner, Adolph. 1857. *Beiträge zur Lehre von den Banken.* Leipzig: Leopold Voss.

Wieser, Friedrich. 1903. "Der Geldwert und seine geschichtlichen Veränderungen. Antrittsvorlesung gehalten am 26. Oktober 1903 an der Wiener Universität." *Zeitschrift für Volkswirtschaft, Sozialpolitik und Verwaltung,* pp. 43–63.

3

MALAVIKA NAIR

Böhm-Bawerk's Influence on Mises's Typology of Money

INTRODUCTION

THIS YEAR MARKS THE HUNDREDTH anniversary of the publication of Mises's (1981) book *The Theory of Money and Credit*. While monetary and financial instruments have evolved and grown in multifarious ways since it was first published, the theoretical concepts and analysis in the book still provide us with tremendous explanatory power over the real world today. This fact in no small way attests to the greatness of the book. This chapter aims at providing a deeper understanding of the background for Mises's typology or classification of money. Mises develops his typology of money in the early chapters of the book and uses it consistently throughout the entirety of its analysis. In particular, this chapter is concerned with Mises's distinction between money and money substitutes. This distinction is crucial since it allows Mises to further distinguish between money certificates (fully backed money substitutes) and fiduciary media (unbacked money substitutes), concepts that lie at the heart of his theory of the business cycle.

This chapter is divided into two sections. The first part of the chapter summarizes a recent debate regarding the nature of token coins and

MALAVIKA NAIR is an assistant professor of economics at the College of Charleston.

their classification between Selgin (2009) and Nair (2011). A close reading of Mises's distinction between money and money substitutes helps clarify issues raised by Selgin (2009) regarding the keeping of full reserves against token coins, thus highlighting the continuing relevance of Mises's typology for doing economic history. The second half of the chapter delves into the connection between Mises's typology and Böhm-Bawerk's work on the distinction between goods and claims to goods. While Mises cites Böhm-Bawerk's work on rights and claims while setting up his own distinction between money and money substitutes, he does not elaborate upon the connection. The aim in this chapter is to fill in that link between Böhm-Bawerk's own theorizing and Mises's classification.

MISES'S TYPOLOGY OF MONEY AND THE STUDY OF ECONOMIC HISTORY

Selgin (2009) puts forth a challenge to those who support 100 percent reserve banking by questioning the practicality of the same reserve requirements as applied to small change. Historical evidence from the private coinage episodes in eighteenth century England shows that as a result of coin shortages, mine owners and private minters started producing their own small denomination coins to pay as wages to workers. Selgin (2009) opines that requiring a rule of 100 percent reserves would have proved to be too costly for the private producers and hence burdensome for the economy. The producers of these small or "token coins" bore the cost of minting the coins as well as guaranteed redemption on demand for standard money to the holders of these coins. Thus, to Selgin (2009), these coins represent market issued fiduciary media, and requiring a 100 percent reserve rule against these tokens would be cumbersome for the minters and producers and hence would slow down growth in the economy.

For not only would the producers have to bear the cost of production and minting but also keep an equivalent amount of standard money always at hand (100 percent reserved), hence making it impractically costly for entrepreneurs to venture into the coin production business. The need for keeping reserves at all arises from the fact that private minters made these coins "redeemable" or "payable on demand" in the standard money of the realm.

Selgin (2009) explains his reasoning with this example:

> Suppose that the cost of one dollar's worth of custom-made token coins, including that of their constituent metal, is 50

cents. Under the 100 percent rule, not only must the retailer bear this cost, but he (or his redemption agent) must keep on hand gold reserves equal to the full nominal value of any tokens placed into circulation. Finally, the retailer must pay any fees charged for keeping his gold under safe storage. Even if, following White (reference suppressed) we suppose that the latter fees are as modest as that charged by modern gold storage services, that is, one percent per annum, it will cost our retailer $1.51 to place just one-dollars' worth of tokens into circulation for one year.

Hence, Selgin (2009) interprets the private coins as fiduciary media or partially backed money substitutes. Since it was too costly for any producer to keep 100 percent reserve backing against them, the only way they could actually circulate was if they were partially backed. In interpreting the small coins as fiduciary media, Selgin is also indirectly interpreting them as money substitutes. For according to Mises's typology of money, only money substitutes (redeemable claims to money) can be either fully backed (money certificates) or partially backed (fiduciary media), money itself cannot be interpreted as being fully or partially backed. This subtle point proves to be crucial for the argument in Nair (2011).

Nair (2011) argues against Selgin's (2009) particular interpretation of the events. Using the careful theoretical distinction that Mises provides of money and money substitutes, Nair (2011) argues for the small coins to be seen as money proper rather than money substitutes. The important distinguishing factor for Mises is that redeemable claims to money that are valued by holders only for being claims and for no other purpose deserve to be included in the category of money substitutes. Mises (1980, p. 65) writes:

> Claims are not goods; they are means of obtaining disposal over goods. This determines their whole nature and economic significance. They themselves are not valued directly, but indirectly; their value is derived from that of the economic goods to which they refer. Two elements are involved in the valuation of a claim: first, the value of the goods to whose possession it gives a right; and, second, the greater or less probability that possession of the goods in question will actually be obtained. Furthermore, if the claim is to come into force only after a period of time, then consideration of this circumstance will constitute a third factor in its valuation.

Hence, Mises states that any other factor present in addition to a claim being valued as a claim must lead us to not classify it as a money substitute. Only those claims that are pure claims to money can thus be money substitutes.

Using this distinction, Nair (2011) uses Selgin's (2008) historical work on the private coinage episodes to show that there is indeed evidence that points to the coins being valued for reasons other than their redeemability. In particular, evidence shows that workers valued the coins for their metallic content as well as for the redemption guarantees that they held. Thus, Nair (2011) reinterprets the private small coins as money proper, commodity money that was stamped with a buy-back guarantee (redemption pledge). Seen in this light, the question of needing to keep 100 percent reserves does not arise, since the goods in question are money proper not money substitutes. If the redemption pledges are buy-back guarantees, the level of "reserves" that the issuer must keep becomes a purely entrepreneurial decision, one that depends upon his expectation of future redemption demand. One example of a piece of evidence provided by Nair (2011) is presented below. It refers to a case in which workers refused to accept "lightweight" coins from their master Wilkinson, hence indicating that workers actually did value the metal content of the coins. Selgin (2008, p. 54) writes:

> Instead, he originally assigned his coins, which bore no express denomination, a value of one penny despite the fact that they only weighed half as much as Druid pennies. . . . Wilkinson's workers and tradesmen where his works were located refused to accept the great ironmaster's tokens at the rate he assigned to them, forcing him to cry them down, as it were, to half their originally intended value. Considered as half pennies, the Willeys were as good as their Druid counterparts, and only at this rating did they first gain widespread acceptance. Wilkinson had inadvertently discovered an important difference between commercial and regal coins: that while the royal mint could take advantage of its copper coins' limited legal tender status to make them as light as it wished, commercial coins could be lightened only subject to the public's approval, without which they could not circulate.

Mises was thus extremely careful when setting up the distinction between money and money substitutes. For if it were true that any good that bore a redemption pledge for an equivalent amount of money could be classified as a money substitute, it would lead us to the seemingly absurd conclusion of having to put goods like cars, milk bottles, and televisions in that category. For all these goods and many others come with a promise to exchange an equal amount of money (typically the purchase price) at any time if the customer is unhappy with the product. However, using Mises's careful distinction, since goods like cars and milk bottles serve ends of their holders independent of the fact that they bear redemption guarantees, leads us to classify them as regular goods that have an added benefit of a buy-back guarantee. The same analysis applies to a money good, just as it is possible for a producer to offer a buy-back guarantee on a car, so it is possible to do the same for a metal coin. The next section turns to the analysis of the connection between Böhm-Bawerk's work on claims and legal rights and Mises's distinction between money and money substitutes.

BÖHM-BAWERK'S DISTINCTION BETWEEN CLAIMS AND GOODS

Mises cites Böhm-Bawerk's (1962) essay titled "Whether legal rights and relationships are economic goods?" in his exposition laying out the differences between money and money substitutes. Specifically, the citation appears in the following passage Mises (1980, p. 52):

> Claims are not goods; they are means of obtaining disposal over goods. This determines their whole nature and economic significance. They themselves are not valued directly, but indirectly; their value is derived from that of the economic goods to which they refer.

The relevant phrase "claims are not goods" refers to Mises's characterization of money substitutes as pure claims to money, deriving their entire significance and value from the underlying money asset. Hence, they are not to be understood as a separate class of goods, in anyway embodying distinct goods-value to their holder other than the value he attaches to the actual money itself. This short phrase forms the entire subject of Böhm-Bawerk's essay. In the essay, Böhm-Bawerk lays out the problem as he sees it of regarding claims as distinct goods and then provides theoretical reasons for why it should not be so. The rest of this chapter lays out his argument while focusing on its most relevant aspects.

Böhm-Bawerk begins by analyzing a question present in the works of Henry Dunning Macleod and John Law. The question goes as follows: If *A* lends to *B* a sum of money for three months, in return for which *B* issues a claim (an IOU) to *A* stating that *A* will once again hold the money in three months' time, has total wealth in the economy doubled as a result of the loan? Writers such as Henry Dunning Macleod and John Law put forth theories claiming that such increases in the amount of credit actually do have the effect of veritably doubling the total wealth in the economy through a doubling of goods. Since *B* now has in his possession the sum of money while *A* has a claim that is worth the amount of money loaned, effectively society is now twice as rich. This account of the matter is wholly unsatisfactory to Böhm-Bawerk however, he writes:

> It will doubtless be generally accepted today that the basic prin-
> ciple of that view is in error. It is all too patent that it involves
> an erroneous duplication in that it posits as a good not only
> the object which is conveyed on credit but also the right or
> legal claim which arises from the transaction. . . . In spite of
> the complete self-assurance with which Macleod's doctrine was
> advanced, it encountered virtually universal and unanimous
> rejection.

Böhm-Bawerk sees the problem stemming from unresolved issues within the theory of goods. The problem, as he sees it, lies in the premise of accepting claims of all sorts as legitimate economic goods. For once they are accepted as legitimate economic goods; Macleod's conclusions about the doubling of wealth as a result of a credit transaction follows naturally. Hence, Böhm-Bawerk turns his attention to the theory of goods.

He provides a brief survey of the development of the theory of goods by highlighting the major periods, culminating in Menger's exposition of what constitutes economic goods. The theory of goods first included only tangible or material goods and only then slowly came to incorporate imma-terial goods such as services. Adam Smith's distinction between "produc-tive" and "unproductive" labor was seen to imply the importance of mate-rial or tangible goods as genuine goods to the exclusion of all intangible services. It was J.B Say who extended the category of wealth or "richesse" to include services provided by physicians, lawyers, actors and the like whose product though not tangible in the physical sense still fulfilled important purposes. Hence, economists came to accept both physical tangible goods as well as intangible services under the rubric of economic goods. It is at this point that Böhm-Bawerk believes economists went too far so as to include also intangible objects such as claims and legal rights as goods.

Using Menger's conditions for the requirements of qualifying as a genuine good, Böhm-Bawerk next stresses the subjective valuation of con-cerned individuals as crucial for economic significance. Things and ser-vices possess value and hence achieve goods status only if they can be used as means to fulfill certain subjective ends for valuing actors. In other words, it is the "renditions of service" provided by tangible and intangible objects that elevates them to true goods status. Hence, it becomes clear how a physical house as well as the services of a doctor both deserve the status of genuine economic goods. Renditions of service however, are not the only crucial factor for Menger. Other conditions are that the thing or service in question must be objectively adapted or able to fulfill a certain end, man must recognize and be aware of such an adaptability, he must also possess the knowledge and skill necessary in order to utilize its capability and last but not least he must have power of disposal over the thing in order for it to be classified as a good. To understand why the last of these conditions is important, Böhm-Bawerk provides the example of how gold mines on the moon or exceedingly attractive building lots on undiscovered islands are not economic goods since no man has the power of disposal over them. To these conditions, Böhm-Bawerk adds another condition of his own, that a good can be a good to a valuing person only if *all* of Menger's preconditions are present at the same time. Even one of the foregoing conditions being absent must disqualify a thing from being classified as an economic good.

Armed with the pre-requisites of goods character, Böhm-Bawerk turns his attention to claims and legal titles to goods. Since claims or even legal titles do not by themselves provide power of disposal over actual goods, but only promises of future power of disposal, they cannot be awarded genuine goods status by themselves. For example, an IOU issued by a borrower is a claim to a future payment and does not afford its holder any power of disposal over the actual money borrowed in the present. That power of disposal lies for the time being with the borrower himself. Hence the money or loan signifies economic goods character for the borrower while it does not do so for the lender. Similarly, a claim or legal title to a house, by itself, does not provide its holder with any power of disposal or ability to satisfy his subjective ends the way the actual house can. Hence legal titles are not to be regarded as distinct goods, independent from the physical house that is the real subject of individuals' ends. In this regard Böhm-Bawerk (1962, p. 59) writes:

> A legally based power of disposal alone without the natural, physical power would be inadequate because factual objective enjoyment of a good cannot be derived from that good without the natural physical control over it. Not until they are combined do legal and physical control constitute that fully assured power

of disposal which is demanded by our economic interests and which, as we have already seen, bestows on the useful things in question their goods-character and makes them for us genuine goods.

Hence, to Böhm-Bawerk, credit transactions do not double the wealth of any society and the claims or IOUs ought not to be regarded as independent sources of wealth.

Yet, Böhm-Bowerk is acutely aware of the fact that in practice and accounting, one does in fact list claims, IOUs, loans, and legal titles to things under the assets category or as wealth. Hence, even though such items are not independent goods in the economic sense of the term, they do end up in the *computation of wealth* for society and its members. This does not present a special problem however; just merely a peculiarity stemming from the fact that man's computation of wealth is always *future oriented* and hence includes those goods that are not yet within his power of disposal. Thus, even though claims to goods enter into the computation of wealth, they do not embody distinct economic goods nature. Once again Böhm-Bawerk (1962, p. 89) provides a powerful example which illustrates his point:

> There are two colonists, A and B, both devoid of wealth, but both industrious and able bodied; they live at a point remote from the rest of their community. A, in consideration of a service done him by B, promises B a sum of money "when his ship comes in." Now this promise has a sound basis in the economic soundness of the debtor; it could as justifiably be accounted by B a part of B's wealth as could the bond of a solvent government or private individual by a European, a man-of-independent-means living on the income from his securities. And thus in that small colonists' "circle" an amount of wealth will have come into existence where there is a complete absence of any factual supply of goods. In this manner, by the method of anticipation of the future, goods and values are taken up into a computation of wealth before they have even begun to exist.

This brings Böhm-Bawerk to put forth a new terminology that is helpful in overcoming this seeming difficulty. He distinguishes between the *materials of wealth* and *forms of wealth*. Materials of wealth are the genuine economic goods that possess within themselves the power to satisfy subjective ends. Forms of wealth on the other hand are embodied in rights and relationships to genuine economic goods, including payment claims and IOUs, that do not provide power of disposal by themselves over genuine goods, yet are included in the computation of wealth owing to practical considerations. Hence, forms of wealth do not deserve independent goods status; they are merely forms or embodiments of the underlying economic good and to award them such status would result in double counting.

To conclude, the following analogy he provides of material objects and their shadows superbly highlights the differences between materials of wealth versus forms of wealth (1962, p. 115):

> In a sense, rights *are* shadows—the juridical shadows which real corporeal goods cast upon the image of our wealth. For where there is no corporeal object to which a right pertains, there can be *no right*. The more substantial and the more distinct these shadows are (and they can be so only because the corporeal thing that casts the shadow stands, substantial and distinct, in close proximity) the more indubitably are they recognizable *as shadows*. The more vague, the more indistinct and the more unrecognizable the corporeal thing is which casts the shadow, the weaker, the more nebulous the shadow consequently is, the more easily is it possible for us to fail to recognize it as a shadow, and the easier it is to consider the shadow to be an independent entity.

CONCLUSION

Mises appears to have advanced Böhm-Bawerk's theory of claims and goods. By differentiating between money and money substitutes, Mises applies Böhm-Bawerk's reasoning to claims that are redeemable at any time, not just claims that are coming due sometime in the future. Money substitutes are hence defined as "absolutely secure and immediately convertible claims to money." Böhm-Bawerk only deals with claims or IOUs issued as a result of explicit loans, claims that may be redeemed for money only at a fixed date in the future. As a result of this, the value of the claim may differ from the underlying money loaned. This is not so in the case of money substitutes. The value of a money substitute (bank note or checking deposit) must always be equal to the actual money to which it lays claim, as a direct result of instant redeemability. Hence, through Böhm-Bawerk's reasoning, money substitutes do not represent goods independent of the underlying money asset and the issuing of money substitutes does not increase the wealth of a society.

Even so, Mises is aware that money is a unique good and that an instantly redeemable claim to money is theoretically capable of performing all the functions of money itself. If people trust the issuer of a bank note or checking deposit well enough, it is possible they utilize the money substitute in multiple exchanges without ever thinking of redeeming it for money proper. In this regard he writes (1980, p. 50):

> A claim to money may be transferred over and over again in an indefinite number of indirect exchanges without the person by whom it is payable ever being called upon to settle it. This is obviously not true as far as other economic goods are concerned, for these are always destined for ultimate consumption.

Yet, he sticks steadfastly to Böhm-Bawerk's thinking in this matter and steers clear of the temptation to include money substitutes in the category of money itself. A claim to money cannot have any value to its issuer if the promise of redemption does not stand good. Herein lays the crux of the matter. Hence, even though money substitutes are capable of performing all the functions of money, they are not to be seen as independent goods that provide value to their holders for any reason other than being redeemable in real money.

It is apt to conclude with the following passage from Mises (1980, p. 53) where he defends his strategy and leaves it ultimately to the readers to judge whether it is the right one.

> It may be pointed out, for instance, that the significance of perfectly secure and liquid claims to money is quite different from that of claims to other economic goods; that whereas a claim on a commodity must sooner or later be liquidated, this is not necessarily true of claims to money. Such claims may pass from hand to hand for indefinite periods and so take the place of money without any attempt being made to liquidate them. It may be pointed out that those who require money will be quite satisfied with such claims as these, and that those who wish to spend money will find that these claims answer their purpose just as well; and that consequently the supply of money-substitutes must be reckoned in with that of money, and the demand for them with the demand for money. It may further be pointed out that whereas it is impossible to satisfy an increase in the demand, say, for bread by issuing more bread-tickets without adding to the actual supply of bread itself, it is perfectly possible to satisfy an increased demand for money by just such a process as this. It may be argued, in brief, that money substitutes have

certain peculiarities of which account is best taken by including them in the concept of money. Without wishing to question the weight of such arguments as these, we shall on grounds of convenience prefer to adopt the narrower formulation of the concept of money, supplementing it with a separate concept of money-substitutes. Whether this is the most advisable course to pursue, whether perhaps some other procedure might not lead to a better understanding of our subject-matter, must be left to the judgement of the reader. To the author it appears that the way chosen is the only way in which the difficult problems of the theory of money can be solved.

REFERENCES

Böhm-Bawerk, Eugen von. 1962. *Whether Legal Rights and Relationships are Economic Goods*. Grove City, Penn.: Libertarian Press.

Nair, Malavika. 2011. "Money or Money Substitutes: Implications of Selgin's Small Change Challenge." *Quarterly Journal of Austrian Economics* 14, no. 2.

Mises, Ludwig von. 1981. *The Theory of Money and Credit*. Indianapolis, Ind.: Liberty Fund.

Selgin, George. 2009. "100 Percent reserve Money: The Small Change Challenge." *Quarterly Journal of Austrian Economics* 12, no. 1: 3–16.

Selgin, George. 2008. *Good Money: Birmingham Button Makers, the Royal Mint, and the Beginnings of Modern Coinage, 1775–1821*. Ann Arbor: University of Michigan Press.

4

Mateusz Machaj

Mises and Value Theory

INTRODUCTION

VALUE THEORIES ARE MURKY WATERS in economic science, because the word "value" denotes several meanings. In some works it aspired to be "Value" with capital "V." The key economic variable, a universal fundamental, is to explain prices, exchanges, equilibrium paths, perhaps even social relations, and unavoidable laws of history. We plan to show Ludwig von Mises did not adhere to this view, yet still believed that the theory of value (without capital "v") plays an important role in economics. The first section briefly describes the importance and definitional nature of the problems of value. The second section recaps the connection between Mises and Čuhel on the theory of value. The third section reviews Mises's criticism in *Theory of Money and Credit* of one of the founders of neoclassicism, Irving Fisher. The fourth section examines the relation between value and price formation. The last section offers concluding comments.

Mises's theory of value, in a nutshell, can be found in his first major work, *The Theory of Money and Credit* ([1912] 1981, pp. 51–60). It was further developed and then shaped into full form in *Epistemological Problems of Economics* ([1933] 2003, pp. 155–93), where he carefully filled in the

MATEUSZ MACHAJ is an assistant professor at the Institute of Economic Sciences at the Univesity of Wroclaw.

gaps and corrected errors by Carl Menger and Eugen von Böhm-Bawerk. The final phase of Mises's work was *Human Action* (1966, pp. 327ff.; or its German forerunner *Nationalökonomie*) where he fully integrated his theory of value with the pricing process.[1] Here we deal with the roots of his theory, which can be found in his treatise on money.

THE ROLE OF VALUE IN ECONOMIC THEORY

"Value" is one of the most used, and overused terms, in economic reasoning, despite the fact that it is an indirectly observable quantity. Its role has been highlighted by many economic writers, and much discussed before the modern era. "Value" in many of its versions served as an explanation for market prices. In a way it could be called a "driving force of the market." Even though economic writers differed in their understanding of "Value," and in their definition of "Value," all the theories had one thing in common: "Value" was supposed to serve as a market price explanator.

Obviously all prices depend upon each other. The price of iron influences the price of the hammer produced from it. The price of the hammer has an indirect influence on prices of other consumption goods, because there is interdependency in the area of market prices. At the same time there is uncertain dynamics of market prices. They change continually and so the entrepreneurs constantly make attempts to adjust them. There is nothing eternal in prices. One feature of prices is: no price is everlasting and perfectly foreseeable. Every single price will be altered in the future in one way or another.

Endless and indeterminate movements of all prices could lead one to conclude that no economic science is possible. If prices are modified in an unpredictable manner, how can one say anything universal about them? Any discipline, which aspires to be "scientific," has to recognize and describe "universal" principles governing particular phenomena. Without such general rules, which identify "universalities" in various differing cases, the discipline cannot be scientific. Only by discovering common and repeatable threads, which on the surface are poles apart, can one build science. Therefore, if prices are to be subjected to scientific analysis, and if economics is to be a science, there has to be a universal force driving the

---

1   On the role of value theory in Mises's evolution, see Hülsmann 2003. On *Human Action* as the final stage in Mises's thought, see Salerno 1999.

prices. Even if they move in different directions and at different speeds, they have to share some universal qualities.

In the classical era the determining "force" of prices was Value. Value as an ultimate factor explains the mechanisms of price movements. Various theories of value share this commonality. Austrians, Marxists, Neoclassicals, and the Classics, they all believed that their value theory has to be a starting point for economic theory, since Value needed to be a vital *explanatus* for otherwise chaotic monetary prices. Henceforth not surprisingly, if clashing schools of thought offered radically dissimilar explanations for monetary prices, their theories of value had to radically differ. Additionally, because Value is not a directly visible or an obviously noticeable quantity, even their definitions of Value had to differ. Most of the debates about "Value" could be settled by understanding this simple fact.

A worthy example is shown by the disagreement between Condillac and Jean Baptiste Say. Say sincerely believed that in commerce two commodities of equal value were exchanged between the parties. Condillac, on the other hand, argued that trade encompasses a value increase, since both parties expect to benefit from the transaction. For Say this could not be the case, because it would need to involve a form of fraud. If there were no equivalence of values, a seller would play a rogue, and a buyer would become a fool (Say [1880] 2001, p. 28). "Value" once created had to circulate in economic relations, and had to be a setting force behind the market. In the case of physics and conservation laws, in market exchanges equal value is given for equal value. For the modern reader, a close investigation of the Condillac-Say clash ends with the conclusion there was no real controversy between them. It was all about the chosen definition and understanding of what Value really meant. Condillac understood that people exchange goods, because they expect a subjective profit, hence some value increase must happen. For Say on the other hand, trade was an activity in which both sides are on an equal level. Agreed price sets a market equivalence of values. If wine is traded for 10 silver coins, then both the seller and the buyer agree that wine is "worth" 10 silver coins. In modern times people constantly use the word "worth" in this way (even the Austrians do so). Both Say and Condillac may well be right. One reflection does not undermine the other; only their definitions collide.

St. Clair commented on the debate:

> Lord, how these economists do misunderstand one another! Condillac does not suggest that the wine merchant is a rogue and the customer a fool; he does not suggest that the merchant

> robs either the consumer or the producer; his doctrine is that
> products increase in utility and value by being transferred from
> the producer to the consumer. (quoted in Rothbard 1995, p. 20)

Probably the best example of definitional war could be shown by controversies over Marx's labor theory of value. Marx wanted to offer an analytical inquiry on how market prices are driven by the amount of ("necessary") labor hours. His main goal was vindication of the "proletariat" and downplay of the positive roles of capitalists. A natural fruit of this approach was the "labor theory of value." Its main proposition was that working hours are a true source of Value, which in turn determines how market prices are formed in the long run (Marx 1887, pp. 29–32).

The market prices of goods do not correspond to the amount of labor time necessary to produce those goods. Karl Marx was well aware of this undeniable fact and throughout the first and the third volumes of *Das Kapital* he tried to address this issue. The notion of discrepancy could not be contested, since all empirical observations demonstrated that profits of capitalists have, in the long run, a tendency to equalize. If labor is a true source for market prices, then labor-intensive sectors should reap higher profits than capital-intensive sectors. In reality no such difference between the sectors exists. The return on capital has a tendency to be equalized throughout the economy without any form of discrimination against more industrialized firms. The great Eugen von Böhm-Bawerk (in *Karl Marx and the Close of His System*) was one of many who brilliantly pointed out the shortcomings of Marx's proposals in trying to solve this puzzle.

The labor theory of value could not therefore aspire to be an elucidation for market prices. Apparently labor efforts (however understood) could not explain long-run dynamics of economic systems. Prices were the result of something else. Labor power and effort were not the philosopher's gemstone that Marx was looking for. Labor could not be "Value" in the universal sense. It had to be something other than the ultimate market price determinant. Marxian sociologists went to great lengths to reinterpret Marx and to argue what his "Value" *may* really, really mean. Whatever it does mean, it is no longer an explanation for prices.

On this definitional quarrel Alexander Gray comments:

> In particular, there is no one to tell us what Marx thought he
> meant by "value." And indeed, what all these conjectures reveal
> is somewhat astounding, and, one would like to think, unique.
> Capital is, in one sense, a three-volume treatise, expounding a
> theory of value and its manifold applications. Yet Marx never

> condescends to say what he means by "value," which accord-
> ingly is what anyone cares to make it as he follows the unfolding
> scroll from 1867 to 1894. (Gray 1946, p. 321)

Why bother with the notion of Value at all? Why not simply study market prices? Philip Mirowski (1989) seems to have provided the answer: because Value to economics in the nineteenth century was like Energy to physics. In physics, Energy was a fundamental variable, ultimate potential for physical movements or emissions. In economics, Value was a fundamental variable, which after creation circulated in the economic system. This Value-centered view is especially noticeable in the works of Quesnay and his followers, Marx included.

Through history economic discipline aspired to become an "exact" science, hence theorists searched for a general factor, which would describe dynamics of the market system. "Value" became this factor. Just as in physics a law of conservation of energy represents our double entry bookkeeping way of thinking, so it was supposed to be with Value in economics. Unfortunately it could not be objectively recognized as something directly measurable and separate from market prices. Despite tremendous efforts, Value was not a real tool establishing exact and eternal economic laws; it was only a smokescreen to do so. It is no surprise then, that against the mainstream of economic thought an alternative tradition flourished. A tradition, started by Turgot and Condillac, could be seen as a deconstructivist approach. From the mainstream perspective followers of the tradition could be seen as denialists of Value (Mirowski 1989, p. 163).

SUBJECTIVISM AND ČUHELIAN DECONSTRUCTIVISM

The tradition was subjectivism. The essence of subjectivism is that value (or something matching that: utility) is "subjective"; that it depends on personal preferences, which cannot be reduced to any objective and generally valid denominator. Value and utility are matters of individual likings and decisions. Sometimes it is said that values cannot be "interpersonally compared." This seems to be an overstatement. One can compare anything to anything else in any way. The point is that values and utilities cannot be measured in universal units as "objectively" as physical quantities.

This subjectivist tradition evolved in two stages. The first stage recognized the role of personal and individual wants in determining use-values of goods and services. "Value" was to be nothing inherent in the thing being possessed. Nothing which could be inferred from labor hours, or from kilograms of natural resources. It purely resulted from a connection between man's mind and the owned good. Carl Menger was one of the economists who contributed to this by emphasizing the relationship between needs and resources (Menger [1871] 1994, p. 116).

Yet the more radical was the second stage, which grew as a natural conclusion of the previous one. If values are subjective, then it follows that objective measurement is impossible. They cannot be subjected to a truly "scientific" analysis (as in natural sciences). This radical conclusion was put forth by the important Czech economist Franz Čuhel (1907). His insights could be portrayed as deconstructivist for most value theories, for they attacked any price theory which was grounded in utility or value measurements. Čuhel's sweeping investigation was immediately accepted by Mises as fundamentally sound, despite the fact that value measurements were used by the Austrian School representatives (Mises 1981, p. 54). Although Menger did not use them, his framework did not preclude such possibility. Böhm-Bawerk used utility measurements frequently in his writings. He was even criticized by Čuhel himself and admitted that he only believed in soft measurability of sensations.[2]

Values cannot be subjected to measurements, but they can be compared to each other. One can assign importance to any single good according to subjective preference rankings. Those rankings can change and goods can change places as actors decide whether one allocation is better than the other. Mises, following Čuhel, argued that value always consists of comparisons (Mises 1981, p. 52; Mises 2003, p. 158). Value exists because of a triangular relationship between possessed good and at least two (or more) possible goals that can be achieved by employment of the good (Hülsmann 2003, pp. xxxvi–xxxvii).[3] In other words, value comes from choice. It is necessarily linked to the notion of opportunity costs. Some things are more or less valuable, because people allocating them have different perceptions and ideas of how to satisfy their subjectively chosen aims. No inherent Value with capital "V" exists.

---

2   In his own words "I never maintained the practical realizability of exact, objectively correct measurement of such intensities, but merely the existence of processes that subjectively estimate, no matter how erroneously and imprecisely, the intensity of feelings" (Böhm-Bawerk 1959, vol. III, p. 136).

3   In neoclassical analysis utility is also a triangular phenomenon (indifference curves are used in order to compare at least two options).

Expected consequences of this inference are both radical and potentially disruptive for policy recommendations. Values cannot be quantitatively estimated for any person, therefore there is nothing to be compared
between the individuals. No auxiliary process can be performed in order to
arrive at a meaningful concept of "total social welfare." Or perhaps it is better to state that in terms of economic science anything named "total social
welfare" has to be subjective for any observer, and any person is free to con-
struct his own such index (for example, according to his ethical beliefs).

At times many economists following Mises and Čuhel use phrases
which are contrary to the idea of non-measurability. Even Mises himself
makes such mistakes. He claimed the following:

> . . . with an unchanged supply, the marginal utility of several
> units taken together is not equal to the marginal utility of one
> unit multiplied by the number of units, but necessarily greater
> than this product. The value of two units is greater than, but not
> twice as great as, the value of unit. (Mises 1981, p. 57)

It is understandable what the message is. Yet the formulation is in clear
contrast to the statements a few pages earlier that "subjective use-value is
not susceptible of any kind of measurement" (p. 55). If no measurement is
possible, we cannot perform an act of "multiplication," since there is nothing to be multiplied. Multiplication is only possible with cardinal numbers,
and those ones were excluded from utility analysis by Čuhel's revolutionary ideas. Obviously Mises did not have in mind a mathematical operation. What he probably meant was the following. Suppose that an actor can
satisfy 5 needs with his 5 units of bread. If he satisfies all of them, then he
will gain more than if he satisfies only the fifth need, but *somehow* does it
five times. This is the meaning hidden in Mises's formulation of "multiplying." Nevertheless it stands in opposition to his radically realistic notion of
marginal analysis in the praxeological background. The reason for this is
that an individual cannot satisfy the same need five times. Our "somehow"
in italics in the previous sentence leads to a praxeological oxymoron.

Mises in his article on the impossibility of socialism referred similarly
to the idea of utility multiplication:

> Marginal utility does not posit any unit of value, since it is obvi-
> ous that the value of two units of a given stock is necessarily
> greater than, but less than double, the value of a single unit.
> (Mises 1990, p. 11)

Again, if as Mises correctly states, utility does not posit any value unit, then it is not possible to "double" something which does not exist.[4] What Mises in fact means is that the second satisfied need is less important than the first need, because by the act of choice it is less urgent. The proposition of decreasing marginal utility can be phrased this way. One does not have to refer to any mathematical tools. No multiplications, doubles, or any forms of additions are needed. They do not enrich the analysis significantly, but instead encounter the danger of smuggling in mistakes.

As in the case of *Theory of Money and Credit*, the quote about doubling in no way represents a conscious violation of the rule that utility is subjective and ordinal. Mises did stay faithful to Čuhelian insights. He was not open to possibilities of value measurements. Imprecise statements about values are merely linguistic inconveniences, not truly formal mistakes, undermining the strength of praxeological formulations. Utility comes with human conscious choice that merely establishes grades and scales, not cardinal numbers.

The consequences of Čuhelian deconstructivism go well beyond welfare analysis, and are particularly important for the theory of "imputation." This theory explains how the prices of producers' goods are formed in the market by consumer preferences, or morphologically speaking, how prices are "imputed" from consumer goods to production goods.

In some cases a physical metaphor in economics went so far as to argue that values or utilities represent potential backward imputation. Such a perspective can be inferred from another Austrian thinker, Friedrich von Wieser (1891, pp. 112–13). Just as energy was transformed within the physical world, utility was to change forms and move within the economic sphere. Wieser was among thinkers who believed in such utility imputation (see also Ekelund 1992, pp. 181–82). Mises accepted the contrary idea.

---

4   Mises proves that when he attacks Schumpeter, who made a statement that he could get satisfaction from consumption a "thousand times as great" as some other satisfaction. To which Mises replied ". . . a few words must be devoted to Schumpeter's attempt to set up as a unit the satisfaction resulting from the consumption of a given quantity of commodities and to express other satisfactions as multiplies of this unit. . . . Is there really anybody on earth who is capable of adumbrating such mental images or pronouncing such judgments? Is there any sort of economic activity that is actually dependent on the making of such decisions? Obviously not" (Mises 1981, p. 58). Qualitatively there is no difference between multiplying two and a thousand times. Mises criticized Schumpeter partially because of the scale (1000 is certainly bigger than 2), but his criticism is qualitative and general. Therefore it applies also to multiplications smaller than 1000.

Utility cannot be measured, and consequently there is no auxiliary process, which could describe the market in terms of utility imputations (or Value imputations).[5] The traditional approach to utility could only lead to conclusions that some choices for subjective reasons are favored over the others. Yet the importance of various needs could only be presented in the framework of existing monetary prices.[6]

As a result, Mises's theory of value is very short and requires little explanation. It is only a minor part of his work, as it was a short chapter in the *Theory of Money and Credit*. There is no reason to write a lengthy book about it, as there would be lots of reasons to write such a book about the neoclassical theory of value. More important in the realm of Mises's value theory is continuity of Čuhelian deconstructivism: it is more vital to use the proper theory of value to spot errors in the works of other thinkers and demonstrate why their sophisticated value theories are incorrect. Sophisticated and complicated theories of values are at most times a sign that something is wrong.

MISES VERSUS FISHER ON VALUE

One of the proponents of a sophisticated and complicated value theory was Irving Fisher. His publication *Mathematical Investigations in the Theory of Value and Prices* is a major building block in neoclassical theory. The book contains the essence of modern consumer theory (1892, pp. 25, 70–75). Mises devotes only a few pages in his chapter on value to Fisher's insights, and only in order to defend Čuhel's achievements.

Fisher admitted that there are problems with utility (or value) measurements. According to Fisher one can avoid this difficulty by inventing some form of "util." A util is when two subjective utilities are compared to a third utility (Fisher 1892, pp. 14–16).[7] Let us assume we are interested in

---

5   Wieser stated that direct measurement of utilities is impossible, but still believed it could be done in some indirect way by comparing goods against each other (Wieser 1927, p. 124). He was similar to Fisher in this belief. For Fisher see below.

6   As stated earlier, Böhm-Bawerk also used utility measurements in his approach. Rothbard's great project in *Man, Economy, and State* was integration of Böhm-Bawerk's production theory with Mises's theory of money. Rothbard replaced utility numbers with money prices and consequently added money market considerations to Böhm-Bawerk's illustration. In effect he created an amazing textbook which integrated Austrian theory of production with Mises's monetary writings.

7   Wieser thought so, too.

arriving at the ratio of utility between the 100th loaf of bread and the 150th loaf. Fisher advises us to contrast them with (say) the utility of B gallons of oil. He further assumes that utility of the 100th unit of bread is equal to the utility of the last unit of B, and the utility of the 150th unit of bread is equal to B/2 unit of gallons of oil:

Utility of 100th loaf = utility of B; and Utility of 150th loaf = utility of B/2.

From these two equations Fisher infers that he is capable of arriving at such a ratio that the 100th loaf is two times more useful than the 150th loaf. Thus:

Utility of 100th loaf : utility of 150th loaf = utility of B : utility of B/2 = 2.

Now the same process can be repeated for all the goods, and the *util* is thus provided (Fisher 1892, p. 18). In this way even though utilities are subjective and ordinal, utilities of various goods can be expressed in terms of each other. One good provides the standard. Every other good's utility is expressed as a multiplication or a division of this basic good.

The mistake in this thinking is quite clear, the final result, "2," is a *non sequitur*. There is no reason to believe that the supply of B gives two times more utility than half of that supply,[8] unless one is implicitly assuming such a thing. But if that is the case, then Fisher did not arrive at a proper ratio of utilities from ordinal rankings. Instead he assumed that there is some form of measurement that can be performed. Mises recognized this and commented: "Just as justifiably as he assumes that the utility of B is equal to twice the utility of B/2, he might have assumed straightaway that the utility of the 150th loaf is two-thirds of that of the 100th" (Mises 1981, p. 56).

These considerations, even if relevant, appear as minor details. Evidently there are other theoretical issues of much greater importance. Something more here is at stake: consumer theory. The above is not merely a quarrel over nonexistence (or half-existence) of a *util*. Fisher was interested in arriving at ratios in terms of continuous functions, which could be used to describe consumer preferences, and choices. He was noticeably interested in mimicking physics, since he recognized that concepts such as equilibrium, stability, elasticity, expansion, inflation, force, level, distribution, reaction, and friction are directly inspired by the science of mechanics. At

---

8   Actually there is a simple omission in Fisher's book. Suddenly "utility of B : utility of B/2" is changed into "B : B/2." Certainly the latter is "2," but the former is not.

the same time he was dissatisfied with the fact that hardly anybody went far enough in the mechanical metaphor to describe economic equilibrium (Fisher 1892, p. 24).

Fisher's book is filled with continuous functions, derivates, and water cisterns. Cisterns particularly match his liking. Just as "water seeks its own level" a similar case is with the economic world, where "marginal utilities" are equalized (Fisher 1892, p. 28). Under such economic equilibrium something additional happens. With arrival at proportionality of all marginal utilities, the continuous ratio becomes the scale of prices of goods and services (ibid., p. 37). The economic system has therefore some regular tendencies to move toward equilibrium, even though it is never achieved, because preferences change (Fisher 1892, p. 21). The device works as a physical system:

> This corresponds to the mechanical equilibrium of a particle the condition of which is that the component force along all perpendicular axes should be equal and opposite . . .
>
> The above is completely analogous to the laws of composition and resolution of forces.
>
> If the marginal utilities and disutilities are thus in equilibrium "gain" must be a maximum. This is the mere application of the calculus and corresponds exactly to the physical application of the calculus which shows that at equilibrium the balancing of forces implies that energy is at maximum. Now energy is force times space, just as gain is marginal utilities times commodity. (Fisher 1892, p. 85)

If Mirowski's thesis could be verified, Fisher's work would amount to perfect evidence for it. The whole purpose of Fisher's neoclassical theory (taught in a modified form in modern microeconomics) is to portray economic systems as mostly systems independent of human will and activity (human action is either nonexistent or negligible). Each individual becomes a particle positioned by external forces which determine various equilibriums.

Mises opposed such methods of calculus, which dealt with infinitesimal quantities, stating two arguments. According to the first argument, infinitesimals are inapplicable to economic problems, because an individual valuing goods and services has to reckon them significantly important enough to value them. If things become infinitesimal, they cannot affect any judgment, and cannot explain actor's behavior. They are too insignificant. The second argument is that even assuming away the previous problem, "it is obviously impossible to find the proportion between two finite marginal utilities by equating them with two infinitesimal marginal utilities" (Mises 1981, p. 57).

The second argument is either invalid, or a repetition of the first one. Mathematically it is certainly possible to find a ratio between two finite numbers, which will be equal to a ratio between two infinitesimal numbers. On the level of pure arithmetic there are no obstacles to that. What Mises meant was an economic content in the two ratios, but then this second argument is the same as the first one: infinitesimals cannot be related in a praxeologically meaningful way to real human activities.

The discrepancies between Mises and Fisher are traced back to differences between Menger and Walras. Even though it is being said that both of these thinkers dealt with "marginal" utilities and units, they have radically different things in mind. For Walras "marginal" meant negligible, infinitesimal quantity, which cannot affect economic decisions.[9] For Menger on the other hand "marginal" unit was the last relevant unit affecting people's decisions. It was not a matter of differences in language, but a clear difference in content (Jaffé 1976, p. 521).

Fisher was well aware of criticism raised against calculus in economics by Mises (and others). Infinitesimals are not under consideration by economic actors. Yet similar objections could be raised for other applications of calculus. After all, the whole world is discontinuous. Even water that appears to be fluid and full of a infinite number of particles, consists as a finite number of particles which are physically extended. They are not infinitely small (Fisher 1892, p. 22). Despite that, continuous models of physical reality have useful applications in the real world analysis. Similarly, neoclassical functions of consumer behavior can be good approximations of economic "forces." In discussing the limitations of sciences Fisher even admits that indifference curves are based on a flawed idea, since two utilities can never be equal (ibid.; henceforth the notion of indifference is anti-empirical).

Mises did not incorporate a response to this counterargument. Almost no phenomenon is infinitesimal, but physical models use such mental constructs. Why should this be justified in the natural sciences, and not in the social sciences? The answer: physical models do work, and have direct application to the real world. Functional relationships in physics are operational

---

9   Actually in Walras there was no difference between marginal and submarginal, since the two are equal (Stigler 1937, p. 241). It does not matter whether we add or subtract a "marginal" unit.

(Jabłecki 2007, pp. 14–17). This is not the case with neoclassical models of consumer behavior. Certainly physical models abstract from various insignificant factors, as economic models desperately try to do the same. In the neoclassical framework the abstraction goes far because it omits significant factors, such as the relevance of marginal unit for satisfaction of a particular need, or the individual's power to influence valuations and market prices. Blaug (1986, p. 297) considered this to be a minor detail, whereas Stigler (1946, p. 81) thought that continuity is indispensible for economics. As Menger and his followers demonstrate both of those statements are questionable.

Neoclassicism also fails, because it narrows the world down to two goods, as if the consumer could only choose between them. Fisher argues that the model could be built with n axes representing n amount of goods, for example, 50 axes for 50 goods (Fisher 1892, p. 79). Matters become clearly much more complicated, but "this space is simply the 'economic world' in which we live" (ibid., p. 80). Fisher was not aware of the fact that mapping all possible preferences (and solving the maximization criteria) for 50 goods would take a supercomputer over three years. The fastest possible human being (limited only by the speed of neurons) would take longer than the universe's age.[10] And yet, a normal human being is capable of going into the store and choosing the proper item for himself in a much shorter amount of time. Without using continuous indifference curves (he does not even act "*as if*" he was using those curves). This is well described by laying praxeological foundations (with concepts of demonstrated preference, understanding, ranking, appraisement, categorization, etc.), not by mathematical economics (simplified functions).

Fisher is right that infinitesimals are used in physics despite the finite nature of all molecules, but this is not an argument for using them in economics. It is astonishing that such unrealistic consumer theory, as the neoclassical theory, survived wide criticism and is taught in almost all modern courses, despite the fact that it cannot help in explaining real consumer behavior.

Mises's rejection of the functional approach to value theory paved the way for his much bigger contribution. This is already indicated in the chapter on value where we learn that value "can rightly be spoken of only with regard to specific acts of appraisal" (Mises 1981, p. 60). Value exists in relation to

---

10   The author learned this example from Professor Steve Keen's lecture (2012).

appraisal, and there is no value without the process of valuation performed by particular individuals. It also leads, *contra* Fisher, to the conclusion that prices are consciously formed by acts of appraisals, which cannot be reduced to any functional relation-mimicking physics.

MONETARY CALCULATION AND VALUATION

If values are formed deliberately and are not transferring any inherent economic energies in the economic system, then prices are formed deliberately, too, and they do not act as water levels in connected cisterns. As acts of valuation are done subjectively by actors, so is the case with pricing of goods and services. Yet even though the act of pricing is done "subjectively," it is done in objective numbers, i.e., monetary prices. The "subjective" nature of prices comes from the fact that there is no objective source for monetary prices disconnected from the subject's mind.[11]

In physics gravitational forces can be reduced to other variables and constants. This cannot be done with prices, because they are purposeful decisions. Will is the ultimate cause. That is why prices have their objective and subjective features. They are objective, because they are expressed in terms of an accepted medium of exchange (therefore can be compared *vis-à-vis* each other). They are subjective, because their cause is always an act of individual (and unique) choice.

Mises rejected the idea of units of utility, and consequently utility imputation. He still thought that the market process can be described in terms of imputation, but monetary imputation, not value imputation. Values are subjective and cannot be imputed in numerical terms. Only money units can be imputed in such a way (from consumer prices to factor prices), and in a subjective manner:

> . . . in monetary theory, as in every other branch of economic investigation, it will never be possible to determine the quantitative importance of the separate factors. Examination of the influence exerted by the separate determinants of prices will never reach the stage of being able to undertake numerical imputation among the different factors. All determinants of prices have their effect only through the medium of the subjective estimates of

11   Even Hayek fell for this narrative approach to prices and believed that prices are approximations of some primary "production functions" and "values" (e.g., Hayek 1982, p. 137).

individuals; and the extent to which any given factor influences these subjective estimates can never be predicted. (Mises 1981, p. 218)

Fisher's neoclassical approach allowed for the possibility of value imputation. Fisher acknowledged that mathematical theory of pricing cannot, of course, predict prices, and that no mathematical economist ever tried to do this (Fisher 1982, p. 118). At least that was the case when he wrote the book. This gap was later filled by the writings of socialist economists working in the Walrasian tradition. "Calculus" and imputation could be performed theoretically by the proper usage of carefully selected equations. Even Oskar Lange (1967), in his later years, believed that his market socialism model could be disposed of in favor of supercomputers which can solve all the necessary equations to impute values directly from consumer preferences.

Later in his life Mises opposed such attempts to impute value: any such value imputation is based on past conditions. Economic activity is directed toward the future. Current conditions are related to current disequilibrium, therefore they cannot directly help us to establish future equilibrium conditions (Mises 1966, pp. 712–13). Since all actions require speculation about the future state of affairs, the only way to "solve" the problem is to constantly speculate about future prices. Or to be precise, the problem can never be "solved," because nobody knows for sure the future state of the markets. Entrepreneurs just attempt to "solve" the problem by constantly speculating.

Here lies one of the misfortunes of economic language. To describe entrepreneurial activity Mises used the term "economic calculation." This term can be very misleading. Why? Because for some it may mean a form of calculus, computation, or accounting (as it did for Mises's opponents). "Calculation," on the other hand, means an appraisal and subjective monetary valuation in terms of cardinal units as was later explained in *Human Action*:

> Cost accounting is therefore not an arithmetical process which can be established and examined by an indifferent umpire. It does not operate with uniquely determined magnitudes which can be found out in an objective way. Its essential items are the result of an understanding of future conditions, necessarily always colored by the entrepreneur's opinion about the future state of the market. (Mises 1966, p. 349)

The successful undertaking of a particular economic project does not become a question of arithmetic. Surely one can add "costs" together and subtract them later from summed up revenues. The challenge of proper economic "calculation" is different. When the entrepreneur is "calculating" he is not operating on existing cardinal numbers. The objective cardinal numbers he has at hand are of two categories: (1) past market prices, which represent past conditions, and, (2) current price offers, which represent current market expectations about the future. This objective information is not sufficient to perform economic "calculation." The biggest part of that activity is speculation and guessing about the future state of the market.

To use a neoclassical analogy, consider the famous rule that marginal revenue has to equal marginal cost (MR=MC), so profits are maximized (or losses minimized). Assuming away many problematic features of this analysis, one essential issue remains. To some extent the curve of MC can be drawn on the graph, because it is based on current price offers; the curve of MR cannot, because it is a derivate of future consumer choices, therefore it cannot be drawn. Rather than that, many various possible MR curves could be drawn, and each of them with assigned case probabilities (immeasurable probabilities). The true graph of neoclassical maximization criteria would therefore have to present only MC curve and a blurred cloud of many possible MR scenarios. That would be a much truer illustration of the problems that entrepreneurs face constantly.

In many of his writings Mises acknowledged the fact that economic calculation is possible, because of cardinal numbers and double entry bookkeeping. The main benefit to society is that those numbers are being used by private entrepreneurs. Numbers are not sufficient and in themselves mean nothing. The whole point of economic calculation is not "calculation" at all. It is the possibility of finding the common denominator for entrepreneurial competition in the realms of private-property arrangements.

This is the only way to "socially appraise" (and value) capital goods, in order to employ them to the best extent possible. No other successful process for this aim has been provided by any theory of value or Value. Despite many undertakings to do so. The alternate choice is abolition of social appraisement process in favor of dictatorship and political decrees (even if they are based on the form of cost accounting).

Reaching this conclusion, Mises combined Čuhelian deconstructivism in the field of value theory with his constructive and positive approach to price analysis. He also achieved something else: economic science is possible without Value. Ironically he was attacked by Lange for that and almost got accused of being a *Schmollerite*! Lange (1936, p. 55) was surprised to learn Mises thought that successful appraisements could be tied to specific institutional set ups (private property). After all, if one believed in aprioristic and universal economic science, one also had to believe that there is universally penetrating phenomenon of Value (natural, or inherent, or whatever . . .), which could be recognized under any institutional set up, couldn't it?[12]

Not really. And that is the whole point of Mises's pathbreaking contribution.

CONCLUSION

It may be tempting to reduce the clash between Austrian theory of value and neoclassical theory value to narrower technical issues of measurement of utility (or quasi-measurement). As the discussion between Mises and Fisher proves, it is definitely more. It is about how the behavior of economic agents is being portrayed and described in detail. The main goal of value theories was to be a proper basis for the explanation of monetary prices in the real world. To Mises the ultimate given in value theory is human choice (a source for value), that is, the potential for deliberate value judgments and for the appraisal of things we call "goods." To manifest this full potential a specific legal framework (private-property arrangements) is necessary. In the neoclassical framework "value" (not choice) seems to be something ultimately given, independent of institutional arrangements, which can be imputed throughout the economic system. Henceforth, we see that the essence of the socialist calculation debate can be hidden somewhere in the realm of value disputes.

LITERATURE

Blaug, Mark. 1986. *Economic Theory in Retrospect*. Cambridge: Cambridge University Press.

Böhm-Bawerk, Eugen von. 1959. *Capital and Interest*. Three Volumes. South Holland, Ill.: Libertarian Press.

Böhm-Bawerk, Eugen von. 1962a. "Karl Marx and the Close of his System." In *Shorter Classics*. South Holland, Ill.: Libertarian Press.

---

12   As Wieser (1891, pp. 119–20) thought.

Čuhel, Franz. 1907. *Zur Lehre von den Bedurfnissen*. Innsbruck: Wagner.

Ekelund, Robert. 1992. "Power and Utility: the Normative Economics of Friedrich von Wieser." In *Eugen von Böhm-Bawerk (1851–1914) and Friedrich von Wieser (1851–1914)*, Blaug, ed. An Elgar Reference Collection.

Fisher, Irving. 1892. *Mathematical Investigations in the Theory of Value and Prices*. Transactions of the Connecticut Academy. Vol. IX (July).

Gray, Alexander. 1946. *Socialist Tradition. Moses to Lenin*. London: The Ballantyne Press.

Hayek, Friedrich August von. 1982. "Two Pages of Fiction." *Economic Affairs* (April).

Hülsmann, Jörg Guido. 2003. "Introduction to the Third Edition: From Value Theory to Praxeology." In Mises 2003.

Jabłecki, Juliusz. 2007. "Continuum in Economics. On the Significance of the Realism of Assumptions in Economic Theory." Working paper, available at: http://www2.gcc.edu/dept/econ/ASSC/Papers2007/infinities_in_economics.pdf

Jaffé, William. 1976. "Menger, Jevons, Walras De-homogenized." *Economic Inquiry* XIV (December).

Keen, Steve. 2012. *Lecture from "Advanced Political Lectures."* Video available at: http://www.youtube.com/watch?v=ont_HLhIXQQ&list=PL303D52E352C0B7D9&index=6&feature=plpp_video

Lange, Oscar. 1936. "On the Economic Theory of Socialism: Part One." *The Review of Economic Studies* 4, no. 1.

Lange, Oscar. [1967] 1994. "Computer and the Market." In *Economic Theory and Market Socialism*. Tadeusz Kowalik, ed. Aldershot: Edward Elgar.

Marx, Karl. 1887. *Capital. A Critique of Political Economy. Volume I*. Online Edition. http://www.marxists.org/archive/marx/works/download/pdf/Capital-Volume-I.pdf

Menger, Carl. [1871] 1994. *Principles of Economics*. New York: New York University Press.

Mirowski, Philip. 1989. *More Heat than Light: Economics as Social Physics, Physics as Nature's Economics*. Cambridge: Cambridge University Press.

Mises, Ludwig von. [1949] 1966. *Human Action. A Treatise on Economics*. Chicago: Contemporary Books.

Mises, Ludwig von. [1912] 1981. *Theory of Money and Credit*. Indianapolis: LibertyClassics.

Mises Ludwig von. [1920] 1990. *Economic Calculation in the Socialist Commonwealth*. Auburn, Ala.: Ludwig von Mises Institute.

Mises, Ludwig von. [1933] 2003. *Epistemological Problems of Economics*. Auburn Ala.: Ludwig von Mises Institute.

Rothbard, Murray N. 1995. *Classical Economics: An Austrian Perspective on the History of Economic Thought*. Brookfield, Vt.: Edward Elgar.

Rothbard, Murray N. 2004. *Man, Economy, and State with Power and Market*. Auburn, Ala.: Ludwig von Mises Institute.

Salerno, Joseph. 1999. "The Place of Mises's *Human Action* in the Development of Modern Economic Thought." *Quarterly Journal of Austrian Economics* 2, no. 1.

Say, Jean Baptiste. [1880] 2001. *A Treatise on Political Economy; or the Production, Distribution, and Consumption of Wealth*. Kitchener: Batoche Books.

Stigler, George J. 1937. "The Economics of Carl Menger." *Journal of Political Economy* 45, no. 2.

Stigler, George J. 1946. *Production and Distribution Theories: The Formative Period*. New York: Macmillan.

Wieser, Friedrich. 1891. "The Austrian School and the Theory of Value." *The Economic Journal* 1, no. 1.

Wieser, Friedrich 1927. *Social Economics*. New York: Adelphi.

5

JOSEPH T. SALERNO

Ludwig von Mises as Currency School Free Banker

1. INTRODUCTION

THE CENTENNIAL OF THE PUBLICATION of the first German edition of Ludwig von Mises's *The Theory of Money and Credit* (1981)[1] offers an excellent opportunity to address a long-standing controversy that has beset Austrian monetary economics for the past three decades. The controversy revolves around the question of whether Ludwig von Mises favored 100-percent gold reserve banking imposed by law or free banking based on gold as the ideal monetary system. There exists sufficient ambivalence in Mises's writings on this point to provide support to the claims of the proponents of both positions. I suggest that this debate is fundamentally misfocused and conflates means and ends. As I argue in this paper, Mises advocated free banking as the most suitable means for achieving the goal of completely suppressing the issue of additional fiduciary media, that is, bank notes and deposits unbacked by gold. In effect, Mises looked forward to a marginal 100-percent reserve ratio on the issue of bank notes and deposits as the outcome of the operation of a free banking regime.

JOSEPH T. SALERNO is professor of economics at the Lubin School of Business, Pace University, New York.

1   The English edition was translated from the second German edition published in 1924 (Mises 1924).

The framing of the debate in terms of Mises's stance on free banking versus 100-percent reserves obscures a much deeper issue dividing Austrians that pertains to Mises's theoretical perspective on the relationship between money and the banking system. Throughout his body of work on monetary economics, Mises steadfastly proclaimed his adherence to the basic doctrines of the mid-nineteenth century British Currency School and, in fact, upheld its "currency principle" as the essence of his own conception of sound money. According to the currency principle, the ideal monetary system was one in which the supply of money, comprising circulating gold plus bank notes and deposits redeemable in gold, should be made to behave exactly like the supply of a pure gold money. Lately, some members of the modern Free Banking School, as it has come to be called, have denied that Mises was a follower of the Currency School or that his vision of sound money was defined by the currency principle. The free bankers base their claim on the fact that Mises was a vigorous proponent of free banking. In contrast, they point out, most prominent members of the original Currency School opposed free banking and favored a central bank as the means to enforce the currency principle on the banking system. Thus, the free bankers conclude that Mises, as a free banker, must have supported their "monetary equilibrium" principle, according to which the supply of money should adjust to offset fluctuations in the demand for money and would automatically do so under a free banking regime.

The argument of this paper is twofold. First, I contend that Mises was indeed an admirer and follower of the Currency School, and that he deliberately attempted to revise and improve its doctrine and apply it to contemporary conditions. Second, I review Mises's strong support for a free banking system and argue that it was based on his view that free banking would result in the almost total suppression of the issue of new fiduciary media and thus produce a money supply that functioned exactly as a "purely metallic currency" (in the terminology of the Currency School). Thus the reason for Mises's preference for a free banking system contrasts sharply with the view of modern free bankers, who predict that the regime of free banking would lead to continual expansion of fiduciary media to the point where gold would be completely expelled from circulation among the public, remaining in the monetary system as merely an interbank clearing asset (White and Selgin 1989). With the dawning of this "mature" stage of free banking the supply of money would therefore be essentially identical to the supply of bank notes and deposits, which the banking system would then continually and automatically adjust so as to prevent departures from monetary equilibrium induced by "money demand shocks."

In arguing that Mises was a proponent of both the currency principle *and* free banking and that he viewed the latter as the indispensable means to achieve governance of the money supply by the former, I seek to reframe the debate on Mises's monetary views in a more meaningful way. My hope is that such a reframing will enhance mutual understanding between Austrians of the neo-Currency School and those who sympathize with the modern free banking movement.[2]

The paper is divided into eight sections. The next section introduces the British Currency School and describes the currency principle. Section 3 deals with the modern Free Banking School, describing the monetary equilibrium principle which it upholds as the norm for optimal monetary policy. Throughout his career Mises held the analytical achievements of the Currency School in high esteem while recognizing and correcting the two crucial errors that vitiated the implementation of its policy in Great Britain in the mid-nineteenth century. This claim is documented in section 4. In section 5, Mises's defense of free banking is closely scrutinized, and it is demonstrated that Mises advocated free banking as the most effective means of eliminating the issue of fiduciary media and implementing the currency principle as the regulator of the money supply. Section 6 is devoted to Mises's analysis of the market mechanisms that would suppress credit expansion and fractional reserve banking under a regime of free banking. Mises's strong opposition to the issue of bank notes—whether fully backed by cash reserves or not—which has been completely ignored in the literature is noted in section 7. Some concluding thoughts are presented in section 8.

2. SOUND MONEY AND THE CURRENCY PRINCIPLE

Ludwig von Mises is generally considered the foremost proponent of "sound money" in the twentieth century.[3] Mises, however, did not develop

---

2   This does not imply that all free bankers are Austrians. For example, Lawrence H. White does consider himself an Austrian, while George Selgin rejects the designation as a description of his own views.

3   Mises's emphatic and unwavering support for the classical gold standard even led Joseph Schumpeter (1968, p. 288, n. 3), an otherwise perceptive doctrinal scholar, to mistake Mises's "practical metallism" for "theoretical metallism," although Schumpeter (1968,

this principle himself, although he undoubtedly perfected it. He learned about sound money from a group of British bankers, merchants, and economists who wrote during the mid-nineteenth century. This group came to be famously known as the "Currency School." Its most prominent members were Robert Torrens, George Norman (Lord Overstone), and William Lloyd.[4]

According to the principle of sound money developed by the Currency School—which was then called the "currency principle"—a nation's money supply, defined to include gold coin and bullion plus bank notes immediately redeemable in gold, should be made to behave precisely as a "purely metallic currency." In practice, this meant: first, that changes in the supply of bank notes must be rigidly linked with changes in the supply of gold; and second, that, therefore *additional* bank notes could be issued only in exchange for deposits of gold of equal denomination. Thus, under an international gold standard, variations in an individual nation's money supply would be determined strictly by the net inflow or outflow of gold through the balance of payments or, if the nation possessed gold mines, also by production of new gold. Issue of additional "fiduciary media," i.e., notes and deposits unbacked by gold, thus would be totally suppressed. Consequently, prices would move in lockstep with world prices, and cyclical fluctuations in prices and output and the accompanying balance of payments crises would be abolished. Secular variations in the purchasing power of money would, of course, still occur but would depend solely on market forces affecting global gold supply and demand.

While the currency principle may seem like an alien doctrine in today's world, it is actually the principle that governs changes in the money supplies of different regions that use the same currency, such as the individual states composing the United States. Assuming that the overall supply of dollars is fixed, the supply of dollars in California, for example, would increase if the residents of the state become more productive and prosperous and demand more dollars by increasing their net exports of products to the rest

---

p. 289) himself points out that the two positions "need not go together." In fact, Mises (1981, pp. 518–24) explicitly rejected "theoretical metallism." See also the tribute to Mises as the foremost twentieth-century advocate of the gold standard by the Ordo-liberal economist Wilhelm Röpke (1969).

4   For a detailed treatment of the historical background and doctrine of the Currency School and of its famous controversy with the rival British "Banking School," see: Fetter 1978, pp. 165–97; Viner pp. 218–89; Wu 129–41; Daugherty 1942 and 1943; and Rothbard 1995, pp. 225–74 and the extensive literature on the topic that he cites in his bibliographical essay (pp. 489–91).

of the country in exchange for dollars. California's money supply may also change if another state, say Michigan, suffers a decline in its industry and income and requires fewer dollars to finance its reduced transactions. In this case Michigan residents would exchange their redundant dollars for more imported products from California and the other states. Michigan's money supply would therefore decline and California's increase. Thus, where institutional arrangements permit the currency principle to operate, it ensures that market forces alone determine the overall quantity and value of money as well as the distribution of the money supply among different nations, states, regions, towns and even families participating in the market economy. [5]

In addition, when variations in the money supply of a region or country that is part of a larger currency area is determined exclusively according to the currency principle, the change in the money supply is automatic and *exactly* equal to the inflow or outflow of money through the balance of payments. For example if Michigan experiences a balance of payments deficit of $1 billion there is no need for its banks to increase the interest rate and contract the money supply by a multiple of this amount, because the money outflow reflects a decrease in market demand for money and is strictly self-limiting. It is not caused by a bank-induced expansion of the money supply accompanying a deliberate cheap money policy, so there is no tendency for an artificial boom followed by a gold outflow and deflationary depression, as there is when fixed exchange rates exist between fractionally backed currencies issued by independent national central banks. Rather the causation is the other way: the contraction in Michigan's money supply is the natural response to a fall in output and income that results from lagging productivity or a shift in U.S. demand away from Michigan's products.

Likewise, the influx of $1 billion dollars into a prospering state like California does not necessitate a decline in interest rates and an induced expansion of the state's money supply beyond the amount of the original balance of payments surplus. That is, there is no "imported inflation" that creates an unsustainable boom followed by a bust in California. People have become relatively wealthier in California and demand to hold more cash to make additional transactions. Just as the market adjusts prices and

---

5   Even if the Fed were concurrently increasing the money supply, this interregional distribution process driven by demand side forces would continue to operate, although its effect would be diluted to a lesser or greater extent by the injections of new dollars into the economy via open market operations.

incomes to reflect the new pattern of supplies and demands, it also, as part of the same process, redistributes the supply of dollars from Michigan to California—or more accurately, transfers dollar notes and bank deposits, one for one, from specific households in Michigan whose incomes and purchases are shrinking to those in California whose incomes and purchases are expanding. Moreover, assuming that intertemporal consumption preferences have not changed in either state, there is no reason to assume that inverse changes in interest rates (up in Michigan, down in California) must accompany the movement of money from one state to the other. [6]

Members of the Currency School thus believed that an international gold standard undisturbed by the issue of fiduciary media would operate in much the same way as a homogeneous domestic currency. They formulated the currency principle, which would force the actual mixed currency of gold and convertible bank notes to behave as a pure metallic currency, as a means of abolishing the political and banking influence on the supply, value, and distribution of money.

By the time Mises published his treatise on *The Theory of Money and Credit* in 1912, the Currency School and its doctrines had long been discredited and were almost completely ignored by his fellow monetary economists. [7] One of Mises's primary aims in this treatise and in his later writings on money was to revive the currency principle and to demonstrate its truth and practical application by giving it a firm foundation in modern monetary theory. Mises also developed the Currency School's seminal theory of boom and bust into what came to be famously known as the "Austrian theory of the business cycle." In an important sense, Mises was the founder of the neo-Currency School, which includes many contemporary Austrians. [8]

---

6   For a detailed analysis of the differences between the balance-of-payments adjustment process operating under an internationally homogeneous, "pure" commodity currency and that operating under "mixed currencies" organized along national lines and including notes and deposits issued by fractional-reserve banks, see Hayek 2008, pp. 337–66. Hayek was especially emphatic in pointing out that movements of interest rates and "secondary" bank-induced inflation and deflation of the money supply were not characteristics of the balance-of-payments adjustment mechanism under a homogeneous international currency.

7   As Hülsmann (2007, p. 207) points out, the English translation of the title is significantly misleading; a more correct translation of the title of the German edition is *The Theory of Money and Fiduciary Media*.

8   On the neo-Currency School, see Salerno 2010, pp. 497–533.

3. THE FREE BANKING SCHOOL AND THE MONETARY EQUILIBRIUM PRINCIPLE

According to the principle of monetary equilibrium, the supply of money must be continually expanded and contracted by the banking system in order to accommodate any changes in the demand to hold money.[9] Following New Keynesian and other modern macroeconomists, modern free bankers use the term "aggregate demand shock" to characterize a situation in which people voluntarily choose to increase or decrease their holding of cash by spending less or more of their income on goods and services.[10] Let me focus on the case in which individuals demand to hold more cash and therefore reduce their overall demand for goods and services below what it was in the previous time period. In this case, "monetary equilibrium" would be disturbed and the demand for money would suddenly exceed the supply of money. If nothing else changed, total spending would fall and there would be a corresponding decline in the scale of prices and incomes. As a result, the value of money would tend to rise but, since prices are not perfectly flexible and are subject to "nominal rigidities," the appreciation would occur slowly and excess demand for money would persist.[11] According to the free bankers, this protracted increase in the value of money would be calamitous, causing unemployment and recession. Thus they advocate that any "excess demand" for money be offset by an equal

---

9   The "monetary equilibrium principle" is a policy norm derived from the monetary disequilibrium theory of macroeconomic fluctuations. Of modern proponents of the theory, Leland Yeager is the most prominent. See Yeager 1997 for his seminal contributions to the theory. Selgin 1988 and Horwitz 2000 attempt to weave parts of the theory into a theoretical foundation for free-banking policy conclusions. For a comprehensive exposition of monetary disequilibrium theory, see Rabin 2004.

10   See for example Selgin 1997, pp. 35–40.

11   This description of the monetary adjustment process will not be contested here. Suffice it to say that it is based on the New Keynesian theory of nominal price rigidities. This Keynesian approach ignores the step-by-step monetary adjustment process articulated by Mises (1998, pp. 337–43a) and Hayek (2008, pp. 351–59). In the Mises-Hayek analysis the protracted adjustment of the value of money to a change of its demand or supply has nothing to do with price rigidities (although it does not assume that prices are perfectly flexible) and is not marked by persistent shortages or surpluses of money. Rather it is a result of the fact that a change of the demand for money does not affect all goods' markets at once. For a detailed analysis of the Mises-Hayek monetary adjustment process that focuses on its methodological suppositions and constructs see Salerno 2010 (pp. 93–103); also see Davidson 2012.

increase in the supply of money. This would preserve monetary equilibrium, maintain the aggregate flow of spending constant, and prevent the purchasing power of money from increasing.

In modern macroeconomic jargon, the monetary equilibrium principle is nothing but a "nominal income target," although free bankers prefer that the target be achieved by a competitive banking system rather than Fed policy. However, until a free banking regime is implemented, free bankers propose that the Fed target a constant nominal income under the rubric of the "productivity norm."[12] It is not surprising, then, that most modern free bankers, including Larry White and George Selgin, favored one or both of the Fed's "quantitative easing" programs.[13] They believed that these unconventional expansionary monetary policies were necessary to offset the fall in consumption and investment expenditures caused by people's demand for greater cash balances to deal with the heightened uncertainty and risks associated with the financial crisis.

The Free Banking School, as its name implies, prefers an institutional arrangement in which a central bank does not exist, and unregulated private fractional-reserve banks compete with one another in issuing bank notes and deposits convertible into gold (or silver). In the free bankers' view, a financial system of this kind would automatically ensure that the money supply always varies in a way that neutralizes money demand shocks and preserves monetary equilibrium. Competitive fractional-reserve banks

---

12   According to Selgin (1997 p. 34), "Formally, the argument here is essentially the same one found in many recent proposals and assessments of nominal income (GNP or GDP) targeting." Nominal income targeting was first proposed in the 1970s by orthodox Keynesian monetary economist Benjamin Friedman (1975; 1977). It later piqued the interest of New Classical and New Keynesian economists. See, for example, Hall and Mankiw 1994.

13   On free bankers endorsing the Fed's quantitative easing programs, see Bagus 2011; Harrison 2011; and Clougherty 2011. None of the free bankers who advocates a nominal income target for the Fed has seriously addressed the question of precisely how "monetary equilibrium" produced spontaneously by a competitive banking industry could be achieved as a policy objective in the institutional context of a central banking regime. While sympathetic to free banking, Butos (2012) is extremely dubious that the competitive outcome of a free banking system can be legitimately translated into a policy norm for a monopolistic central bank to follow, because the latter operates under radically different institutional conditions from those framing a competitive banking system. In particular, the specific knowledge, incentives, and access to economic calculation that powerfully shape the behavior of free banks are for the most part unavailable to central monetary planners.

would accomplish this by issuing just the right amount of new notes and checking deposits to fully satisfy the increased demand for money. Since these additional notes and deposits would be unbacked by gold, the monetary equilibrium principle, in sharp contrast to the currency principle, implies that the issuing of fiduciary media is not only economically benign but critically necessary to the proper functioning of a market economy. Thus, by characterizing Mises as a monetary equilibrium theorist, the free bankers attribute this position to him also.[14]

4. MISES AND THE CURRENCY SCHOOL

Throughout his writings, Mises recognized and lauded the lasting contributions of the Currency School to monetary and business cycle theory and policy. In his first complete presentation of the Austrian theory of the business cycle, published in 1928, Mises (2006, pp. 101, 128) stated:

> Of all the theories of the trade cycle, only one has achieved and retained the rank of a fully-developed economic doctrine. That is the theory advanced by the Currency School, the theory which traces the cause of changes in business conditions to the phenomenon of circulation credit [that is, the issue of fiduciary media].[15] . . . Every advance toward explaining business fluctuations to date is due to the Currency School. We are also indebted to this School alone for the ideas responsible for policies aimed at eliminating business fluctuations.

In his earlier treatise, *The Theory of Money and Credit*, Mises credited the Currency School as the main inspiration for the development of

---

14   At the outset of the modern free banking movement, some free bankers maintained that Mises either rejected the monetary equilibrium doctrine altogether (Selgin 1988, pp. 61–62) or had an "ambiguous relationship" with it (Horwitz 2000, pp. 77–78). Others, most notably Larry White (1992, p. 522), argued that Mises viewed the issuance of fiduciary media as "a natural and desirable development in a free society." Partly in response to the present author (2010b and 2010c), both Horwitz (2010a and 2010b) and Selgin (2010) later abandoned their earlier views and more or less defended White's interpretation of Mises as a monetary equilibrium theorist.

15   Mises (1981, pp. 296–300) distinguished between "circulation credit," which is produced by bank credit expansion, and "commodity credit," which involves the bank purely as an intermediary facilitating the transfer of credit from savers to investors. Fritz Machlup (pp. 224, n. 4, 231–32) used the terms "created credit" and "transfer credit" respectively to more clearly denote these two different types of credit.

modern business cycle theory. There Mises (1981, pp. 282–83) commented that the Currency School "propounded a theory, complete in itself, of the value of money and the influence of the granting of credit on the prices of commodities and the rate of interest." While noting that the school's doctrines were based on the erroneous value theory of the classical school and a mechanical version of the quantity theory, Mises yet maintained, "Within its own sphere of investigation," the Currency School "was extremely successful." "This fact," he observed, "deserves grateful recognition from those who, coming after it, build upon the foundations it laid."

Mises, however, did not allow his admiration for the Currency School to blind him to the two key errors it committed. In fact he was eager to expose and correct these errors because they were the reason that the currency principle failed on the policy level when it was implemented in Great Britain by the Bank Act of 1844, more popularly known as Peel's Act.[16] The first error was an analytical one. Unlike the opposing and inflationist Banking School, the Currency School failed to recognize that bank deposits were perfectly interchangeable with bank notes in exchange and, as such, were part of the money supply. Consequently, the currency principle's rigid restriction on the creation of fiduciary media was tragically weakened because Peel's Act applied only to bank notes, while banks were left free to create new, unbacked demand deposits *ad libitum*.

The second, practical flaw in the program of the Currency School was its insistence that power to enforce the currency principle be centralized in a bank with monopolistic legal privileges—in this case the Bank of England. This quasi-central bank, in which most of the system's gold reserves were held, would then have the means and the power to enforce the currency principle for the banking system as a whole. In effect, the authors of Peel's Act unwittingly created the template for the modern inflationary and crisis-prone monetary and financial system. In the modern system, a central bank such as the Fed is legally empowered to issue its own fiat notes and deposits which serve as the reserves for the commercial banks. The commercial banks, in turn, are permitted to create fiduciary media by pyramiding their own bank deposits on these Fed liabilities.

The economic effects of Peel's Act were predictable: the British economy experienced recurring episodes of inflation which culminated in the crises and depressions of 1847, 1857, 1866, and 1890. During each of these

---

16   For a discussion of Peel's Act and its aftermath, see Fetter 1978 (pp. 194–224) and Rothbard 1995 (pp. 248–66).

crises, Peel's Act was suspended. Before the end of the nineteenth century, the currency principle and the entire Currency School program had fallen into disrepute. Of course with each "emergency" suspension of Peel's Act by the British government, moral hazard became more pervasive and deeply ingrained in the British financial system, making future crises and suspensions even more likely.

Mises, nevertheless, believed that the currency principle embodied a seminal truth about the prevention of cyclical fluctuations and argued that its fatal neglect of bank deposits was easily corrected. Thus Mises (1981, pp. 407–08) brushed aside the critics of the Currency School who sought to discredit its core doctrine by referring to its confusion over the nature of bank deposits:

> [T]he doctrine of the Currency School does not stand or fall by
> its views on the nature of checks and deposits. It is enough to
> correct it on this one point—to take its propositions concerning
> the issue of notes and apply them also to the opening of deposit
> accounts—to silence the censures of those who adhere to the
> banking principle.

When Mises wrote the foregoing words in the second edition of his *Theory of Money and Credit* in 1924, he still had reservations concerning the Currency School's aim of eliminating all further issue of fiduciary media. Mises (1981, p. 408) referred to this goal as a "heroic remedy with a vengeance" and pointed out that it would mean "renouncing all attendant advantages" of stabilizing the purchasing power of money. And yet, he wound up strongly affirming the currency principle at the very end of the book. Mises (1981, p. 447) did so in a long passage that he quoted from the first (German) edition of his book:

> [I]t is obvious that the only way of eliminating human [i.e.,
> political and banking] influence on the credit system is to sup-
> press all further issue of fiduciary media. The basic conception
> of Peel's Act ought to be restated and more completely imple-
> mented . . . by including the issue of credit in the form of bank
> balances within the legislative prohibition.

Mises (1981, p. 448) continued, "It would be a mistake to assume that the modern organization of exchange is bound to continue to exist. It carries within itself the germ of its own destruction; *the development of the fiduciary medium must necessarily lead to its breakdown*"[17] (emphases added).

By 1928, however, there was no longer ambivalence: Mises had become a hard-line proponent of the currency principle. Near the end of his 1928 monograph on business cycle policy Mises (2006, p. 150) proposed a revised Currency School program to abolish cyclical fluctuations:

> The most important prerequisite of any cyclical policy, no mat-
> ter how modest its goal may be, is to renounce every attempt
> to reduce the interest rate, by means of banking policy, below
> the rate which develops on the market. That means a return to
> the theory of the Currency School, which sought to suppress
> all future expansion of circulation credit and thus all further
> creation of fiduciary media. However, this does not mean a
> return to the old Currency School program, the application of
> which was limited to banknotes. Rather it means the introduc-
> tion of a new program based on the old Currency School theory,
> but expanded in the light of the present state of knowledge to
> include fiduciary media issued in the form of bank deposits.
>
> The banks would be obliged at all times to maintain metal-
> lic backing for all notes—except for the sum of those outstand-
> ing which are not now covered by metal—equal to the total
> sum of the notes issued and bank deposits opened. That would
> mean a complete reorganization of central bank legislation. The
> banks of issue would have to return to the principles of Peel's
> Bank Act, but with the provisions expanded to cover also bank
> balances subject to check. . . . By this act alone, cyclical policy
> would be directed in earnest toward the elimination of crises.

And Mises (2006, p. 150) intended this policy to be applied not only to central banks but also to commercial banks that issued demand deposits. Thus he asserted: "In those countries where checking accounts at private commercial banks play an important role in trade—notably the United

---

17   Compare Mises's Currency School view of fiduciary media with the conditions White and Selgin envision under a "mature free-banking system" in which fiduciary media might completely displace the money commodity not only from circulation but from all monetary use. According to White and Selgin (1989, p. 235): "[A]t the limit, if inter-clear-ing-house settlements were made entirely with other assets [than gold] . . . and if the public were completely weaned from holding commodity money, the active demand for the old-fashioned money commodity would be wholly nonmonetary." Of course, in such a scenario it would be absurd to speak of fiduciary media at all; all bank note and deposit "liabilities" would be privately issued fiat money.

States and England—the same obligation must be exacted from those banks also."

The evidence is clear, then, that even before the Great Depression, Mises championed the cause of the Currency School and viewed the suppression of the issue of fiduciary media as the main prerequisite for the abolition of cyclical fluctuations. But if this is indeed the case, then how is it that Mises could advocate free banking, an institutional arrangement that legally permits the creation of fiduciary media by competitive private banks completely unregulated by legislation or a monopoly central bank?

5. FREE BANKING: TOWARD THE ELIMINATION OF FIDUCIARY MEDIA

As I noted above, modern free bankers point to Mises's defense of free banking as strong evidence that Mises favored the issue of fiduciary media as a means of adapting the money supply to continual fluctuations in the demand for money. This monetary equilibrium principle was advocated, in much cruder form, by the British Banking School, whose members opposed the currency principle that changes in the money supply should be rigidly governed by changes in the supply of gold.[18] Mises (1981, p. 406) explicitly rejected the banking principle, which he described as "the contrivance of an adjustment between the stock of money and the demand for money."

Mises first discussed free banking in the final chapter of the *Theory of Money and Credit*, which dealt with the problems of credit. Mises began the chapter by noting that, since the time of the Currency School, governments in Europe and the United States had recognized the need to restrict banks in their issue of fiduciary media in order to avoid economic crises. Following Great Britain, these governments adopted various legislative policies to restrict the issue of unbacked bank notes. After surveying these policies, Mises (1981, p. 410) concluded: "None of these many systems of limiting the note circulation has proved [sic] ultimately capable of interposing an

---

18   The Banking School appealed to the inane "principle of reflux" as the mechanism maintaining continuous equality between money supply and money demand. For a description and critique of the principle, see: Viner 1937, pp. 234–38; Wu 2007, pp. 135–38; and Rothbard 1995, p. 244. While modern free bankers reject the principle of reflux, they argue that, under free banking, the "adverse clearing mechanism," which will be discussed below, would prevent persistent departures from monetary equilibrium.

insurmountable obstacle in the way of further creation of fiduciary media." Mises (1981, p. 411) then pointed out that the only effective limit to the issue of fiduciary media was the failure of central banks to cooperate or collude in expanding credit: "So long as the banks do not come to an agreement among themselves, concerning the extension of credit, the circulation of fiduciary media can indeed be increased slowly, but it cannot be increased in a sweeping fashion."[19] It was on this insight that Mises built his case for free banking as the most effective method of eliminating the further issue of fiduciary media.

Although he did not go on to make a sustained argument for free banking in *The Theory of Money and Credit*, Mises (1981, p. 435) did suggest that the experience of government regulation of banking "has been incomparably more unfavorable than experience of uncontrolled private enterprise." More important for my purposes here, Mises had formulated the problem that is to be solved by free banking as one of suppressing further creation of unbacked bank notes and deposits.

Mises discussed the topic of free banking in a little more detail in 1928 in his monograph on business cycle policy. There he made three key points regarding the limitation on the expansion of fiduciary media under free banking. To begin with, individual banks would learn to exercise extreme caution in issuing fiduciary media because no legal tender laws would exist to force their acceptance among the public. The public, on their part, eventually would learn the difference between trustworthy and inferior brands of notes and deposits. Thus, if a bank engaged in imprudent and reckless credit expansion, its brand of notes and deposits would suffer a loss of reputation and ejection from circulation. They would no longer qualify as money substitutes that are generally acceptable at face value in exchange. In the course of time, according to Mises (2006, p. 124), "solvent and highly respected banks would emerge . . . whose fiduciary media would enjoy the general confidence essential for money-substitute quality." This would be the case because the managers of these banks "would have learned from past experiences."

This brings us to his second point. Mises (2006, p. 125) contended that once a solid core of banking institutions had gained widespread trust and become well-established, the less responsible banks would be compelled to "follow suit" and become more prudent in issuing and lending their own

---

19   Outside the Anglo-American countries, central banks were the main issuers of fiduciary media at the time that Mises wrote this.

brands of fiduciary media. Any bank that issued its notes and deposits in relative excess compared to the most conservative institutions would soon find itself with a negative balance on interbank clearings. That is, the volume of its own notes presented to it for payment by other banks would exceed in nominal value the volume of notes issued by other banks that it had accumulated and was presenting for exchange. It would have to make up its deficit on note clearing by paying in gold and this would result in a loss of cash reserves and a deteriorating reputation. If the irresponsible bank did not promptly restrict its emission of fiduciary media, losses of reserves would become chronic and provoke a loss of confidence and a bank run by its own depositors and note-holders.

Mises concluded his discussion by making his third, and most important, point: the overall evolution of the free banking system tended toward the ideal of the Currency School. Wrote Mises (2006, p. 125):

> In the course of the development of a banking system with fiduciary media, crises could not have been avoided. However, as soon as bankers recognized the dangers of expanding circulation credit, they would have done their utmost, in their own interests, to avoid the crisis. They would then have taken the only course leading to their goal: the extreme restraint in the issue of fiduciary media.

6. Limits on Fiduciary Media: Adverse Clearing versus Brand Extinction

It was not until *Human Action*, first published in 1949, however that Mises fully spelled out the market mechanisms by which free banking would come to impose rigid limits on the emission of fiduciary media. Significantly, Mises (1998, pp. 431–45) discussed free banking in the section entitled: "The Limitation of the Issuance of Fiduciary Media." Throughout this section, Mises emphatically reiterated his view that free banking is the most effective monetary arrangement for stifling the creation of fiduciary media. For example, Mises wrote (1998, p. 439): "The establishment of free banking was never seriously considered precisely because it would have been too efficient in restricting credit expansion." Mises (1998, p. 439, n. 17) then continued in a footnote to this passage:

> The notion of "normal" credit expansion is absurd. Issuance of additional fiduciary media, no matter what its quantity may be,

always sets in motion those changes in the price structure the description of which is the task of the theory of the trade cycle.

In another passage, Mises (1998, p. 440) argued:

> Free banking is the only method available for the prevention of the dangers inherent in credit expansion. It would . . . not hinder a slow credit expansion, kept within very narrow limits, on the part of cautious banks which provide the public with all information required about their financial status. But under free banking it would have been impossible for credit expansion with all its inevitable consequences to have developed into a regular . . . feature of the economic system. Only free banking would have rendered the market economy secure against crises and depressions.

I quote one last statement from Mises (1998, pp. 437–38):

> If the governments had never interfered for the benefit of special banks, if they had never released some banks from the obligation, incumbent upon all individuals and firms in the market economy, to settle their liabilities in full compliance with the terms of the contract, no bank problem would have come into being. The limits which are drawn to credit expansion would have worked effectively. Considerations of its own solvency would have forced every bank to cautious restraint in issuing fiduciary media. Those banks which would not have observed these indispensable rules would have gone bankrupt, and the public, warned through damage, would have become doubly suspicious and reserved.

Any reasonable interpretation of the foregoing passages and their context suggests that Mises held firmly to two positions. First, the creation of fiduciary media *in any amount* precipitates a cyclical boom and bust. Second, free banking is an effective remedy for business cycles precisely because its operation would result in rigid limitation, if not complete suppression, of bank credit expansion.[20]

---

20   In fact, in an early work, Selgin (1988, p. 62) seemed to attribute precisely this second position to Mises when he wrote: "Indeed, Mises's support for free banking is based in part on his agreement with Cernuschi, who . . . believed that freedom of note issue would automatically lead to 100 percent banking." Cernuschi was a nineteenth-century French economist who, as we shall see below, was favorably cited by Mises.

But what was the origin and nature of the limits on credit expansion that Mises referred to in his writings on free banking? Mises's answer to this question was that the forces restricting the creation of fiduciary media are inherent in the very concept of a "money substitute." Mises (1998, p. 429) defined money substitutes as "claims to definite sums of money, against a debtor about whose solvency and willingness to pay there does not prevail the slightest doubt." Besides "undoubted solvency and willingness to pay on the part of the debtor," these claims need to embody the additional quality of "daily maturity" in order to qualify as a money substitute. That is, the issuer must be ready and willing to redeem the claim for money on demand and without charge to the holder. Finally, even if a claim embodied both these qualities, it would render the same services as money to an individual *only if* all the parties that he exchanged with were "perfectly familiar" with the qualities of the claim.

Historically most money substitutes have taken the form of bank notes and demand deposits, which may or may not have been fully backed by actual money. Mises was only concerned with limiting the issue of fiduciary media, that is, the fraction of money substitutes that is unbacked by cash or "money proper."[21] For it is only the issue of unbacked bank notes and deposits that expand the money supply, diminish the purchasing power of money, and artificially reduce the loan rate of interest below the natural rate determined by the market. The emission of notes and deposits fully backed by money proper, which are called "money certificates," have no effect on market phenomena. They merely replace the actual gold in circulation with a title to an equal amount of gold now stashed in bank vaults, leaving the money supply unchanged.

In analyzing the potential limits on the creation of fiduciary media, Mises (1998, pp. 432–36) presented two scenarios. In the first scenario, there is a single bank whose clientele includes all households and firms either in the entire world or in a single isolated country. Even in this case

---

21   Mises (1998, pp. 429–31) distinguished between "money proper" and "money in the broader sense." The supply of money proper referred to cash, e.g., gold coin and bullion under the gold standard or Fed-issued currency notes and reserve deposits under the current fiat-dollar standard. The supply of money in the broader sense comprised money proper plus that fraction of money substitutes unbacked by cash, i.e., fiduciary media in the form of commercial bank notes and deposits. In current jargon these two monetary aggregates are roughly equivalent to base money and M1, respectively. However, Mises's crucial emphasis on bank notes and deposits as money substitutes is missing in the modern literature.

there is a broad limit that is imposed by the necessity of maintaining the public's confidence in the bank, because a loss of confidence would precipitate mass redemption of bank notes and deposit withdrawals. The bank thus must avoid any action that arouses suspicion among the public. How far it can extend its issue of fiduciary media and expand the money supply, especially if its clients start to expect price inflation to accelerate, depends on unpredictable psychological conditions.

In Mises's second scenario there co-exists a "multiplicity of independent banks," but the banks do not collude in expanding credit. It is further assumed for simplicity that no firm or household is a client of more than one bank. Now suppose that one bank alone creates additional fiduciary media, while all other banks refrain from expansion. The borrowers who receive the loans from this bank are now in a position to bid for additional goods and services on the market. This increase in demand causes prices to rise and goods to be redistributed to the clients of the expanding bank, forcing clients of all other banks to cut back on their purchases. As a result, a balance of payments deficit develops for the clients of the expanding bank as they now must make greater aggregate payments to non-clients than they receive from them. However, the deficit cannot be paid for with the newly issued money substitutes from the expanding bank *because they are not recognized and treated as such by the non-clients.* That is, the notes and deposits of the expanding banks do not function as money substitutes in these transactions. Payments to non-clients thus must take the form of actual money. Consequently, the expanding bank is forced to redeem its bank notes and checkable deposits in cash for its clients, which causes its gold reserves to diminish. The bank must eventually cease its credit expansion or run the risk that its reserves will plummet to zero, at which point it would be unable to redeem the remainder of its money substitutes outstanding and become insolvent.

Modern free bankers stress this "principle of adverse clearing" as the primary, if not the only, mechanism by which the issue of fiduciary media by an individual free bank is limited (Selgin, 1988, pp. 40–47; White 2010). For Mises, however, long before the reserves of the relatively expansionary bank have been exhausted by the adverse balance of payments faced by its clients, another factor would operate to extinguish the character of its notes and deposits as money substitutes. This factor is a loss of confidence on the part of its *own* clients in the bank's ability to discharge its debts in a timely manner. This loss of "good will" would cause its clientele to shrink rapidly. This means that fewer and fewer people would be willing to accept and hold the bank's notes and deposits as money substitutes. Even if everyone were still willing to accept the discredited notes in loans and payments rather than forego the loan or sale, they would all rush to spend them as soon as possible rather than hold them in their cash balances. The notes would thus begin to trade at a discount and those who accepted these discounted notes would earn an arbitrage profit by returning them to the issuing bank for payment at full face value in cash. At this point a bank run would become inevitable.[22] But, for Mises, the note brand *qua* money substitute vanishes prior to the reserve drain and precipitates it.[23]

Mises believed that this latter mechanism, which derives from the inherently precarious position of money substitutes under free banking, would act swiftly and effectively to rigidly constrain the issue of fiduciary media among free banks. It is worth quoting Mises at length (1998, p. 436) describing what may be called the "mechanism of brand extinction":

> It is very easy for a bank to increase the number of people who are ready to accept loans granted by credit expansion and paid out in an amount of money-substitutes. But it is very difficult for any bank to enlarge its clientele, that is, the number of people who are ready to consider these claims as money-substitutes and to keep them as such in their cash-holdings. To enlarge this clientele is a troublesome and slow process, as is the acquisition of any type of good will. On the other hand the bank can lose its clientele very quickly. . . . It was a serious blunder to believe that the reserve's task is to provide the means for the redemption of those bank notes the holders of which have lost confidence in the bank. *The confidence which a bank and the money-substitutes it has issued enjoy is indivisible. It is either present with all its clients or it vanishes entirely.* If some of the clients lose confidence the rest of them lose it too. No bank issuing fiduciary media and granting circulation credit can fulfill the obligations which it has taken over in issuing money-substitutes if all clients are losing

22   In the earlier literature, the loss of gold reserves to a bank's clients was called an "internal drain," and was distinguished from the "external drain" of gold reserves associated with the price-specie-flow or adverse clearing mechanism. See Viner 1937, pp. 161–64.

23   Although Mises never used the term "brand" in his discussion, a money substitute, as he construes it, can exist only as a branded entity. An unbranded money substitute, that is, one that does not identify a specific issuer, defies economic logic. In contrast, all other "products" on the market could conceivably perform their intended function in satisfying wants without being branded. Curiously, in his own treatment of discrimination between note brands, Selgin (1988, pp. 42–47) fails to cite Mises's path breaking contribution.

confidence and want to have their banknotes redeemed and
their deposits paid back. *This is an essential feature or weakness
of the business of issuing fiduciary media and granting circulation
credit.* (emphases added)

Now, this does not mean that Mises ignored the adverse clearing
mechanism; but he did assign it a secondary role as an economic feedback
mechanism for a bank that exercised extreme restraint in issuing fiduciary
media and had already established its note (and deposit) brand as a viable
money substitute.[24] For such banks an adverse clearing balance signaled
an issue of notes in excess of what its clients wished to hold in their cash
balances that required immediate redemption. But in the event of a "loss of
confidence" in a particular brand of money substitute, the bank's reserves
would be "futile" in securing "the prompt redemption of banknotes and the
prompt payment of deposits" (Mises 1998, p. 436). In other words, Mises
held that a high or low reserve ratio is not *directly* relevant to the stability
of a bank. It is simply one of the objective data that the bank's clients take
into account in formulating their subjective judgment concerning whether
the banks notes and deposits are or are not money substitutes. These objective data also include past performance of the bank's loan and investment
portfolio, its customer service, its physical facilities, the qualifications and
experience of its managerial staff, its geographical accessibility, etc.

In short Mises argued that a fractional-reserve bank's "stability" con-
sisted of a binary set of possibilities: either the bank's note brand is perceived as possessing all the qualities of a money substitute or the brand
becomes extinct. Indeed, technically it is even inaccurate to speak of a
brand *becoming* extinct or of a *process* of brand extinction, despite the fact
that it takes more or less time for the bank's reserves to be exhausted. The
brand *is* extinct the instant its clientele begins to distrust the bank's ability
to fully discharge its note liabilities on demand.[25] As Mises (1998, pp. 442,
444) emphasized

---

24   For the rest of this discussion, I will use the term "bank" interchangeably with
"issuers of money substitutes," and the term "bank notes" to denote all of a bank's demand
liabilities.

25   As Jeff Herbener (2002, p. 83) has perceptively noted, in Mises's view:

> [P]eople only demand money-substitutes, not fiduciary media, and
> their demand exists only when they have confidence in full redemp-
> tion based on the issuers' practice of full redemption. People could not
> demand fiduciary media because they cannot distinguish between a

> What makes a banknote a money-substitute is the special kind
> of good will of the issuing bank. The slightest doubt concern-
> ing the bank's ability or willingness to redeem every banknote
> without any delay at any time and with no expense to the bearer
> impairs this special good will and removes the banknote's char-
> acter as a money-substitute. . . . One must not forget that every
> bank issuing fiduciary media is in a rather precarious position.
> Its most valuable asset is its reputation. It must go bankrupt as
> soon as doubts arise concerning its perfect trustworthiness and
> solvency.

It is important to note that in the foregoing passages Mises does not
distinguish between the "illiquidity" and "insolvency" of a fractional
reserve bank, as modern free bankers do. The quality of its loan and investment portfolio is an objective factor that does not *directly* affect the status
of its demand liabilities as money substitutes. It is the "special good will"
Mises speaks of that induces a bank's clients to forebear at every successive
moment from immediately exercising their contractual right to redeem
their notes for cash and that therefore permits the issuer of money substitutes to continue in business. Thus good will, for Mises, is the solvent bank's
"most valuable asset" that, in effect, bridges the inherent gap between, on
the one hand, the sum of the bank's cash reserves plus the *liquidation value*
of its loans and investments and, on the other, the value of its demand
liabilities.

Mises's analysis of this point has an important, and heretofore unno-
ticed, implication for the appropriate accounting procedure for issuers of
money substitutes. In order to reflect the reality of the special contractual
obligation assumed by banks, all assets should be carried on their books at
liquidation value.[26] Thus for fractional-reserve banks there is no meaningful distinction between "illiquidity" and "insolvency."[27]

---

money-substitute that is a money-certificate and one that is a fiduciary
medium. If they could make such a distinction, then fiduciary media
would not be viable.

26   The market value of a bank's loans and investments is potentially extremely volatile and may fluctuate greatly with economic and financial conditions. However, at any
given moment, good will is a binary variable: its value is either sufficient to maintain the
bank's assets equal to the total nominal value of its demand liabilities or it is zero—meaning
negative net worth and insolvency. There is never any intermediate state of "illiquidity" for
a fractional reserve bank.

27   The liquidation value of cash reserves of course is always equal to their par value.

Now it is important to emphasize that, unlike Murray N. Rothbard (2008, pp. 85–110) Mises was not arguing that fractional-reserve banks are inherently bankrupt. Mises's point was rather that a fractional-reserve bank is a uniquely and inherently unstable market institution, whose solvency depends on acquiring and maintaining a special intangible factor that is liable to vanish instantly. This special good will is a specific, non-isolable, and non-exchangeable factor required in the production function of every firm issuing money substitutes.

We might speculate briefly on why there is no discussion in the free banking literature of the brand extinction mechanism, or of anything akin to it, despite the fact that it plays such a prominent role in Mises's analysis of free banking. While this issue would require a separate paper to fully disentangle, I suggest that it lies in the fact that free bankers reject Mises's concept of money substitute in favor of the inside/outside money dichotomy. For example, White (1986, p. 314, n. 23) criticizes the term money substitutes as "confusing" because the term suggests "nonmoney-ness." However, by substituting the terms "outside money" to denote commodity or fiat money and "inside money" to denote notes and deposits issued by private banks, the free bankers obscure the fact that the "money-ness," if one wishes to call it that, of inside money originates and vanishes according to distinctly different principles than those that apply to outside money. Specifically, the circulation of commodity money or fiat money is not dependent on the existence of special good will attaching to its producer; nor is outside money subject to the principle of brand extinction in the same sense as bank notes and deposits.[28]

As a side note, the adoption of the terms "inside money" and "outside money" by modern free bankers appears paradoxical. The concepts were originally developed in 1960 by Gurley and Shaw (1960), whose aim was to challenge the real balance effect re-introduced into neoclassical monetary theory by Don Patinkin. A highly technical theoretical debate ensued

---

This means that issuers of money substitutes that are fully backed by money proper, i.e., 100 percent-reserve banks, need no "special good will" to maintain balance between assets and demand liabilities. They, of course, require general customer good will like any other ongoing firm that seeks to earn profits.

28   This is not to deny that the *value* of fiat money can be destroyed by hyperinflation or the dissolution of the issuing government by revolution or war; or even that the *value* of a commodity money like gold could conceivably approach zero if a technological advance were to radically alter its conditions of scarcity.

which concluded without a completely satisfactory resolution.[29] The inside/outside money conceptual apparatus quickly fell into disuse and by 1980 the monetary theorist Jürg Niehans (1980, p. 203, n. 9) would declare: "The distinction between inside money and outside money is simply irrelevant. It is part of the analytical fallout from the confusion about real balance effects."

The paradox of free bankers appropriating this defunct distinction lies in the fact that the real balance effect is at the very heart of the monetary equilibrium approach that they champion.[30] But the use of the term in the free banking literature may not be so puzzling when it is considered that the eminent Keynesian monetary theorist James Tobin (1963, p. 410, n. 2) cited Gurley and Shaw's work as important in "originating and contributing" to the "new view" of money of which Tobin was the leading proponent. In brief, according to the "new view," private fractional-reserve banks are just garden-variety financial intermediaries, like insurance companies or pension funds, and are not able to unilaterally create money at the stroke of a pen as almost all money and banking textbooks have taught for decades.[31] And indeed, Selgin (1988, pp. 82–84) favorably cites Tobin's work as supporting his own argument that, absent a "monopoly bank of issue," free banks are purely "credit transferers or intermediaries, and not credit creators."

Our discussion is not intended as a criticism of the free bankers for embracing the distinction between inside and outside money. Rather the aim is to emphasize that the theoretical foundations of the distinction are rooted in a variant of monetary theory that is much closer to the Banking School's view of the function of banks than it is to Mises's Currency School perspective on banking.

---

29   This debate is recounted in Johnson (1967, pp. 75–85).

30   To be fair, Larry White (1999, p. 12, n. 12) says that his use of the "distinction between inside and outside money is different from the one used by Gurley and Shaw." Also, the distinction has been resurrected in more recent monetary literature although it is used for a different purpose, and inside money has a different definition than that originally assigned to it by Gurley and Shaw (Lagos 2006).

31   Stated Tobin (1963, p. 418): "Commercial banks do not possess, either individually or collectively, a widow's cruse which guarantees that any expansion of assets will generate a corresponding expansion of liabilities. . . . Marshall's scissors of supply and demand apply to the 'output' of the banking industry, no less than to other financial and nonfinancial industries."

7. A NOTE ON THE (BANK) NOTE

One aspect of Mises's thought on free banking that has been completely overlooked is his highly skeptical view of the advantages of bank notes and his promotion of free banking as a method of totally suppressing their circulation.[32] The reason for Mises's hostility to bank notes was that they were the main vehicle through which fiduciary media were issued. In continental Europe, checkable deposits were not generally subject to legal reserve requirements. Yet, their creation did not lead to multiple bank credit expansion, because almost all those who received payment by check cashed it immediately and did not redeposit the funds.[33] According to Mises (1998, p. 442), "the public was not ready to treat such bank deposits as money-substitutes." Only a small group of big firms treated checkable deposits at the central bank (but not commercial banks) as money substitutes. The opportunity for bank credit expansion via demand deposits was therefore nonexistent for commercial banks and very narrowly limited for central banks in continental Europe.[34] As Mises (1998, p. 442) noted in 1949, with the exception of countries under the sway of Anglo-Saxon banking methods, "Banknotes were practically the sole instrument of credit circulation and credit expansion." Things were otherwise in the U.S., where "a considerable part of the public looks upon deposits as money-substitutes [making] them what is popularly called checkbook currency." Mises's opposition to bank notes thus stemmed from the fact that in most major countries up to the mid-20th century, bank notes were the primary form in which fiduciary media were created.

---

32   The sole exception that I have come across so far in the literature is Herbener 2002 (p. 86). In this pioneering article, Herbener presents an interpretation of Mises's views on money and banking policy that is close to the one presented here.

33   Explained Mises (1998, p. 443):

As far as payees immediately cash the checks received and withdraw the whole amount from the bank, the method [of paying employees by check] means merely that the onerous burden of manipulating coins and banknotes is shifted from the employers cashier to the bank's cashier. It has no catallactic implications. If all citizens were to deal in this way with checks received, the deposits would not be money-substitutes and could not be used as instruments of credit circulation.

34   In terms of the money supply process taught in modern money and banking textbooks, the currency/deposit ratio was nearly infinite and the deposit multiplier was therefore practically zero.

Indeed, in several statements Mises argued that one of the primary virtues of free banking was that its operation would suppress the issue of all bank notes, *including those fully backed by gold*. His argument was that the business of issuing money certificates was extremely expensive and risky and that a bank's clients may not be prepared to reimburse such high costs through fees paid for the marginal convenience of carrying notes and holding deposits instead of coins. Mises (1998, p. 432) therefore concluded that issuing money certificates, in order to be profitable, would almost inevitably have to be associated with the issuing of fiduciary media:

> Issuing money-certificates is an expensive venture. The banknotes must be printed, the coins minted; a complicated accounting system for the deposits must be organized; the reserves must be kept in safety; then there is the risk of being cheated by counterfeit banknotes and checks. Against all these expenses stands only the slight chance that some of the banknotes issued may be destroyed and the still slighter chance that some depositors may forget their deposits. Issuing money-certificates is a ruinous business if not connected with issuing fiduciary media.

Furthermore, Mises (1998, pp. 443–44) argued, the widespread use of bank notes was invariably a product of government intervention and not of the private market:

> [F]reedom in the issuance of banknotes would have narrowed down the use of banknotes considerably if it had not entirely suppressed it. . . . Governments did not foster the use of banknotes in order to avoid inconvenience to ladies shopping. Their idea was to lower the rate of interest and to open a source of cheap credit to their treasuries. . . . If the governments had never interfered, the use of banknotes and of deposit currency would be limited to those strata of the population who know very well how to distinguish between solvent and insolvent banks. No large scale credit expansion would have been possible.

Mises (1998, p. 444) emphatically concluded:

> Banknotes are not indispensable. All the economic achievements of capitalism would have been accomplished if they had never existed. Besides, deposit currency can do all the things banknotes do.

Once we recognize Mises's opposition to the bank note *per se*, and not just as a form of fiduciary media, his approving quotation of the famous statement by French economist and free banker Henri Cernuschi takes on a different meaning than previously ascribed to it. Taken in its full context it is clear that Mises's point is that free banking would not merely restrict the emission of unbacked bank notes, but would result in wholesale brand extinction of nearly *all* bank notes. Declared Mises (1998, p. 443):

> [F]reedom in the issuance of bank notes would have narrowed down the use of bank notes considerably if it had not entirely suppressed it. It was this idea that Cernuschi advanced in the hearings of the French Banking Inquiry on October 24, 1865: "I believe that what is called freedom of banking would result in a total suppression of banknotes in France. I want to give every-body the right to issue banknotes so that nobody should take any banknotes any longer."

Mises's attitude toward the bank note as expressed in his analysis of free banking may partially explain a puzzling element in his proposal for post-World War Two monetary reform. Mises's reform program was pub-lished in 1953 as part of the section on "Monetary Reconstruction" that he added to the second edition of *The Theory of Money and Credit* (Mises 1980, pp. 451–500). The central recommendation in this program was for the United States to return to the classical gold standard at a fixed legal parity established at the market price for gold prevailing at the (pre-announced) date of initiation of the reform. He also recommended, in accordance with the Currency School principle, that all further issue of U.S. dollars, in any form, be subject to a strict 100 percent gold reserve requirement. This pro-hibition on issue of fiduciary media would not only apply to new dollar notes which would henceforth be issued by a Conversion Agency subject to a 100-percent gold reserve requirement. Mises (1981, p. 491) also explic-itly applied it to the creation of deposits by commercial banks:

> The total amount of dollar bills, whatever their name or legal characteristic may be, must not be increased by further issu-ance. No bank must be permitted to expand the total amount of its deposits subject to check or the balance of such deposits of any individual customer . . . otherwise than by receiving such cash deposits in legal-tender bank notes from the public or by receiving a check payable by another domestic bank subject to the same limitations. This means a rigid 100 percent reserve for all future deposits. . . .[35]

---

35   Note that Mises's program for postwar monetary reform resembles a currency

Mises (1998, p. 494) was not satisfied with this general quantitative restriction on the issuance of bank notes, however. He went even further and prescribed that the Treasury be mandated "to withdraw from circulation, against the new gold coins, and to destroy within a period of one year after the promulgation of the new legal gold parity of the dollar, all notes of five, ten, and perhaps also twenty dollars." Thus new legal tender notes "must be issued in denominations of one or fifty dollars and upward." In current dollars, this means that aside from the one-dollar bill, which would be tantamount to small change, there would be no note in circulation with a purchasing power of less than $450![36] Now this further restriction on the minimum denomination of currency notes issued was never a part of the original Currency School program. The reason that Mises insisted on it in his postwar monetary reform proposal was to ensure that people who had grown accustomed to using a paper money tenuously linked to gold since the advent of World War One were again familiarized with gold money.[37] But it also reflected his strong conviction that bank notes were not indispensable to economic development and growth, and that the complete suppression of bank note issue would be the ideal outcome of a free banking regime.

8. CONCLUSION

From the abundant and systematic evidence presented in this paper, I believe that it is reasonable to conclude that very early in his writings on monetary and business cycle theory, Mises arrived at two views from which he never deviated for the rest of his career.[38] The first was that the creation of fiduciary media under any and all circumstances causes a divergence of

---

board arrangement, but it went beyond it to legally require that not only the notes issued by the currency board be 100-percent backed by gold, but also that the demand deposits created by commercial banks be subject to the same legal mandate. For a discussion of the similarities and differences between Mises's plan and the modern currency board, see Salerno 2010a, pp. 484–94, 516–27.

36   This figure is calculated by comparing the purchasing power of the dollar between the years 1950 and 2010 using the inflation calculator available at http://www.west-egg.com/inflation/

37   Thus Mises (1998, p. 493) wrote: "Gold must be in the cash holdings of everyone. Everybody must see gold coins changing hands, must be used to having gold coins in his pockets, to receiving gold coins when he cashes his paycheck, and to spending gold coins when he buys in a store."

38   Indeed, as pointed out above (pp. 14–15, 17–18), the seeds of these views were clearly present in 1912 in the first German edition of *The Theory of Money and Credit*.

the loan rate from the natural rate, leading to the sequence of phenomena described by Austrian business cycle theory. The second was that free banking is the best policy available for bringing about the goal of the Currency School and Peel's Act: the eradication of the issuance of fiduciary media. In short, Mises's overarching aim in his work on money and business cycles was to revive, correct, and advance the Currency School's theoretical approach and to formulate a practical program that would effectively achieve its policy goals.

If my interpretation is correct, then the ongoing debate over whether Mises was a "free banker" or an advocate of 100-percent reserves is exposed as superficial and ultimately irrelevant. The proper foci of the debate are the positions that Mises took on two critical theoretical propositions. The first is that *any* increase in fiduciary media generates a business cycle, implying a rejection of a key tenet of monetary equilibrium theory propounded by modern free bankers. The second is that under a system of free banking the behavior of the overall money supply tends to approximate its behavior under a 100-percent commodity money. This paper has provided overwhelming textual evidence that Mises strongly and persistently affirmed both propositions. As a result, it appears that the claim of modern free bankers that Mises was one of their theoretical forerunners is highly implausible.

REFERENCES

Bagus, Philipp. 2011. "Who's Afraid of Deflation?" *Mises Daily* (July 22). Available at http://mises.org/daily/5465

Butos, William. 2012. "Monetary Orders and Institutions: A Hayekian Perspective." *Quarterly Journal of Austrian Economics*. Forthcoming.

Clougherty, Tom. 2011. "Hayek and Monetary Stabilization." *The Cobden Centre* (August 3). Available at http://www.cobdencentre.org/tag/lawrence-h-white/

Daugherty, Marion R. 1942. "The Currency-Banking Controversy, Part 1." *Southern Economic Journal* 9 (October): 140–55.

_____. 1943. "The Currency-Banking Controversy, Part 2." *Southern Economic Journal* 9 (January): 241–50.

Davidson, Laura. 2012. "Against Monetary Disequilibrium Theory and Fractional Reserve Free Banking." *The Quarterly Journal of Austrian Economics* 15, no. 2 (Summer): 195–20.

Fetter, Frank Whitson. 1978. *The Development of British Monetary Orthodoxy, 1797–1875*. Fairfield, N.J.: Augustus M. Kelley Publishers.

Friedman, Benjamin M. 1975. "Targets, Instruments and Indicators of Monetary Policy." *Journal of Monetary Economics* I (October): 443–73.

_____. 1977. "The Inefficiency of Short-Run Monetary Targets for Monetary Policy." *Brookings Papers on Economic Activity*, No. 2. Pp. 293–335.

Gurley, John G., and Edward S. Shaw. 1960. *Money in a Theory of Finance.* Washington, D.C.: The Brookings Institution.

Hall Robert E., and N. Gregory Mankiw. 1994. "Nominal Income Targeting." In *Monetary Policy.* N. Mankiw, ed. Chicago: The University of Chicago Press. Pp. 71 – 94. Available at http://www.nber.org/chapters/c8329.pdfhttp://www.nber.org/chapters/c8329.pdf

Harrison, Edward. 2011. "Lawrence White on Friedrich von Hayek." *Credit Writedowns* (January 21). Available at http://www.creditwritedowns.com/2011/01/lawrence-white-on-friedrich-von-hayek.html

Hayek, F. A. 2008. *Prices and Production and Other Works: F. A. Hayek on Money, the Business Cycle, and the Gold Standard.* Joseph T. Salerno, ed. Auburn, Ala.: Ludwig von Mises Institute.

Herbener, Jeffrey M. 2002. "Ludwig von Mises on the Gold Standard and Free Banking." *Quarterly Journal of Austrian Economics* 5, no. 1 (Spring): 67–91.

Horwitz, Steven. 2000. *Microfoundations and Macroeconomics: An Austrian Perspective.* New York: Routledge.

_____. 2010a. Comment on Peter Boettke. "Mises on Free Banking—Why Is There a Debate?" Coordination Problem Blog (May 7). Available at http://www.coordinationproblem.org/2010/05/mises-and-free-banking-why-is-there-a-debate.html

_____. 2010b. Comment on Joseph T. Salerno. "Selgin contra Horwitz and White on Mises's View of Fiduciary Media." Mises Economics Blog (May 16). Available at http://archive.mises.org/12724/selgin-contra-horwitz-and-white-on-misess-view-of-fiduciary-media/#comment-688782

Hülsmann, Jörg Guido. 2007. *Mises: The Last Knight of Liberalism.* Auburn, Ala.: Ludwig von Mises Institute.

Johnson, Harry G. 1967. *Essays in Monetary Economics.* Cambridge, Mass.: Harvard University Press.

Lagos, Richard. (2006) "Inside and Outside Money." Federal Reserve Bank of Minneapolis Research Department Staff Report 374 (May).

Machlup, Fritz. 1940. *The Stock Market, Credit, and Capital Formation.* Vera C. Smith, trans. London: William Hodge and Company, Limited.

Mises, Ludwig von. 1924. *Theorie des Geldes und der Umlaufsmittel.* 2nd ed. Munich.

_____. 1981. *The Theory of Money and Credit*. 3rd ed. Trans. H. E. Batson. Indianapolis: Liberty Classics.

_____. 1998. *Human Action: A Treatise on Economics*. Scholar's ed. Auburn, Ala.: Ludwig von Mises Institute.

_____. 2006. *The Causes of the Economic Crisis and Other Essays before and after the Great Depression*. Percy L. Greaves, Jr., ed. Auburn, Ala.: Ludwig von Mises Institute.

Montgomery, Michael R. 2006. "The Genesis of an Idea: Classical Economics and the Birth of Monetary Disequilibrium Theory." In *Money and Markets: Essays in Honor of Leland B. Yeager*. Roger Koppl, ed. New York: Routledge.

Nair, Malavika. 2012. "Regulation in a Nineteenth Century Indigenous Banking System as a Bankers' Club." Working Paper.

Niehans, Jürg. 1980. *The Theory of Money*. Baltimore: Johns Hopkins University Press.

Rabin, Alan A. 2004. *Monetary Theory*. Northampton, Mass.: Edward Elgar.

Röpke, Wilhelm. 1969. "The Fight against Inflationism." In idem, *Against the Tide*. Elizabeth Henderson, trans. Chicago: Henry Regnery Company.

Rothbard, Murray N. 1995. *Classical Economics: An Austrian Perspective on the History of Economic Thought, Volume II*. Brookfield, Vt.: Edward Elgar.

_____. 2008. *The Mystery of Banking*. 2nd ed. Auburn, Ala.: Ludwig von Mises Institute.

Salerno, Joseph T. 2010a. *Money: Sound and Unsound*. Auburn, Ala.: Ludwig von Mises Institute.

_____. 2010b. "White contra Mises on Fiduciary Media." *Mises Daily* (May 14). Available at http://mises.org/daily/4389

_____. 2010c. "Selgin contra Horwitz and White on Mises's View of Fiduciary Media." Mises Economics Blog (May 16). Available at http://archive.mises.org/12724/selgin-contra-horwitz-and-white-on-misess-view-of-fiduciary-media/

Schumpeter, Joseph A. 1968. *History of Economic Analysis*. Elizabeth Boody Schumpeter, ed. New York: Oxford University Press.

Selgin, George. 1988. *The Theory of Free Banking: Money Supply under Competitive Note Issue*. Totowa, N.J.: Rowman & Littlefield.

_____. 1997. *Less Than Zero: The Case for a Falling Price Level in the Economy*. London: Institute of Economic Affairs.

_____. 2010. Comment on Joseph T. Salerno. "Selgin contra Horwitz and White on Mises's View of Fiduciary Media." Mises Economics Blog (May 18). Available at http://archive.mises.org/12724/selgin-contra-horwitz-and-white-on-misess-view-of-fiduciary-media/#comment-689126

Tobin, James. 1987. "Commercial Banks as Creators of Money." In idem, *Essays In Economics: Volume 1: Macroeconomics*. Cambridge, Mass.: The MIT Press. Pp. 272–82.

Viner, Jacob. 1937. *Studies in the Theory of International Trade*. New York: Harper & Brothers Publishers.

White, Lawrence H. 1986. "A Subjectivist Perspective on the Definition and Identification of Money." In *Subjectivism, Intelligibility and Economic Understanding: Essays in Honor of Ludwig M. Lachmann on His Eightieth Birthday*. Israel M. Kirzner, ed. London: Macmillan Press. Pp. 301–14.

_____. 1992. "Mises on Free Banking and Fractional Reserves." In *A Man of Principle: Essays in Honor of Hans F. Sennholz*. John W. Robbins and Mark Spangler, eds. Grove City, Penn.: Grove City College Press. Pp. 517–29.

_____. 1999. *The Theory of Monetary Institutions*. Malden, Mass.: Blackwell Publishers.

_____. 2010. "A Response to Salerno on Fiduciary Media." *Division of Labor* (May 17). Available at http://divisionoflabour.com/archives/007130.php

White, Lawrence H., and George A. Selgin. 1989. "The Evolution of a Free Banking System." *Economic Inquiry* 25 (July 1987). Reprinted in Lawrence H. White, *Competition and Currency: Essays on Free Banking and Money*. New York: New York University Press. Pp. 218–42.

Wu, Chi-Yuen. 2007. *An Outline of International Price Theories*. Auburn, Ala.: Ludwig von Mises Institute.

Yeager, Leland B. 1997. *The Fluttering Veil: Essays on Monetary Equilibrium*. George Selgin, ed. Indianapolis: Liberty Fund.

6

MATTHEW MCCAFFREY

The Influence of the Currency-Banking Dispute on Early Viennese Monetary Theory

INTRODUCTION

VIENNA AT THE BEGINNING OF the twentieth century witnessed one of the most remarkable moments in the history of monetary theory. In consecutive years, three young economists in Vienna published treatises involving the problems of money and banking: Rudolf Hilferding's *Finance Capital* in 1910, Joseph Schumpeter's *The Theory of Economic Development* in 1911, and Ludwig von Mises's *The Theory of Money and Credit* in 1912. These works have each achieved significance in their own right, but the purpose here is to examine each in light of a particular dispute in monetary theory and to show that each of these works may be read in light of the Currency-Banking controversy of nineteenth-century Britain.

Although each of these three economists significantly elaborated on their ideas in later works, the focus here is on these early books so as to limit the discussion to manageable length. The three works are also worth grouping together for other reasons. The authors were all personally and professionally familiar with each other at this time, and to some extent at least, address each other through their writings. And although they differed fundamentally in many respects, each author also shared a common

MATTHEW MCCAFFREY is a Ph.D. candidate at the University Angers.

intellectual milieu through the seminar of Eugen von Böhm-Bawerk at the University of Vienna. The treatises themselves also share common themes. Specifically, each expounds a theory of money and banking, and describes the relationship between money, banking, and economic development. Toward this end, each book also contains contributions to the theory of entrepreneurship (McCaffrey 2012).[1]

This chapter is outlined as follows: The first two sections summarize the controversy between the Banking and Currency Schools, discussing the relevant arguments, and distinguishing several fundamental points of contention. The next three sections take the early ideas of Hilferding, Mises, and Schumpeter in turn, discussing how the ideas of the Banking and Currency School theorists exercised an important influence on each, and examining the common threads between the two generations.

THE CURRENCY SCHOOL

Although debates over monetary theory and policy were common in England since the seventeenth century, the mid-nineteenth century (in roughly the periods 1821–1844 and 1844–1865) saw a deliberate and systematic focus on particular issues in banking theory, characterized by a broad division of opinion into two schools of thought which became known as the "Banking School" and the "Currency School."[2] The central disputes between the two schools can be divided into their theoretical and political (policy) segments. On the one hand are concerns about the theo-

---

1   Not all of the authors devote the same space to each of these topics: Schumpeter focuses on entrepreneurship and development. But, as has been pointed out (Rothbard 1987), money and banking are vital for Schumpeter's entrepreneur (at least in *The Theory of Economic Development*).

2   In 1821 the United Kingdom resumed payments after more than twenty years of inconvertible paper currency (although the legislation concerning the resumption was actually passed in 1819). The period following the return saw the publication of innumerable works on the nature of money and on prescriptions for banking policy. The Bank Charter Act, popularly known as "Peel's Act," after Sir Robert Peel, was passed in 1844. In the mid-twentieth century a significant secondary literature on the dispute began to appear. For a summary of the debate, cf. Robbins (1958), Smith ([1936] 1990), and Daugherty (1942; 1943). For expositions in regard to particular problems, cf. Viner (1937, esp. chap. V) and Wu ([1939] 2007, esp. pp. 129–41) in relation to international trade and price theories, respectively. For particular emphasis on the "real bills doctrine," cf. Mints (1945, esp. chaps. VI and VII). For a discussion of the dispute in light of the relatively neglected Free Banking School, cf. White (1984) and Smith ([1936] 1990).

retical problems of money and money-substitutes, that is, how the economy functions in the presence of a "mixed currency"—one with both gold and convertible paper money used as media of exchange. On the other hand are various problems of economic policy relating to banking institutions and their governance, in particular, the question of how to limit the inflationary expansion of currency issues and curb or eliminate the business cycle. The areas of theory and policy are not mutually exclusive; however, this paper treats mainly theoretical problems.[3] The questions of economic policy, which ultimately reduce to the institutional question of central versus free-banking, are discussed elsewhere (White 1984; Smith [1936] 1990; Salerno 2012), and may be set aside for the moment. And although many points both of theory and policy were debated in this period, I shall discuss mainly the more influential ideas which relate to the early work of Hilferding, Mises, and Schumpeter.[4]

Economic crises in England in 1825, 1836, and 1839 (among others) spurred increasing interest in the workings of the English monetary system and ways to improve it. It was in this intellectual climate that the ideas of the Currency School matured. By the early nineteenth century, a broad consensus had been reached in the British economic community that a mixed currency based on convertibility into gold was the most desirable monetary system. Differences of opinion arose however, as to the exact workings of the monetary system, and how to ensure the proper maintenance of the money supply and the avoidance of economic crises. As opposed to the Banking School, which argued against the restriction of banking operations, the Currency School contended that certain limitations should be placed upon the Bank of England (and any other banks of issue) to prevent an inflationary expansion of the money supply. In what follows it should be remembered that both schools focused exclusively on short-run issues, and it is on these points that disagreement is found, whereas in the long run, both schools tended to agree with Ricardo (Viner 1937, p. 221).[5]

---

3   This point is particularly important when considering the writings of Mises, who while supporting many of the theoretical principles of the Currency School, nevertheless broke sharply with it on the problem of central banking and rules for monetary policy.

4   In particular, I shall mostly bypass the themes of international trade and the regulation of the exchanges, which comprised a significant share of the debate.

5   That is, in the long run the quantity and value of money are determined by the cost of gold production.

I shall deal with each of the following ideas at greater length in relation to the 20th-century economists, but for now a brief survey of Currency
School arguments will suffice. The position of the writers of the Currency
School was built around what became known as the "Currency Principle"
which may be summarized as follows: "A mixed currency would operate
properly only if it operated precisely as would a metallic currency, i.e., only
if any efflux or influx of gold resulted in a corresponding (absolute, not
proportional) decrease or increase in the quantity of the currency" (Viner,
1937, p. 221).[6]

Currency School theorists held that while issues of convertible paper
currency could not be excessive for an indefinite period, they could be excessive to a significant degree "for sufficiently long periods to endanger the
maintenance of convertibility and to generate financial crises" (Viner 1937,
p. 223). The problem that faced the writers of the Currency School was
how to regulate the issue of currency so as to ensure that a mixed currency
would conform to the principles of a purely metallic system. The Currency
School writers maintained that bank money convertibility was a necessary
but, not a sufficient, condition for ensuring the proper maintenance of the
money supply.

In examining this problem, the Currency School focused almost exclusively on the issue of bank notes as opposed to deposits. If the volume of
notes exceeds the amount that would have circulated in a purely metallic
system, this constitutes an "overissue." The problem with such overissue,
according to the Currency School, was threefold. First, it was inflationary, causing a rise in the price level. Second, it resulted in a drain on gold
reserves to foreign nations. Third, it serves as a primary cause of business
cycles. The main concern of the Currency School then was to find methods
of regulating banking practices that could prevent the overissue of notes
and avoid, or at least greatly reduce, the effects of financial panics. Convertibility of the currency was the first important check on overissue, but
the Currency School felt that additional legal stipulations were required to
limit inflationary expansions of the money supply.

---

6   Put another way, "note issues would be correctly regulated if they were made to
fluctuate in volume exactly as a purely metallic currency would have done" (Daugherty
1942). Wu ([1939] 2007) characterizes the principle thus: "There is always a danger of an
over-issue of bank notes, which therefore should be strictly regulated—so regulated that
the notes might become mere tokens for metallic money" (p. 130). This last description
highlights the relevance of the Currency Principle for discussions of monetary policy, particularly regarding fiduciary media.

The Currency School and Banking Schools both favored convertibility of bank notes into specie. Where they differed was on the role that convertibility and other limiting influences played on note issue. The Banking School maintained that convertibility by itself would be sufficient to ensure that banks would not unduly increase the volume of circulation, while the Currency School did not. The problem facing the Currency School was how to regulate bank issues such that convertibility would always be ensured—convertibility functions as a limit to excess issues and represents "an application of the principles of a purely metallic currency" (Daugherty 1942).

The policy solution recommended by the Currency School was to divide the Bank of England into two separate departments, one of which would be responsible for the issue and redemption of bank notes, while the other would oversee demand deposits. According to Peel's Act, bank note issues would be backed by securities held by the bank up to the amount of £14,000,000, and beyond this, there would be a strict 100-percent reserve requirement for all note issue. Deposits, on the other hand, were left completely unregulated, because, in a crucial error of Currency School doctrine, notes and deposits were thought to have entirely different economic functions.[7]

The Banking School

The theories of the Banking School, although possessing intellectual roots in earlier controversies, were developed primarily in response to the Currency School and its support of Peel's Act. However, Banking School doctrine was never systematized to the degree that Currency School doctrine was. As Hayek puts it "The 'Currency School' . . . stepped forward with a well-defined programme. . . . [Whereas] the opposing doctrine of the 'Banking School' developed only gradually and never attained a coherent set of ideas" (1991, p. 230). Despite this lack of unanimity, the influence of the Banking School is still historically important. Several writers stand out as the authoritative voices of the Banking School, in particular Thomas Tooke, John Fullarton,[8] James Wilson, and later and to a lesser extent, John Stuart Mill.

---

7   For an explanation of this view, cf. Robbins (1958, pp. 105–08).

8   As I shall argue, Fullarton exercised an important influence, especially on Hilferding (positively) and Mises (negatively), but he may also have had some influence on

As with the Currency School, it is possible to express the central doctrine of the Banking School in terms of a "Banking Principle," defined thus: "The amount of paper notes in circulation [is] adequately controlled by the ordinary processes of competitive banking, and if the requirement of convertibility was maintained, could not exceed the needs of business for any appreciable length of time" (Viner 1937, p. 223).[9] Therefore overissue of the currency is absolutely impossible given genuine convertibility. This "elasticity" is the fundamental characteristic of bank note issue, and no regulation of the currency is necessary to prevent overissue.

The key to understanding the position of the Banking School, and the doctrine of the impossibility of overissue, is to be found in what is probably its most fundamental principle, the "law of the reflux," an idea developed principally by Fullarton and Tooke, and later repeated by Wilson and Mill.[10] The law of reflux states that so long as the currency is convertible banks cannot overissue their notes, because any issue exceeding public demand would immediately flow back to the bank:

> If the loans or deposits are advanced on proper securities, for short periods, the reflux of the notes, if any have been issued, will be equal to the efflux, leaving the circulation unaltered. If, indeed, the transactions of the district, or the trade of the country generally, require more instruments of exchange, a larger amount of notes would remain out; but this increase would *be the effect of increased transactions and prices, and not the cause of them.* (Tooke [1848] 1962, IV, p. 194; emphasis in original)[11]

Although Banking School theorists supported convertibility, it appears to have been the prevailing opinion that convertibility is relatively unimportant compared to reflux in terms of its ability to prevent an increase in the circulating medium (Fullarton 1845, p. 68; Mints 1945, p. 88). Emphasis is therefore on the "needs of business" in explaining the determination

---

Keynes, who describes Fullarton's *On the Regulation of Currencies* as "most interesting" (1936, p. 364). Although it does not appear that any extensive attempt has been made to trace the influence of Fullarton on Keynes, the reader may notice certain similarities.

9   The word "competitive" here is misleading, because Banking School theorists were not generally concerned with competitive banking or the difference between the impossibility of overissue under free and centralized banking regimes.

10   Cf. Fullarton (1845, pp. 82–98) and Tooke ([1848] 1962, IV, pp. 185–97; [1844] 1959, pp. 60–66).

11   Cf. Fullarton (1845, esp. chap. 5), for the canonical exposition of the law of reflux.

of the circulation. While the writers of the Currency School based their analysis on early versions of the quantity theory[12] of money, members of the Banking School tend to deny altogether the influence of the money supply on the general price level. Prices do not respond to changes in the quantity of money, but rather the amount of the circulation responds to the supply and demand for goods, which explains Tooke's comment above regarding the direction of the causal effect of money on prices.

As a direct result of this theory, Banking theorists looked to real factors for the explanation of financial crises, as opposed to the monetary theory advanced by the Currency School. In terms of policy, the Banking School strongly opposed Peel's Act: in their opinion the supply of the circulating medium could never be overissued, so any additional regulation of issues would at best be redundant, and at worst exacerbate economic crises. The Banking School also denied the Currency School's distinction between notes and deposits, arguing that although they performed the same economic function as media of exchange, neither required explicit limitation.

The theories of the Banking School on the business cycle deserve considerable attention in their own right, but a brief survey of the major points must be sufficient. The Banking School's views on the business cycle were somewhat scattered, but were decidedly non-monetary. Tooke, for example, advanced an overinvestment theory. He often cited exogenous elements, especially the opening or reopening of foreign markets, as the cause of increases in speculation to which correspond the initial prosperity of the cycle (Link 1959, pp. 131–32). The anticipation of new demand incites speculation, which in turn leads to overinvestment in inventories, which is the focus of Tooke's commentaries. On at least some occasions however, speculation takes the form of increased conversion of floating to fixed capital,[13] which is the portion of Tooke's theory which concerns this paper. The boom phase for Tooke is characterized by excessive investment. This sometimes takes the form of "overbanking," or in other words, loans on "insufficient or inconvertible securities, or in too large a proportion to

---

12   It is important to clarify what is meant by "quantity theory" in this context of this paper. The term is used here in a far narrower sense than is typical (e.g., as it is used with regard to the equation of exchange). What it refers to is primarily the *direction of the causal connection between money and prices*. The Currency School believed, correctly, that increases in the supply of money cause increases in the prices of goods, whereas Banking School advocates believed the causal connection ran the opposite direction.

13   Although Link (1959) comments that the focus on fixed capital is not a general feature of Tooke's theory.

the liabilities" ([1848] 1962, IV, p. 262).[14] The exact causes of the depression are not clear, although it appears that rising prices during the boom precipitate the turning point.

The most coherent theory of the business cycle from the Banking School was developed by James Wilson, who developed a non-monetary overinvestment theory of economic fluctuations.[15] In the mature version of his cycle theory, Wilson relied heavily on the idea of overinvestment in fixed capital (as compared to floating capital) to explain cycles. Businesses are susceptible to expanding the supply of fixed capital beyond the level made possible by real savings. This in turn causes problems, because consumption and investment cannot both be satisfied due to insufficient resources. Wilson argues:

> No community can, without the greatest inconvenience and derangement, increase its fixed capital faster than it is able to spare labour from the production of those commodities on which the community relies for its daily subsistence. Under all circumstances it can only be the amount of labour which the savings of the country can command and sustain, that can be applied to the increase of its fixed capital. (1847, p. 125)

Despite the fact that real resources are lacking for the completion of long-term projects, investment in fixed capital continues, and raises the income of wage-earners and thus stimulates consumption. However, this demand cannot be met due to the excessive investment (that is, to the lack of real resources), and the prices of consumer goods begin to rise, as do interest rates. This in turn triggers a fall in fixed-capital investment as projects are abandoned, and the depression is ushered in.[16]

John Stuart Mill also elaborated a theory of the trade cycle which includes themes from both Tooke and Wilson.[17] As with his predecessors, Mill makes reference to exogenous shocks such as poor crops and the opening of foreign markets as the initial impetus of a cycle. He also discusses

---

14   Tooke may mean "reserves" instead of "liabilities."

15   This theory is presented in its most complete form in the collection of Wilson's essays titled *Capital, Currency, and Banking* (1847). For secondary sources, cf. Link (1959) and Boot (1983).

16   Hayek mentions the importance of Wilson's capital-based view of the cycle on several occasions, for example Hayek (1941, p. 425).

17   Forget (1990) and Link (1959) are particularly important for this presentation of Mill's cycle theory.

"overtrading" ([1967a] 2006, p. 75) both in inventories and fixed capital. Mill credits "professional traders" with expanding investment to begin the boom, and "rash speculators" with exacerbating price rises through vigorous speculation (Forget, 1990). With Mill however, redeemable money substitutes begin to play a role in encouraging the initial wave of speculation. They are however, relegated to a secondary role, usually encouraging further speculation but not causing it ([1967b] 2006, p. 191; Forget 1990), although Mill does allow for sudden credit expansion which could cause a speculative boom (Mill [1967c] 2006, p. 275). Like Tooke, Mill is unclear on the causes and consequences of the depression.

As far as consistent themes are concerned, Banking School writers tended to focus on real factors (usually exogenous, international elements) which caused waves of speculation in the economy. Speculation encourages poor investment decisions, particularly in fixed capital. This creates disequilibrium between consumption and investment which leads to the crisis. Although these ideas are developed most clearly by Wilson, they are present in one form or another in Tooke as well, and both writers find a place in Mill's theory.

RUDOLF HILFERDING AND THE BANKING SCHOOL

Rooting himself in the Marxist tradition, Hilferding naturally takes Marx's discussions of money as the starting point for his own theory, and already in Marx's work, we observe the influence of the Banking School. Marx even described Fullarton as "one of the best writers on money," and at the time of Tooke's death, hailed him as "the last English economist of any value."[18] Although critical of certain aspects of Banking School theory, Marx was sympathetic in regard to its monetary doctrines. He was also unfavorable toward the Currency School, and instead of utilizing the "quantity theory," advocated a distinctly Banking-School approach wherein the prices of commodities determine the quantity of the circulating medium.[19]

---

18   Quoted in Green (1987) and Pivetti (1987), respectively.

19   For samples of Marx's opinions on the Currency School, cf. Marx (1972), p. 684, where he refers to the Currency School's "ignorance and . . . complete misunderstanding" of the direction of the causal relation between the quantity of money and prices. For some of Marx's comments on the members of the Banking School, cf. Marx (1972, p. 124, n. 2; 1911, pp. 259–63). On Marx's monetary theory and its development, cf. Arnon (1984). For his views on the quantity of the circulating medium, cf. Marx (1973), where he speaks of "the fundamental law that the mass of the circulating medium, at a definite velocity of cir-

These ideas, and the corresponding Banking School doctrines, are echoed in Hilferding's writings.

The Endogeneity of Money

Money and banking have a special significance in Hilferding's work, and it is not far from the mark to say that monetary issues are the indispensable core of his treatment of 'the latest phase of capitalist development.' *Finance Capital* attempts to build a grand vision of the final stages of capitalism, stages which largely depend upon the structure of the industries of banking and finance. Like Marx, Hilferding introduces money and credit into his analysis from the outset, building a system that thoroughly integrates an analysis of indirect exchange. To that end, Hilferding relied greatly on the traditional Banking School understanding of money and credit, even to the extent that Schumpeter—somewhat contemptuously—remarked that he "drew on it largely and uncritically" ([1954] 1963, p. 725). Hilferding's analysis is still important in the history of thought however, as it represents a relatively rare extension of "pure" Banking School doctrine.

In Hilferding's analysis, money arises out of the necessity, in capitalist society, of having a general standard through which to express the value of all commodities, a standard of value which can express the share each member of society has in the production of goods, i.e., each good's "socially necessary labor time" of production. As Hilferding puts it, "The anarchy of the commodity producing society generates the need for money" ([1910] 1981, p. 39).

The relevant point for this paper, however, is the question as to the determinants of the quantity of money in circulation under a mixed monetary regime. To answer this question, Hilferding begins by denouncing the quantity theory in no uncertain terms, stating that "Ever since Tooke's demonstration, the quantity theory of money has been rightly regarded as untenable" ([1910] 1981, p. 47). As the basis of his monetary theory, Hilferding preferred the Banking School's price-based theory of the circulation.

---

culation, is determined by the prices of the commodities and by the mass of commodities circulating at definite prices" (pp. 789–90). This position is summed up by the dicta, "Trade governs money, not money trade," and "The servant of trade [money] must follow the variations (in the prices) of the other commodities" (p. 870). Cf. also Marx (1973, pp. 186–87), and the discussions of this aspect of Marx's monetary theory in Arnon (1984) and Vorhies (1982), both of which mention the Banking School connection.

While Hilferding argued, following the Banking School, that the quantity theory did in fact apply to cases of inconvertible paper money, he also held that the condition of convertibility nullified the quantity theory. Hilferding concluded from this that, "The crucial test, therefore, is convertibility" ([1910] 1981, p. 63). To support this notion he cites Fullarton at length, presenting two of Fullarton's examples to contrast the possible effect on prices of both inconvertible and convertible monetary regimes ([1910] 1981, pp. 51–53).[20]

Hilferding concluded that, "The quantity of circulating media is determined primarily by the aggregate price of commodities. Given the quantity of commodities, changes in the quantity of money in circulation follow the fluctuations of commodity prices" ([1910] 1981, p. 37). It is clear then that the quantity of the circulation is determined endogenously, with the prices of commodities representing the principal independent variable, and therefore the quantity theory is "rightly regarded as refuted" ([1910] 1981, p. 50). It is also quite obvious from his extensive citations that Hilferding's analysis relies on Tooke and Fullarton's description of money and prices.

Note Issue and "The Law of Reflux"

The Banking School's influence, however, is felt most heavily in Chapter 5 of *Finance Capital*, "The Banks and Industrial Credit," where Hilferding outlines the role of banks of issue in granting credit to industrial enterprises, and the influence which such banks exert on the economic process as a whole. It is here that Hilferding discusses limitations on bank issues, and where he adopts the law of reflux as an explanation of the fundamental limit on overissue. Marx endorsed the Banking Principle almost verbatim,[21] and Hilferding cites Marx' position approvingly ([1910] 1981, p. 38, n. 5), while providing his own presentation of the Principle:

---

20   Hilferding appears to confuse Fullarton's meaning in these citations. Whereas Hilferding means to show that inconvertible paper money can be issued so as to affect prices, while a convertible currency cannot have such an effect, Fullarton is *not* making a distinction between inconvertible and convertible currency in his examples, but between two variations of inconvertible currency. Only after these sections are concluded does he introduce the subject of convertible bank notes and the impossibility of their overissue. Cf. Fullarton (1845), chap. 3.

21   "The issue of paper money must not [read: cannot] exceed in amount the gold (or silver, as the case may be) which would actually circulate, if not replaced by symbols" (quoted in Hilferding [1910] 1981, p. 378, n. 5).

> The volume of paper money must always be kept down to the minimum amount of money required for circulation. This minimum can, however, be replaced by paper, and since this amount of money is always necessary for circulation there is no need for gold to appear in its place. ([1910 1981, p. 38)

Given convertibility, there can be no deviation of the amount of the circulation from the "required amount," that is, from the needs of business. To support this claim, Hilferding turns once more to the Banking School, this time to Fullarton and the notion of the law of reflux.

Hilferding first notes the reflux principle in regard to bills of exchange: "The circulation of bills is limited only by the number of business transactions actually concluded . . . commercial bills can in principle only be issued when a business transaction has been concluded, and for this reason bills cannot be overissued" ([1910] 1981, p. 84). More important for our study however, he applies the reflux analysis to bank notes as well:

> The convertible bank note cannot be issued in excess quantities. . . . A bank note which is not required in circulation is returned to the bank. Since it can be used in lieu of the bill of exchange, the issue of notes is subject to the same laws as is the circulation of bills, and expands along with the latter so long as credit remains undisturbed. (1910, 1981, p. 86)

To emphasize his position, Hilferding quotes the following passage from Fullarton's *On the Regulation of Currencies*:

> I have no hesitation in professing my own adhesion to the decried doctrine of the old Bank Directors of 1810, 'that so long as a bank issues its notes in the discount of good bills, at not more than sixty days' date, it can never go far wrong.' In that maxim, simple as it is, I very strongly believe, there is a nearer approach to the truth, and a more profound view of the principles which govern circulation, than in any rule on the subject, which since that time has been promulgated. ([1910] 1981, p. 86, n. 8)

Given his use of the law of reflux to explain the quantity of bills of exchange and bank notes, and given the positive citation of Fullarton, who refers to the "decried" real-bills doctrine, it is unclear whether Hilferding was conscious of possible differences between the two principles.[22] Nothing in Fullarton's work suggests that he was, and this error appears to be adopted

---

22   For the distinction between the reflux and real-bills doctrines, cf. Glasner (1992).

by Hilferding.[23] The fact remains though that Hilferding sided quite explicitly with the Banking School on these issues, differing significantly only on some points of Marxist terminology and presentation.

Non-Monetary Theories of the Trade Cycle

A final and most important influence exercised by the Banking School on Hilferding concerns his theory of the trade cycle.[24] As mentioned above, the Banking School's views on the causes of the business cycle, inasmuch as they could be defined, were nonmonetary. In similar fashion, Hilferding's theory of the cycle begins with nonmonetary factors. Hilferding's develops a disproportionality theory which focuses on discoordination between capital and consumer goods industries. The cycle begins with large "expansion of production" due to supply or demand shocks ([1910] 1981, p. 258).[25] As a result, profits increase, and so too does investment in fixed capital. The organic composition of capital also increases however, leading to a fall in the rate of profit. As the quantity of fixed capital increases, production time is lengthened, and it becomes increasingly difficult to adapt production to future consumption ([1910] 1981, p. 262).[26] Overinvestment has taken place in long-term production industries which disequilibrates supply and demand. The discrepancy between supply and demand causes the depression, which pushes down prices and profits, as firms which are not able to earn the average rate of profit go bankrupt.

James Wilson's theory anticipates Hilferding. Although Hilferding does not cite Wilson as he does other Banking scholars, his exposition is similar to Wilson's on several important points. As with Wilson, Hilferding's analysis depends primarily on overinvestment in fixed capital. Tooke

---

23   Perhaps this is what Schumpeter was referring to in his above-quoted remark.

24   Unsurprisingly, arguments similar to Hilferding's appear in the work of Tugan-Baranowsky, who was also influenced by the Banking tradition. Hilferding, however, was critical of his contemporary on several points.

25   Rosner (1998) points out important similarities between the business cycle theories of Hilferding and Hayek. One important difference between Hilferding and Hayek's presentation of the business cycle, however, is that Hayek's theory is a monetary theory, similar to that of the Currency School, whereas Hilferding's is a non-monetary, Banking-style theory. Hilferding's theory does presuppose credit markets and does have monetary aspects, but the cycle for Hilferding originates in the real economy, whereas in at least one of Hayek's scenarios, the origin of cycles is monetary policy.

26   For Hilferding, the prices of factors of production only reflect current demand, not anticipated future demand.

also mentioned the possibility of overinvesting in fixed capital, although it was not the emphasis of his theory. Hilferding broadens this theme however, to provide a general theory of the business cycle, whereas Wilson and Tooke had been primarily concerned with explaining specific crises (for the sources cited in this paper, the railroad bubble of the 1840s and the crisis of 1847). Also, while Hilferding does refer to overconsumption, he does not discuss the inadequacy of saving specifically, as Wilson does. The latter theme especially is more appropriate to the cycle theory of Mises.

This theory is an improvement on the Banking approach in at least one sense: Banking theory had difficulties explaining the cause of sudden increases in speculative activities (White, 1984, p. 110–11), whereas Hilferding grounds his theory in identifiable causes of supply and demand shocks, such as, "the opening of new markets, the establishment of new branches of production, the introduction of new branches of production, the introduction of new technology, and the expansion of needs resulting from population growth" ([1910] 1981, p. 258).[27] Tooke's emphasis on new investment opportunities is also relevant. While his thinking on this point was never particularly clear, it is possible he was groping for the more general idea of innovation and shocks to explain initial increases in speculative activity.

Both Hilferding and the Banking School find the origin of economic crises in the real economy, and although credit conditions play a role in exacerbating downturns, they are never their cause. In particular, the universal focus on the opening of new (typically, foreign) markets as an exogenous shock to production is significant. This conclusion is unsurprising considering the opposition of Banking School theories to the monetary doctrines (and the monetary cycle theory) of the Currency School. As Hilferding puts it:

> At first sight a period of prosperity seems to be characterized by general and uniform price rises and a period of depression by a similar fall in prices. This is the reason why the cause of crises has been sought so long and so persistently in changes in the value of money. The superstitious faith in the quantity theory of money draws its strongest support from this view. ([1910] 1981, p. 420, n. 2)

---

27   Compare the above list with Schumpeter's (1934, p. 66) list of the different methods of "introducing new combinations," i.e., the essence of entrepreneurial activity. The obvious similarities are important because each ultimately believes that such innovations are the cause of the business cycle.

Hilferding and the Currency School

Hilferding briefly mentions the topic of legal restrictions on note issue by asserting that "The artificial regulation of the issue of bank notes fails as soon as circumstances require an increased issue" ([1910] 1981, p.85). That is, since the quantity of bank notes in circulation depends upon the demands of business, any restriction seeking to limit the volume of notes must run afoul of shortages in the note circulation whenever the public's demand for notes exceeds the maximum legal issue: "The essence of mistaken banking legislation is that it severely restricts the expansion of circulation credit and prevents it from reaching those limits which would be reasonable from the standpoint of economic laws" ([1910] 1981, p. 277). This was also the position of the Banking theorists, and Hilferding's comment is clearly aimed at Currency-esque regulations of banking practices. In fact, Hilferding goes on to lament what he considered the lack of progress in monetary theory in the nineteenth century:

> The insuperable obstacle to a knowledge of the laws of money and note circulation has been the hostility toward the labour theory of value. This accounts for the triumph of the Currency School in English banking legislation, notwithstanding its reduction to historical and theoretical absurdity in the works of Tooke [and] Fullarton. . . . Capitalism may learn more adequate principles, slowly and laboriously, from the bitter and costly experiences of diverse countries and periods, but it cannot find the power within itself to generalize them, as the maintenance of American, English, and to a lesser extent, German legislation and policies with regard to banks of issue demonstrates. ([1910] 1981, p. 87, n. 7)

This remark, embedded in Hilferding's discussion of money and credit, appears to imply that there is an affinity between the Banking School and the labor theory of value. This historical connection requires further exploration, but one might speculate that Hilferding is claiming that the causal relation of prices on money is a natural conclusion of the labor theory of value. At the same time, Hilferding singles out the Currency School approach, based on an early quantity theory, for censure. Although he does not speculate on the Currency School's influence, as we shall see below, the quantity theory lends itself easily to the monetary analysis of economists such as Mises. Hilferding may be implicitly profiling two distinct threads in the history of economic thought; the Banking School/labor theory tradition, and the Currency School/subjective value tradition.

Hilferding makes this point more clearly in his review of Mises's *The Theory of Money and Credit*. The review is comprised of two major criticisms, both of which are relevant. The first concerns Mises's acceptance of the subjective theory of value, and his application of the theory to the quantity of money:

> Among the [Mengerian marginal utility] school's unsolved problems . . . the monetary problem naturally occupies a place of prime importance. . . . The bankruptcy of the subjective theory of value, its inability to explain the basic problems of economics, could not be more clearly stated (Hilferding [1912] 1993, pp. 179–80).

Second, Hilferding notes Mises's endorsement of the Currency School on overissue and his consequent rejection of the Banking School and the law of reflux:

> He [Mises] lapses completely into the old quantity theory, the inferences of which he not only accepts but its errors also, which he even exaggerates. . . . Incidentally it should be noted that Mises—as a consistent quantity theoretician—champions the view that banks can expand credit arbitrarily without limit. Since he shares the opinion of Böhm that interest is dependent on the size of the national subsistence fund, it is impossible for him to find the specific causes determining the height of the rate of interest. As a result he arrives at an absurdity; the banks, by reducing the interest rate for transactions, can increase to a considerable extent the demands of their customers and also by expanding the emission of fiduciary media they can satisfy these demands. ([1912] 1993, pp. 181–82)

Once again, Hilferding clearly acknowledges two distinct traditions in economic thought, each springing from a specific theory of value, and each developing the principles of different sides of the Currency-Banking debate. Hilferding, although writing within the Marxist tradition, is an orthodox Banking School economist, at least as far as his views on the determinants of the quantity of money (and consequently, on the "quantity theory") and the law of reflux (the possibility of overissue) are concerned.

As we have seen, Hilferding aligns his theory squarely with the Banking School tradition. However, some have claimed that Hilferding's arguments are complementary to the Free Banking School, identified in White (1984) and Selgin (1988). Horwitz (1994), for example, argues that Hilferding's monetary theory should be viewed in the light of the Free Banking

School and its competitive theory of note issue. This view however, may perhaps place too much stress on certain aspects of Hilferding's theory, to the neglect of others.

All of the principles which Hilferding shares with the Free Banking School—rejection of the quantity theory, impossibility of overissue, the law of reflux—are found in the writings of the Banking School as well. In addition, Hilferding expounds his entire theory without reference to any of the members of the Free Banking School, while strongly endorsing orthodox Banking School doctrine, further showcasing his position as a disciple of the latter.[28] There is therefore no reason on these grounds to believe that there is any necessary connection between Hilferding and the Free Banking School.

As Horwitz (1994) observes,

> Hilferding never explicitly indicates that he envisions several banks competitively issuing convertible notes. His discussion of the return of unwanted bank notes could refer to a competitive system or it might refer to a central bank issuing convertible currency. . . . The evidence in *Finance Capital* appears to indicate that he accepted the erroneous claim of the Banking School [regarding the impossibility of over issue].

Yet these are precisely the issues which separate the Banking from the Free Banking tradition. One may then conclude that any similarity with Free Banking is a coincidental result of Hilferding's infatuation with standard Banking School doctrines.

However, another major point of distinction may be drawn between Hilferding and the Free-bankers. One of the central tenets of the Free Banking School has been that competitive banking is not merely an acceptable substitute for, but is actually a system superior to, monopolized banking (see the above sources). The overarching argument of *Finance Capital*, on the other hand, is that the cartelization of the banking system is an evolutionary feature of capitalism (that is, voluntary cartelization, absent legal barriers to entry). By combining industrial capital with banking capital, banks create "finance capital," which is in turn used to control ever more

---

28   A minor point: Horwitz (1994) cites Hilferding as saying Fullarton was "correct" on his critique of the quantity theory, whereas Hilferding's complete quotation reads "interesting and essentially correct," which is not quite the same thing. This is important because this slight misquotation highlights a point made earlier regarding a possible confusion between Hilferding and Fullarton's views. Cf. above, note 20.

of the economic system as a whole, through the centralized direction of investment. As the system is centralized, driven by its own internal logic, a *de facto* socialization of the financial and banking sectors—and thus, of the entire market—occurs, setting the stage for the *de jure* adoption of socialism via a mandate of the state. Hilferding summarizes as follows:

> With the development of banking, and the increasingly dense network of relations between the banks and industry, there is a growing tendency to eliminate competition among the banks themselves, and on the other side, to concentrate all capital in the form of money capital, and to make it available to producers only through the banks. If this trend were to continue, it would finally result in a single bank or a group of banks establishing control over the entire money capital. Such a "central bank" would then exercise control over social production as a whole. ([1910] 1981, p. 180)

Free Banking, for Hilferding, leads necessarily to central banking, as a necessary step in the organic development of the capitalist system. This conclusion is obviously far different from that of the Free Banking School. As has been shown above, Hilferding allies himself with Marx and the Banking theorists, and cannot really be identified with any other tradition in the sphere of monetary thinking.

Ludwig von Mises and the Currency School

A careful examination of *The Theory of Money and Credit* shows quite clearly that Mises not only considered himself an intellectual successor to the Currency School, but that he considered the Currency-Banking dispute to be *the* event in the development of nineteenth-century money and banking theory ([1924] 1953, pp. 342, 345).[29] Mises even describes his theory of the business cycle as "an elaboration and continuation of the doctrines of the Currency School" ([1924] 1953, p. 24). However, while Mises regards himself as a member of the Currency tradition, he is concerned not merely with restating received wisdom—as Hilferding was—but rather with developing the Currency School's theoretical apparatus. To this end, Mises both elaborates on the Currency School tradition and continues the

---

29   Mises also sees the triumph of the Banking School in some twentieth-century trends in economic policy, such as the practice of providing fiduciary credit as a stimulus for business activity. Cf. Mises ([1924] 1953, p. 439).

theoretical debate with the Banking School, to some extent avoiding the pitfalls of Currency views on monetary policy, and choosing instead to systematically develop a marginalist-inspired version of the Currency Theory.

At the outset, it is important to mention that there is some dispute over how to classify Mises in the history of monetary thought. The difficulty arises from Mises's simultaneous support for both the Currency School and free-banking, which would seem to place him in two irreconcilable traditions in monetary thinking. However, as shown by Salerno (2012), Mises's theoretical and policy positions are entirely compatible. Mises may therefore be categorized as a "Currency School free-banker," a label which signals both his theoretical ties to the Currency tradition and his disagreement on matters of monetary institutions and reform. This distinction is based on a classification first developed by Smith ([1936] 1990, esp. pp. 144–45), and anticipates the possible objection that Mises should not be considered a member of the Currency School due to his opposition to central banking.[30]

Advancing the Currency Theory

It is well known that the Currency School erred greatly in ascribing to bank notes and checking deposits different economic functions, and thus Peel's Act regulated only the issue of bank notes while leaving deposit banking alone altogether. This error was the target of much Banking School writing, but while Mises does not hesitate to acknowledge the Banking School's prescience in grouping notes and deposits together ([1924] 1953, p. 389), this difference of opinion with the Currency School does nothing to lessen Mises's appreciation of its arguments. In Mises's view, the Currency-Banking debate was diverted from theoretical questions to matters of policy by this error:

> The criticism of isolated dogmatic and economico-political errors of the Currency Principle that constituted the essence of most nineteenth-century investigation into the theory of banking and credit led to an emphasis being placed on all the factors that could be used to demonstrate the essential similarity of notes and other media of bank credit, and to the oversight of the important differences that exist between the two groups of credit characterized above [that is, between commodity credit

---

30   White (1984, pp. 103–04) argues that Mises is closer to the Free Banking School than the Currency School (although for somewhat different reasons).

and circulating credit], the discovery of which constitutes one
of the permanent contributions of the Classical School and its
successors, the Currency Theorists. ([1924] 1953, pp. 265–66)

According to this interpretation, this most notable error of the Currency School was overemphasized, while the more fundamental issue of the economic function of fiduciary media was largely neglected. For Mises, the central tenets of Currency doctrine do not stand or fall on their failure to distinguish between notes and deposits ([1924] 1953, p. 369). Thus Mises, in his exposition of the theory of money and banking, is simultaneously developing the theoretical doctrines of the Currency School and engaging in a revisionist analysis of the Currency-Banking dispute.

Mises's theory is based on Menger's theory of individuals' demand for money, combined with the marginal utility approach to value. The result is a systematic refinement of the Currency Theory which avoids pitfalls which hobbled the Classical approach to monetary theory. Mises thus attempts to put the Currency School's version of the quantity theory on firmer ground. While he cannot be considered a quantity theorist generally speaking, as Hilferding claims, Mises is a quantity theorist in a limited sense. That is to say, he argues that a causal link runs from the supply of money to prices, and not the other way around, as the Banking School supposed.

Despite adhering to this type of quantity theory, Mises is quick to distinguish between his version of the theory and that of the Currency School, which Mises describes as "purely mechanical" ([1924] 1953, p. 344). For Mises, the older theory leads to the conclusion—false, in his view—that changes in the quantity of money affect prices in some proportional or deterministic way. Mises's rejection of this view is the first step toward the development of his own theory of the business cycle.

The Currency School, however, never consistently and systematically developed a theory of the trade cycle, choosing instead to focus on the problem of international gold flows. Furthermore, they lacked a theory of capital to assist them in understanding the effects of monetary expansion (Huerta de Soto, 2006, pp. 627–29).[31] Mises viewed his own work as an

---

31   Mises does claim that the Currency School came close to perceiving the central problem of the business cycle: the divergence between the Money and Natural rates of interest. According to him, the Currency School understood the problems of fiduciary media and an artificially low rate of interest, but never made the necessary leap to understand differences between interest rates ([1924] 1953, pp. 398–99). Mises implies that the reason for the Currency School's lack of a systematic cycle theory was due to their belief that it is

attempt to fill this gap in the Currency School's exposition, and considers his own arguments a close parallel to those of the older school ([1924] 1953, p. 365). Mises's attempt to solve the dilemma of the Currency School by bringing together his marginal utility theory of money, Böhm-Bawerk's capital theory, and Wicksell's Natural and Money rates of interest, is vital for his theory of the trade cycle.

The Limitations to Credit Expansion

The heart of Mises's argument, however, is concerned with the economics of uncovered bank notes and deposits, which Mises calls "fiduciary media." In fact, the original German title of *The Theory of Money and Credit, Theorie des Geldes und der Umlaufsmittel*, actually translates to "The Theory of Money and Fiduciary Media." Practically the entire third part of the book is devoted to a refutation of the central tenets of the Banking School. It is possible that the success of *Finance Capital*, and with it Hilferding's restatement of Banking School principles, provided some of the impetus for Mises's attention to the Currency-Banking debate.[32]

Whatever Mises's exact motivation, there is no question that he is a strong opponent of the Banking School. In particular, Mises challenges the fundamental idea of limitations on note issue which defined so large a portion of Banking School writing. Mises does indeed acknowledge that redemption functions as an important check on bank policy, but also argues that if all banks expand their fiduciary issue together, the problem of redemption does not arise ([1924] 1953, pp. 312, 373, 325–26). So long as banks act in concert (or similarly, if a central bank controls fiduciary issue), redemption may not be an adequate check on credit expansion.[33]

---

impossible to "grant credit beyond the available amount of capital" ([1924] 1953, p. 343), and their concern only with problems of non-systematic credit expansion ([1924] 1953, pp. 354–55).

32   Mises does not cite Hilferding's theoretical works, but singles him out for censure in a note to the second edition of *The Theory of Money and Credit*, criticizing his understanding of the value of money and comments that "It was certainly an evil fate for Germany that its monetary and economic policy in recent years [i.e., during the hyperinflation of 1923] should have been in the hands of men like Hilferding and Havenstein, who were not qualified even for dealing with the depreciation of the mark in relation to gold" ([1924] 1953, p. 200, n. 1).

33   Although Mises does recognize certain policy tools which might be used to (incompletely) restrict note issues, such as requiring cover for notes in the form of short-term bills ([1924] 1953, pp. 313–14). Despite the fact that Mises opposes the Banking School

Mises singles out Tooke and Fullarton as the most important expo-
nents of the law of reflux (and of the Banking School in general), and devotes serious attention to their analysis of fiduciary issue. His remarks are
worth quoting *in extenso*:

> Tooke, Fullarton, Wilson, and their earlier English and German
> disciples, teach that it does not lie in the power of the banks-
> of-issue to increase or diminish their note-circulation. They
> say that the quantity of notes in circulation is settled by the de-
> mand within the community for media of payment. . . . Expan-
> sion and contraction of the quantity of notes in circulation is
> said to be never the cause, always only the effect, of fluctuations
> in business life. It therefore follows that the behaviour of the
> banks is merely passive; they do not influence the circumstances
> which determine the amount of the total circulation, but are in-
> fluenced by them. . . . The fundamental error of the Banking
> School lies in its failure to understand the nature of the issue
> of fiduciary media. When the bank discounts a bill or grants a
> loan in some other way, it exchanges a present good for a future
> good. Since the issuer creates the present good that it surrenders
> in the exchange—the fiduciary media—practically out of noth-
> ing, it would only be possible to speak of a natural limitation of
> the quantity of fiduciary media if the quantity of future goods
> that are exchanged in the loan-market against present goods
> was limited to a fixed amount. But this is by no means the case.
> The quantity of future goods is indeed limited by external cir-
> cumstances, but not that of the future goods that are offered on
> the market in the form of money. The issuers of the fiduciary
> media are able to induce an extension of the demand for them
> by reducing the interest demanded to a rate below the natural
> rate of interest . . . whereas on the other hand the demand for
> fiduciary media would be bound to cease entirely as soon as the
> rate asked by the bank was raised above the natural rate . . .

> That demand for money and money-substitutes which deter-
> mines the exchange-ratio between money and other economic

---

doctrine of reflux, he also holds that a system of competitive banking would place limits on
the issue of fiduciary media. Under such a system, each bank depends on its own reputation, which is destroyed whenever the slightest doubt concerning its solvency arises. He
argues that simultaneous expansion would be impossible, because it would require banks
with a greater reputation for solvency to ally with banks of lesser reputation, thus risking a
loss in reputation (Mises 1998, pp. 441–45; Salerno 2012).

goods achieves expression only in the behaviour of individuals when buying and selling other economic goods. Only when, say, money is being exchanged for bread is the position of the economic goods, money and commodity, in the value-scales of the individual parties to the transaction worked out and used as a basis of action; and from this the precise arithmetical exchange-ratio is determined. But when what is demanded is a money loan that is to be paid back in money again, then such considerations do not enter into the matter. Then only the difference in value between present goods and future goods is taken into account, and this alone has an influence on the determination of the exchange-ratio, i.e., on the determination of the level of the rate of interest.

For this reason the Banking Principle is unable to prove that no more fiduciary media can be put into circulation than an amount determined by fixed circumstances not dependent on the will of the issuer. It has therefore directed its chief attention to the proof of the assertion that any superfluous quantity of fiduciary media will be driven out of circulation back to the issuing body. Unlike money, fiduciary media do not come on to the market as payments, but as loans, Fullarton teaches; they must therefore automatically flow back to the bank when the loan is repaid. This is true. But Fullarton overlooks the possibility that the debtor may procure the necessary quantity of fiduciary media for the repayment by taking up a new loan. ([1924] 1953, pp. 305–08)

It is easy to see that Mises's argument incorporates the Wicksellian distinction between Natural and Money rates of interest.[34] According to Mises, failing to distinguish between these two rates of interest was a major failing of the Currency School ([1924] 1953, pp. 354–55).[35] It is precisely the banks' ability to issue credit at rates below the Natural rate which induces additional borrowing on the part of business. The demand for credit is not independent of the rate of interest on loans, but is partly determined

---

34   Although Mises supports Wicksell's distinction, he is critical of it in one important regard: Mises denies Wicksell's contention that a tendency exists in the market which obliges the banks to adjust the Money rate to the Natural rate of interest ([1924] 1953, pp. 355–57), preventing any significant divergence between them. This lack of necessary convergence between the two rates paves the way for Mises's theory of the trade cycle.

35   The Banking School, and Tooke especially, did devote attention to the theoretical problems of the interest rate, but also failed to draw the Wicksellian distinction.

by it ([1924] 1953, p. 354). It is important to note that Mises does not argue that undue expansions of bank credit will always occur, but merely that there is no necessary elasticity of the issue of fiduciary media of the sort described by the Banking School. There is no economic principle to explain why excess fiduciary media *must* flow back to the banks if the banks choose simultaneously to expand the supply of fiduciary media together ([1924] 1953, pp. 311–12).[36]

Yet Mises continues, arguing that even if the simple reflux explanation were true, there would still be no substantive reason to believe that fiduciary issues can be restricted:

> The fatal error of Fullarton and his disciples was to have overlooked the fact that even convertible bank-notes remain permanently in circulation and can then bring about a glut of fiduciary media the consequences of which resemble those of an increase in the quantity of money in circulation. Even if it is true, as Fullarton insists, that bank-notes issued as loans automatically flow back to the bank after the term of the loan has passed, still this does not tell us anything about the question whether the bank is able to maintain them in circulation by repeated prolongation of the loan. The assertion that lies at the heart of the position taken up by the Banking School, viz., that it is impossible to set and permanently maintain in circulation more notes than will meet the public demand, is untenable; for the demand for credit is not a fixed quantity; it expands as the rate of interest falls, and contracts as the rate of interest rises. But since the rate of interest that is charged for loans made in fiduciary media created expressly for that purpose can be reduced by the banks in the first instance down to the limit set by the marginal utility of the capital used in the banking business, i.e., practically to zero, the whole edifice built up by Tooke's school collapses. ([1924] 1953, p. 345)

In addition to all this, Mises contends that there is yet another error in the Banking School analysis, namely that the Banking School confused fiduciary media with money certificates (i.e., fully backed money substitutes) ([1924] 1953, p. 281). Mises's theory of money precludes the possibility of the overissue of money certificates, but not of fiduciary media ([1924] 1953, pp. 325–26). Mises also draws a sharp line between a credit transaction, which is simply a present good traded for a future good, and

---

36   Cf. also Mises ([1924] 1953, pp. 343–44).

fiduciary media, the creation of which does not impose any restrictions on the borrower. Whereas in a credit exchange, the lender must necessarily restrict his own consumption so as to lend, in the case of fiduciary media the new money substitutes are created *ex nihilo*, and thus the lender does not have to restrict his present consumption (beyond that required by the physical cost of producing fiduciary media) ([1924] 1953, pp. 264–65).

Mises's theory of money also allows him to criticize another of the more serious Banking School arguments regarding overissue. Fullarton famously argued that hoards of money would absorb excess issue of bank notes when supply exceeded demand, and would release bank notes whenever demand exceeded supply, thus equilibrating the market for fiduciary media.[37] These hoards are idle in the sense that they do not affect economic calculations and prices.

Mises first points out that the Banking School never tried to show *how* the process of storing up and of releasing of hoards would take place, an explanation which is absolutely necessary for this theory of hoards. More importantly however, Mises argues that when viewed through the lens of the marginal utility theory of money, the idea of "idle" stocks of money is untenable. Following Menger, Mises focused on the idea of money as a commodity like any other, in the sense that commodities are always held by individuals, and are still the subject of economic activity even when they are "idle" in the common sense of the word. Every portion of the money supply is always owned by some individual somewhere, and appears as a good on that individual's value scales, and thus is incorporated into the price calculations of the monetary economy ([1924] 1953, pp. 147–50). That is to say, there is no activity "hoarding" which is economically different from holding money in a cash balance. This analysis fits appropriately with the "methodological individualism" of the Austrian school,[38] as opposed to say, Hilferding's theory, which perceives money as reflecting socially necessary labor time of production, and is divorced from any notion of individual value.

Mises thus rejects the theory of endogenous money as espoused by Hilferding and the Banking School. Instead, Mises holds that the supply of fiduciary media may be augmented by the banks of issue (if and so long as

---

37   Mises notes ([1924] 1953, p. 146) that this argument implicitly assumes the correctness of the quantity theory.

38   Although the expression "methodological individualism" comes from Schumpeter ([1908] 2010).

they act in concert),[39] and in particular, by the central bank, and he even goes so far as to describe fiduciary media as, "the indefinitely augmentable product of the arbitrary issuing activity of the banks" ([1924] 1953, p. 285). Banks may therefore be active (as opposed to the purely passive) institutions altering the supply of fiduciary media; that is to say, they may be the exogenous source of fiduciary media, and the ultimate source of increases in the supply of money.[40]

From the above remarks it should be clear that in terms of monetary theory, Mises should be considered an intellectual successor to the Currency School, although his theoretical apparatus is derived using tools unavailable to the Classical economists, namely, marginal utility theory, Böhm-Bawerkian capital theory, and Wicksellian interest rate theory. Nevertheless, there are strong and explicit affinities not only between Mises's positive exposition of the theory of money and banking, but also in his negative appraisal of the Banking School, which demonstrate that Mises viewed himself as a firm advocate of Currency School teaching.

JOSEPH SCHUMPETER AND THE ENTREPRENEURIAL THEORY OF CREDIT EXPANSION

The Theory of Economic Development is not usually remembered as a treatise on money and banking, but rather as a theory of entrepreneurship and development. However, Schumpeter's theory of the entrepreneur in this early work is inextricably entwined with a theory of credit expansion and the forces which govern it. In addition to the well-known traits of innovator and creator, the entrepreneur is also the only recipient of newly-created fiduciary media in the circular flow. The whole question posed by Schumpeter's theory of development relates to how a system with no spare resources can ever economically develop. The answer lies in the creation of bank credit.

While Hilferding and Mises can be classified as successors to the Banking and Currency Schools respectively, Schumpeter occupies a sort of middle ground between the two positions. It is therefore appropriate that *The Theory of Economic Development* appears chronologically as well as

---

39   Cf. note 33.

40   Here I refer to what Mises described as "money in the broader sense," which includes both money and money substitutes. Cf. Mises [1924] 1953, pp. 482–83 for his particular categorization of the different types of money.

theoretically between the works of the other economists. As with his fellow Viennese economists, there is some discussion in *The Theory of Economic Development* concerning bank credit and its effects on the economic process which proves fundamental for the larger theoretical arguments. Monetary theory is not the focus of Schumpeter's book (as it was for Mises), although to some extent it was the foundation upon which Schumpeter constructed a theory of capitalism (as with Hilferding). For Schumpeter, monetary theory is one component of many in the analysis of the capitalist process.[41]

Schumpeter's book represents something of a problem for historians of thought, because it includes few references to the economic literature, and none at all to the Currency-Banking dispute. However, given Schumpeter's other writing in the period,[42] it is clear that he was already thoroughly acquainted with 19th century monetary theory, especially in the British Classical tradition, and that he wished to develop his own theory in light of his studies in the history of economic thought. Also, given the early influence of Hilferding on Schumpeter (Michaelides and Milios, 2005), it is quite possible that Schumpeter is attempting to clarify certain points of Hilferding's theory, including in the field of money and banking.

Credit Means of Payment

Schumpeter's development theory depends on the issue of uncovered notes and deposits, which he calls simply "credit means of payment" (1934, p. 73). Credit means of payment are created exclusively for the entrepreneurs (that is, in the circular flow, no other source of demand for credit means of payment exists, nor are there other uses credit could be devoted to). Schumpeter therefore assigns significant attention to potential problems of credit, especially the problem of inflation.

Even though new credit will be used to finance innovations, Schumpeter notes that the issue of credit does not in itself increase the productive capacity of the economy (1934, p. 108). It does, however, bid the factors of production away from their current uses. This triggers inflationary changes, and prices, specifically those of producers' goods, begin to rise. But this

---

41   Schumpeter's own theory of money was never completed to his satisfaction, although portions of his unfinished manuscript on the subject have been published as *Das Wesen des Geldes* (1970).

42   Cf. the comments scattered throughout Schumpeter ([1912] 1967).

credit inflation is only temporary, and lasts only so long as no new stocks of goods appear on the market.

Schumpeter explains this view of the inflationary process by way of an analogy. Purchasing power, of both the existing stock of money and the supply of bank credit, is like gas circulating in a closed container. When more gas (i.e., more credit means of payment) are pumped into the container, the space allotted to each individual molecule of gas (the command of every unit of purchasing power) decreases proportionately (1934, p. 109). This "compression" of purchasing power constitutes the inflationary process.

Schumpeter's analogy applies both to bank notes and bills circulating as media of exchange, and Schumpeter also accepts the Banking School's point that deposits are credit means of payment in addition to notes and bills (1934, p. 109), thus avoiding the error of the Currency School.

The problem of credit inflation is therefore also temporary and ultimately illusory: at first, credit is extended beyond the available supply of goods, but as soon as the entrepreneurs begin to produce, new goods flood the market, and although the new credit remains in circulation, its effects are cancelled out as prices adjust proportionately.

In fact, Schumpeter goes a step further, arguing that the process of credit creation and innovation may actually have net deflationary effects: "The entrepreneur must not only legally repay money to his banker, but he must also economically repay commodities to the reservoir of goods" (1934, p. 110). But the entrepreneur does more than merely return the economy to its original productive levels; he must actually *increase* the amount of goods available to society. If he succeeds (and at this point Schumpeter is mostly unconcerned with the possibility of failure), he therefore increases the stock of goods beyond the increase in purchasing power (that is, beyond the effects of the increase of credit means of payment) (1934, pp. 74, 233–35). Thus at the end of the period of economic development,

> the equivalence between the money and commodity streams is more than restored, the credit inflation more than eliminated, the effect upon prices more than compensated for, so that it may be said that there is no credit inflation at all in this case—rather deflation—but only a non-synchronous appearance of purchasing power and of the commodities corresponding to it, which temporarily produces the semblance of inflation. (1934, p. 110)

Schumpeter does not dwell on the precise difference between real inflation and the semblance of inflation, but it is implied that the prices of all goods in the economy rise proportionately, and that there are no distorting effects as there are, for example, in the theory of Mises. This is the natural conclusion derived from Schumpeter's gas analogy, which treats the relationship between credit and commodities as strictly proportional on net, and does not allow for the uneven alterations in the prices of producers' goods which incite errors in the pattern of production.[43]

The deflationary effects of development are, according to Schumpeter's theory, actually quite severe, because only income in the form of entrepreneurial profit and interest remain in the economy, while credit means of payment return to the bank and are removed from circulation, thus exacerbating the deflation (1934, p. 111). However, Schumpeter provides two reasons why the extent of deflation will be limited in actual banking practice. First, as Mises also pointed out, there is the possibility of prolonging loans, thus keeping credit means of payment (i.e., bills, notes, and deposits) in circulation beyond the period of innovation. Although this would not solve the problem permanently, it does explain how deflationary tendencies could be temporarily limited (1934, p. 111).

Second, Schumpeter argues that credit means of payment can remain permanently in circulation, because after the introduction of new commodities, the effects of credit are neutralized by new commodities, and credit actually loses its effect on prices altogether. Thus it is benign from the point of view of inflation, and there will be no special need to reduce the circulation. In fact, there may be an impetus to maintain it, because the previously new credit is now incorporated into the circular flow, and may be used to cover further economic activities, although any such activities are not development in Schumpeter's sense, but ordinary production (1934, p. 112).

This view of credit expansion is something of a cross between the Currency and Banking views: while credit expansion is inflationary in the Currency sense in the short run, in the longer run, which allows for the completion of production, expansion of the supply of credit beyond the supply of commodities is essentially impossible. This latter position is closer to the Banking School, although it does not depend upon the strict reflux theory of Fullarton to explain the lack of inflationary problems.

---

43   In fact, Schumpeter rejects malinvestment theories of the business cycle of the sort Mises would advance (Schumpeter 1934, p. 231).

Schumpeter's Supply-and-Demand Theory of Credit Issue

Schumpeter uses a simple supply-and-demand theory to explain the determinants of the quantity of money in the economy. He treats the quantity of money as exogenous, with new credit being issued exclusively by banks (1934, pp. 74, 195), but nevertheless the system is not without limits to expansion. The banker is not a passive agent as in the Banking School view, but rather "the capitalist par excellence" (1934, p. 74), the ultimate gatekeeper of all economic change.

With a redeemable commodity standard, limits are set both by calls for redemption, and the export of gold. In this sense Schumpeter says nothing too different from the Currency School. Nevertheless, there are limits to these limitations, and room exists for the banks to cautiously increase the supply of credit means of payment, so long as "the resulting inflation is really temporary and moreover remains moderate" (1934, p. 113). Schumpeter argues that there are two limitations to the supply of credit means of payment. First, the possibility of entrepreneurial failure limits the amount banks will be willing to issue, by requiring the banks to exercise discretion in their lending policies (1934, p. 114). But Schumpeter largely dismisses this limit by pointing out that the prices of loans will simply include a risk premium so as to avoid the problem of default (1934, pp. 195–96).[44]

Second, there is the risk of the depreciation of money substitutes through needless issue. As noted above, such inflation can only be "temporary" if new goods are introduced to counter the increase in the supply of credit. Because the process of development does not occur synchronously with increases in the supply of goods, there will be periods of inflation during production. A bank of issue must therefore keep certain reserves (taken from ordinary savings) in order that they remain solvent during these periods. This reserve is a further limit on the expansion of credit.

These arguments lead Schumpeter to the conclusion that the limitations on the supply of money, while not rigid or quantitatively definable, are nevertheless significant:

> Therefore, even if we cannot, in the nature of things, state the
> limit to the creation of purchasing power . . . and even if the lim-
> it must vary according to the mentality of the people, legislation,
> and so on, yet we can state that there is such a limit at any time

---

44   The problem of bad credit risk was also typically assumed away by the Currency and Banking Schools, as well as by Hilferding and Mises.

and what circumstances normally guarantee its maintenance. Its existence neither excludes the creation of purchasing power in our sense nor alters its significance. But it makes its volume at any time an elastic, though nevertheless definite, magnitude. (1934, pp. 113–14)

Once again, Schumpeter walks a fine line between the position of Hilferding and the Banking School who altogether deny the possibility of over-issue, and Mises and the Currency School, who hold that limitations on issue were often lacking. Although he does not delve deeply into the problem, Schumpeter also recognizes that banks acting together can permanently increase their issues and thus also the price level (1934, pp. 114–15). He notes in passing, in accordance with the Currency position, that because of this ability, "special legal restrictions and special safety-valves are actually necessary in practice" (1934, p. 115) in order to prevent excessive issues.

Concerning the demand for bank credit, Schumpeter introduces an interesting challenge to Banking-style interpretations of the "needs of trade." Whereas the requirements of business had been viewed in the Banking tradition as definite limits to the ability to issue new bank credit, Schumpeter argues that the demand for credit means of payment comes from entrepreneurs, who will only wish to produce (that is, innovate) if they can earn a profit (1934, p. 196). Schumpeter also points out that the number of potential innovations at any point in time is for all practical purposes unlimited. There is therefore no strict limit to the quantity of credit entrepreneurs might demand (1934, p. 197).[45] Limitations are therefore restricted to the supply side of the money market, and the elasticity of the quantity of credit is dependent almost entirely on these factors.

Schumpeter's analysis of the early stages of the boom is in a sense similar to Mises'. Both economists agreed that the creation of credit means of payment would put excess purchasing power in the hands of individuals seeking to purchase producers' goods. In fact, Schumpeter (erroneously) attributes to Mises the coining of the expression "forced saving" to refer to the rise in prices in producers' goods industries which characterizes the boom phase of the business cycle (1934, p. 109, n. 1).[46] It is possible,

---

45   Remember that, unlike some other equilibrium constructs, in Schumpeter's circular flow model the interest rate is zero.

46   Mises and Schumpeter appear to have different points in mind with this common phrase (i.e., overconsumption vs. involuntarily restricted consumption). On this and other issues relating to the different meanings of "forced saving," cf. Machlup (1943). This note of

however, that Schumpeter's seemingly positive reference to Mises in regards forced saving is made in the context of the first German edition of Mises's book (Schumpeter does not provide the bibliographic citation). In the earliest edition of *The Theory of Money and Credit*, Mises made several remarks which were removed from later editions, and which cast his early writing in a somewhat different light, in the sense that they are incompatible with his later views on monetary theory (Gertchev 2004; Hülsmann 2012). Inconsistencies in the different versions of the text, as well as the fact that *The Theory of Money and Credit* was only the first major step in Mises's thinking on money, have led to confusions on certain issues. One of these relates to the concept which later became known as "forced saving" (although Mises never uses this term). Mises occasionally makes claims which, taken outside the context of his later writings, might appear to make his views on forced saving ambiguous (Mises [1924] 1953, pp. 208, 347–348, 350). Specifically, Mises seems to imply that forced saving might encourage sustainable capital formation. Regardless of Mises's actual intentions, this point may have seemed quite Schumpeterian at the time it was first written. Nevertheless, it may explain why there seems to be an affinity between these earlier writings of Mises and Schumpeter.

But despite Schumpeter praising the "power and originality" of *The Theory of Money and Credit*,[47] potential agreement is quite limited. Credit creation for Schumpeter is both necessary for economic development and benign in terms of the negative effects of inflationary expansion. For Mises, however, the issue of fiduciary media is a matter to some extent at the discretion of the banks, and its overissue sets in motion malinvestments which lead inevitably to the bust, and not to sustainable growth.

On the one hand, Schumpeter's analysis of the limitations on the creation of credit means of payment resembles the Currency School, in the sense that he does not perceive serious limitations to a dedicated attempt to expand credit. On the other hand, his theory of development explicitly incorporates an expansion of the quantity of bank credit which, although exogenously determined, is not only not harmful, but is in fact beneficial. This aspect of the theory is thus closer to the Banking School notion of an "elastic" currency responding to the needs of trade (although, as mentioned above, different in some key respects). Schumpeter's theory,

---

Schumpeter's appears in the second edition of *The Theory of Economic Development*, which was published only after the first edition of *The Theory of Money and Credit*.

47   Quoted in Hülsmann (2007, p. 208).

however, focuses less on past influences than it does on his theory of economic development.

The Development Theory of the Business Cycle

A certain resemblance also exists between Schumpeter's innovation-based theory of the business cycle and the Banking School approach. This is especially true of Schumpeter's earliest presentation in *The Theory of Economic Development*. Schumpeter, Hilferding, and the Banking School—although Schumpeter's theory is more original than either—share a non-monetary approach to business cycles.

Innovation and development are the causes of the trade cycle. Entrepreneurs "introduce new combinations" and compete for means of production (fixed capital). As is the case in similar theories, there is a lag between investment and the sale of finished goods. Thus the prices of factors rise in the inflationary boom, increasing the costs of older (non-innovating) firms and thus threatening their position in the market, causing bankruptcies (1934, pp. 232–33). The failure of firms causes a decline in capital investment, which in turn leads to a collapse of the rate of interest, money incomes, and the demand for consumers' goods (1934, p. 237).

Much of Banking theory appears in Schumpeter, although it plays a different role than in the original Banking Writings. For example, Schumpeter notes in passing the prevalence of what he deems "psychological" aspects of the business cycle, such as speculative mania and subsequent panics, but claims that these are not the essence of the cycle (1934, pp. 213, 219, 227–28). Like Hilferding, Schumpeter seeks a deeper explanation of the psychological characteristics of the cycle, as opposed to simply taking them as given. For Schumpeter, such events can only be effects, and not causes of prosperity and depression, which are only attributable to the efforts of entrepreneurs to radically alter the state of production (1934, pp. 227–28). Likewise, disproportionality between economic sectors and overproduction exist in the business cycle, but are also effects, never causes (1934, pp. 227–28).

Both Schumpeter's theory and Tooke's cite essentially exogenous innovations as the ultimate cause of business cycles. The new firm (with its innovations) "does not grow out of the old but appears alongside it" (1934, p. 216). Schumpeter's entrepreneur "introduces new combinations," such as:

> (1) [A] new good . . . or of a new quality of a good. (2) The introduction of a new method of production. . . . (3) The opening of a new market. . . . (4) The conquest of a new source of supply of

raw materials or half-manufactured goods. . . . (5) The carrying
out of the new organization of any industry. (1934, p. 66)

The disequilibrating effect of such innovations, especially the influence
of new foreign markets, was stressed by the Banking School. Although it
is not obvious whether Tooke exercised any positive influence on Schumpeter's theory, this aspect of Tooke fits squarely into Schumpeter's exposition, although Schumpeter's theory of the cause of cycles is more specific
than Tooke's. Schumpeter acknowledges, for instance, that cycles may be
caused by bad harvests, but regards this sort of cause as secondary to his
development theory (1934, p. 220).

Mill too observed that rapid increases in the amount of productive
innovations (in other words, increases in fixed as compared to circulating
capital) could cause economic fluctuations, but he dismissed this possibility as empirically unlikely ([1967d] 2006, p. 97). Mill claimed instead that
increases in the amount of fixed capital are financed through profits and
not through circulating capital, and in any case occur slowly. However, in
Schumpeter's circular flow there are no profits from which to draw, and
so entrepreneurial resources must be financed through credit expansion.
Although Schumpeter often avoids using the words "fixed capital" specifically (for example, 1934, p. 241, n. 1),[48] he is clear that the innovations of
the entrepreneurs require serious long-term investment, i.e., a sufficient
stock of fixed capital.

Mill and Schumpeter both perceived business fluctuations as periodi-
cal, cyclical events which occur in the capitalist economy. In his *Business
Cycles: A Theoretical, Historical, and Statistical Analysis of the Capitalist
Process* (1939), Schumpeter would fully develop his multi-cycle schema,
but in *The Theory of Economic Development* he utilizes a one-cycle model,
as does Mill. Mill however, thought cycles were due primarily to erroneous
and morally reprehensible speculation, which he hoped one day could be
eliminated from the economy ([1967a] 2006, pp. 77–78), whereas Schumpeter viewed the cycle as a natural and necessary part of capitalist economic development.

---

48   It is possible that Schumpeter takes this route to avoid spurious association with
the older overinvestment theories, concerning which Schumpeter is rather cautious (1934,
pp. 219, 239–40).

We can see then that Schumpeter's theory may be expressed in the terminology of the Banking School (and of Hilferding), but is not a direct descendent of that tradition. As Schumpeter explains:

> The unsaleableness of commodities already produced, still more of those producible, at prices which cover costs calls forth the well known further phenomenon of the tightness of money, possible insolvency, which is so typical that every theory of the business cycle must be in a position to explain it. Ours does so... but it does not employ this typical fact as a primary and independent cause. This overproduction is accentuated by [a] skewness of the boom. . . . This circumstance on the one hand, and the discrepancy between effective supply and effective demand which must occur in many industries during the depression on the other, make it possible to describe the external form of depressions in the language of the various disproportionality theories. . . . For us, disproportionalities between quantities and prices of goods . . . is an intermediate phenomenon just like overproduction and is not a primary cause. (1934, pp. 239–40)

As is typical of his theoretical work, Schumpeter's early theory of the business cycle is consistent with other theories, and owes much to other traditions in economics, although it cannot be said to belong to one in particular.

CONCLUSION

The dispute between the Currency and Banking Schools had a profound impact on at least three distinct approaches to economics, as exemplified by Hilferding, Mises, and Schumpeter. What is most striking is the fact that this influence was felt by economists with such wide-ranging differences: differences which serve as an appropriate testament to the importance of the earlier Schools. By focusing on the nature of dynamic change in the economy, Hilferding, Mises, and Schumpeter each introduced theories which complement and, in their particular ways, complete the theories of the earlier schools. Through their respective analyses of money and credit, each economist attempted to explain a part of the process of economic change in capitalist society. The enduring worth of these arguments may be seen from the fact that there is still much investigation and debate on the theoretical and empirical questions raised by these writers, debate which appears not yet to have borne all the fruit of which it is capable.

REFERENCES

Arnon, Arie. 1984. "Marx's Theory of Money: The Formative Years." *History of Political Economy* 16, no. 4: 555–75.

Boot, H. M. 1983. "James Wilson and the Commercial Crisis of 1847." *History of Political Economy* 1, no. 4: 567–83.

Daugherty, Marion R. 1943. "The Currency-Banking Controversy, Part II." *Southern Economic Journal* 9, no. 3: 241–51.

———. 1942. "The Currency-Banking Controversy, Part I." *Southern Economic Journal* 9, no. 2: 140–55.

Fullarton, John. [1845] 1969. *On the Regulation of Currencies; Being an Examination of the Principles on Which it is Promised to Restrict, Within Certain Limits, the Future Issues on Credit of the Bank of England and of the Other Banking Establishments Throughout the Country.* 2nd ed. Reprint, New York: Augustus M. Kelley.

Gertchev, Nikolay. 2004. "Dehomogenizing Mises's Monetary Theory." *Journal of Libertarian Studies* 18, no. 3: 57–90.

Glasner, David. 1992. "The Real-Bills Doctrine in the Light of the Law of Reflux." *History of Political Economy* 24, no. 4: 867–94.

Green, Roy. 1987. "John Fullarton." In *The New Palgrave: A Dictionary of Economics.* John Eatwell, Murray Milgate, and Peter Newman, eds. London: Macmillan.

Haberler, Gottfried. 1951. "Schumpeter's Theory of Interest." *The Review of Economics and Statistics* 33, no. 2: 122–28.

Hayek, F.A. 1991. "The Dispute Between the Currency School and the Banking School, 1821–1848." In *The Collected Works of F.A. Hayek,* Volume III. W.W. Bartley III and Stephen Kresge, eds. Chicago: University of Chicago Press.

———. 1941. *The Pure Theory of Capital.* London: Routledge & Kegan Paul.

Hilferding, Rudolf. [1910] 1981. *Finance Capital.* London: Routledge.

———. 1912. "Review of *Theorie des Geldes und der Umlaufsmittel.*" *Die Neue Zeit* 30 (2): 1024–27. Reprinted in *Mises: An Annotated Bibliography.* Bettina Bien Greaves and Robert W. McGee, eds. Irvington-on-Hudson, N.Y.: Foundation for Economic Education. 1993.

Horwitz, Steven. 1994. "Complementary Non-Quantity Theory Approaches to Money: Hilferding's *Finance Capital* and Free Banking Theory." *History of Political Economy* 26, no. 2: 221–38.

Huerta de Soto, Jesús. 2006. *Money, Bank Credit, and Economic Cycles*. Auburn, Ala.: Ludwig von Mises Institute.

Hülsmann, Jörg Guido. 2007. *Mises: The Last Knight of Liberalism*. Auburn, Ala.: Ludwig von Mises Institute.

——. 2012. "The Early Evolution of Mises's Monetary Theory." In *Theory of Money and Fiduciary Media: Essays in Celebration of the Centennial*. Jörg Guido Hülsmann, ed. Auburn, Ala.: Ludwig von Mises Institute.

Keynes, John Maynard. 1936. *The General Theory of Employment, Interest, and Money*. New York: Harcourt, Brace, & World.

Forget, Evelyn L. 1990. "John Stuart Mill's Business Cycle." *History of Political Economy* 22, no. 4: 629–42.

Link, Robert G. 1959. *English Theories of Fluctuations, 1815–1848*. New York: Columbia University Press.

Machlup, Fritz. 1943. "Forced or Induced Saving: An Exploration into Its Synonyms and Homonyms." *The Review of Economics and Statistics* 25, no. 1: 26–39.

Marx, Karl. 1973. *Grudrisse*. Trans. Martin Nicolaus. New York: Vintage Books.

——. [1930] 1972. *Capital*. 2 vols. Eden and Cedar Paul, eds. Reprint, London: J.M. Dent & Sons.

——. 1911. *A Contribution to the Critique of Political Economy*. N.I. Stone, trans. Chicago: Charles H. Kerr.

McCaffrey, Matthew. 2012. "Conflicting Views of the Entrepreneur in Turn-of-the-Century Vienna." Unpublished Manuscript.

Michaelides, Panayotis and John Milios. 2005. "Did Hilferding influence Schumpeter?" *History of Economics Review* 41: 98–126.

Mill, John Stuart. 1967a. "Paper Currency and Commercial Distress." In *The Collected Works of John Stuart Mill*, ed. J.M. Robson. 4: 71–123. Reprint, Indianapolis: Liberty Fund 2006.

——. 1967b. "The Currency Juggle." In *Collected Works* 4: 181–92.

——. 1967c. "Of the Influence of Consumption on Production." In *Collected Works*. Vol. 4: 262–79.

——. 1967d. *The Principles of Political Economy with Some of their Applications to Social Philosophy*. In *Collected Works*. Vols. 2–3.

Mints, Lloyd W. 1945. *A History of Banking Theory in Great Britain and the United States*. Chicago: University of Chicago Press.

Mises, Ludwig von. 1998. *Human Action: The Scholar's Edition*. Auburn, Ala.: Ludwig von Mises Institute.

——. [1924] 1953. *The Theory of Money and Credit*. New Haven, Conn.: Yale University Press.

Pivetti, Massimo. 1987. "Thomas Tooke." In *The New Palgrave: A Dictionary of Economics*. John Eatwell, Murray Milgate, and Peter Newman, eds. London: Macmillan.

Robbins, Lionel. 1958. *Robert Torrens and the Evolution of Classical Economics*. London: MacMillan & Co.

Rosner, Peter. 1988. "A Note on the Theories of Business Cycle by Hilferding and by Hayek." *History of Political Economy* 20, no. 2: 309–19.

Rothbard, Murray N. 1987. "Breaking Out of the Walrasian Box: The Cases of Schumpeter and Hansen." *The Review of Austrian Economics* 1, no. 1: 97–108.

Salerno, Joseph T. 2012. "Mises as Currency School Free Banker." In *Theory of Money and Fiduciary Media: Essays in Celebration of the Centennial*. Jörg Guido Hülsmann, ed. Auburn, Ala.: Ludwig von Mises Institute.

Schumpeter, Joseph A. [1908] 2010. *The Nature and Essence of Economic Theory*. Bruce A. McDaniel, ed. New Brunswick, N.J.: Transaction.

——. [1939] 1982. *Business Cycles: A Theoretical, Historical, and Statistical Analysis of the Capitalist Process*. Philadelphia: Porcupine Press.

——. 1970. *Das Wesen des Geldes*. Göttingen: Vandenhoeck & Ruprecht.

——. [1954] 1963. *The History of Economic Analysis*. New York: Oxford University Press.

——. 1942. *Capitalism, Socialism, and Democracy*. New York: Harper and Brothers Publishers.

——. 1934. *The Theory of Economic Development*. Redvers Opie, trans. Cambridge, Mass.: Harvard University Press.

——. [1912] 1967. *Economic Doctrine and Method*. R. Aris, Trans. New York: Oxford University Press.

Selgin, George A. 1988. *The Theory of Free Banking: Money Supply under Competitive Note Issue*. Totowa, N.J.: Roman and Littlefield.

Smith, Vera C. [1936] 1990. *The Rationale of Central Banking*. Indianapolis: Liberty Fund.

Tooke, Thomas. [1848] 1962. *A History of Prices and of the State of the Circulation from 1972 to 1856*. Vol. IV. Series of Reprints of Scarce Works on Political Economy No. 16. London: London School of Economics and Political Sciences.

——. [1844] 1959. *An Inquiry into the Currency Principle; the Connection of the Currency with Prices, and the Expediency of a Separation of Issue from Banking*. 2nd ed. Series of Reprints of Scarce Works on Political Economy No. 15. London: London School of Economics and Political Science.

Viner, Jacob. 1937. *Studies in the Theory of International Trade*. New York: Harper and Brothers Publishers.

Vorhies, Francis W. 1982. "Marx and Mises of Money: The Monetary Theories of Two Opposing Political Economies." Ph.D. Dissertation, University of Colorado at Boulder.

White, Lawrence H. 1984. *Free Banking in Britain: Theory, Experience, and Debate, 1800–1845*. New York: Cambridge University Press.

Wilson, James. 1847. *Capital, Currency, and Banking; Being a Collection of a Series of Articles Published in the* Economist *in 1845, on the Principles of the Bank Act of 1844, and in 1847, on the Recent Monetarial and Commercial Crisis; Concluding with a Plan for a Secure and Economical Currency*. London.

Wu, Chi-Yuen. 1939. *An Outline of International Price Theories*. Reprint, Auburn, Ala.: Ludwig von Mises Institute, 2007.

7

GARY NORTH

The Regression Theory
as Conjectural History

MENGER ON THE ORIGIN OF MONEY

CARL MENGER'S LAST published work during his lifetime was an 1892 essay, "On the Origins of Money." He introduced it by pointing out how odd it was in his era that the precious metals, gold and silver, were universally used as money. That coins should circulate widely seemed strange to investigators in his day.

> But that every economic unit in a nation should be ready to exchange his goods for little metal disks apparently useless as such, or for documents representing the latter, is a procedure so opposed to the ordinary course of things, that we cannot well wonder if even a distinguished thinker like Savigny finds it downright "mysterious."[1]

One explanation of the origin of money is that the civil government declared precious metals coins as money. Sovereignty is therefore the source of money's acceptance and therefore its value.

GARY NORTH holds a Ph.D in history from the University of California, Riverside and is the editor of GaryNorth.com.

1   Carl Menger, "The Origin of Money," *Economic Journal* II (1892): 239. Available: School of Comparative Individualism: http://www.cooperativeindividualism.org/menger-carl_on-the-origins-of-money-1892.html

To assume that certain commodities, the precious metals in particular, had been exalted into the medium of exchange by general convention or law, in the interest of commonweal, solved
the difficulty, and solved it apparently the more easily and naturally inasmuch as the shape of the coins seemed to be a token
of state regulation. Such in fact is the opinion of Plato, Aristo-
tle, and the Roman jurists, closely followed by the mediaeval
writers. Even the more modern developments in the theory of
money have not in substance got beyond this standpoint.[2]

No Historical Documentation

Menger rejected this hypothesis. He offered this explanation for his
rejection: there are no historical records of such a transition from local
value to widespread value by means of fiat dictate.

An event of such high and universal significance and of noto-
riety so inevitable, as the establishment by law or convention
of a universal medium of exchange, would certainly have been
retained in the memory of man, the more certainly inasmuch as
it would have had to be performed in a great number of places.
Yet no historical monument gives us trustworthy tidings of any
transactions either conferring distinct recognition on media of
exchange already in use, or referring to their adoption by peo-
ples of comparatively recent culture, much less testifying to an
initiation of the earliest ages of economic civilization in the use
of money.[3]

His rejection of a historical explanation was based on the absence of primary source evidence. There should be records in some archive of such
a transition, given the widespread use of precious metal coins. He called
such a theory of money created by state decree unhistorical: ". . . the pre-
supposition is unhistorical."

Nor do even the theorists above mentioned honestly face the
problem that is to be solved, to wit, the explaining how it has
come to pass that certain commodities (the precious metals
at certain stages of culture) should be promoted amongst the
mass of all other commodities, and accepted as the generally
acknowledged media of exchange. It is a question concerning

---

2   Ibid., "Attempts at Solution Hitherto," part 2.

3   Ibid.

not only the origin but also the nature of money and its position in relation to all other commodities.[4]

When an explanation for the origin of any private practice or institutional arrangement is based on historical events that lack any substantiating historical evidence, we could call this thesis conjectural or hypothetical. It is an explanation of the way things must have occurred. It seems logical that this was the way that they did occur. So, they *must* have occurred this way.

The Most Marketable Commodity

Menger came to a conclusion regarding the function of money. Money metals were adopted because they were subject to widespread demand. This made them eminently saleable.

> The theory of money necessarily presupposes a theory of the saleableness of goods. If we grasp this, we shall be able to understand how the almost unlimited saleableness of money is only a special case,—presenting only a difference of degree—of a generic phenomenon of economic life—namely, the difference in the saleableness of commodities in general.[5]

Two decades later, Ludwig von Mises defined money as the most marketable commodity.

> The greater the marketability of the goods first acquired in indirect exchange, the greater would be the prospect of being able to reach the ultimate objective without further maneuvering. Thus there would be an inevitable tendency for the less marketable of the series of goods used as media of exchange to be one by one rejected until at last only a single commodity remained, which was universally employed as a medium of exchange; in a word, money.[6]

This was a recapitulation of Menger's argument. Menger had written,

> Hence it is also clear that nothing may have been so favourable to the genesis of a medium of exchange as the acceptance, on the part of the most discerning and capable economic subjects,

---

4   Ibid.

5   Ibid., "The Problem of the Genesis of a Medium of Exchange," part 3.

6   Ludwig von Mises, *The Theory of Money and Credit* (New Haven, Conn.: Yale Universuty Press, [1912] 1953), pp. 32–33.

for their own economic gain, and over a considerable period of time, of eminently saleable goods in preference to all others. In this way practice and a habit have certainly contributed not a little to cause goods, which were most saleable at any time, to be accepted not only by many, but finally by all, economic subjects in exchange for their less saleable goods; and not only so, but to be accepted from the first with the intention of exchanging them away again.[7]

In Part 8, Menger offered an explanation that served as an alternative to the conjectural history of the origin of money as the product of state decree. Precious metals came into use as money because of their uses as ornaments. He devoted a total of one sentence to this explanation.

There is no centre of population, which has not in the very beginnings of civilization come keenly to desire and eagerly to covet the precious metals, in primitive times for their utility and peculiar beauty as in themselves ornamental, subsequently as the choices materials for plastic and architectural decoration, and especially for ornaments and vessels of every kind.[8]

At this point, we expect some historical documentation. There is none. This creates a tactical problem. A defender of the fiat dictate theory of money's origin can invoke the same argument against Menger as he had invoked against the critic's ideological peers. Each side declares that the origin of money was rooted in a particular institutional arrangement. What seems reasonable to one commentator does not seem reasonable to the other.

ECONOMIC VALUE: FORWARD AND BACKWARD

Mises offered a more detailed treatment of the transition from commodity-for-use to commodity-for-exchange. He began Chapter II of Part Two of *Theory of Money and Credit* with a consideration of this problem.

Mises argued for subjective economic value. This process of subjective imputation of economic value applies to all factors in the economy. Money is no exception. Then what accounts for the use of any commodity as money? Two things: expectations of future exchange value and historical memories

---

7   Menger, "On the Genesis of Media of Exchange," part 6.

8   Menger, "How the Precious Metals became Money," part 8.

of past economic value. People impute value to scarce assets in the present because they believe that others will impute value to these similar assets in the future. But, in making these forecasts, they look to the past. Has a particular commodity maintained its objective exchange value? If so, buy it. It will function as money. But this raises a theoretical problem. Why did a commodity gain value in exchange yesterday? It does no good to appeal it its value the day before yesterday. That would lead to infinite regression. "It's turtles all the way down." Mises understood this.

> To trace back the value that money has to-day to that which it had yesterday, the value that it had yesterday to that which it had the day before, and so on, is to raise the question of what determined the value of money in the first place. Consideration of the origin of the use of money and of the particular components of its value that depend on its monetary function suggest an obvious answer to this question. The first value of money was clearly the value which the goods used as money possessed (thanks to their suitability for satisfying human wants in other ways) at the moment when they were first used as common media of exchange. When individuals began to acquire objects, not for consumption, but to be used as media of exchange, they valued them according to the objective exchange-value with which the market already credited them by reason of their "industrial" usefulness, and only as an additional consideration on account of the possibility of using them as media of exchange.[9]

He spoke of "an obvious answer." But the answer which he provided was not based on a detailed study of historical sources in a wide range of societies. Yet it also lacked the quality of certainty which Mises referred to in *Human Action* as "apodictic certainty," meaning a category of human action.[10] As he wrote, "Apodictic certainty is only within the orbit of the deductive system of aprioristic theory. The most that can be attained with regard to reality is probability."[11] So, with respect to the transition from value-in-use to value-in-exchange, the most that we can say is that this transition was probable.

---

9   Mises, *Theory of Money and Credit*, pp. 109–10.

10   Ludwig von Mises, *Human Action: A Treatise on Economics* (New Haven, Conn.: Yale University Press, 1949), pp. xvi, 15.

11   Ibid., p. 105.

The historian asks, "How probable?" When he asks this, given the non-mathematical training of most historians, he really does not mean statistically probable. Neither did Mises ask such a thing of records from the distant past, with the accumulated data governed by some algorithm. The historian means something like this. "Do we have sufficient documentary evidence to judge the nature of this transition in a representative sample of widely dispersed societies?" If money is as universal as Menger asserted, then there should be some trace of the supposed pattern of the transition from barter to money.

Yet, because of the nature of the transition, there will not be such documentation. While the archeological records of ancient mercantile civilizations are heavily weighted by tablets relating to commerce, these documents came from societies that had highly developed monetary arrangements. This is why the records are so extensive. The mind-numbing similarity of these tablets within a collection leads translators to cease translating after about 10 percent of the documents are translated.[12] What the historian wants is a collection of records of trade before money, with records of gold and silver as ornaments. This would mean barter. Then, at some point, records would show more transactions using gold and silver as tools of exchange. That would require sustained continuity of record-keeping and record-preservation. To find documentary evidence on transition from metal as ornamental to metal as money would be a remarkable discovery. To find such records in a dozen societies in several time periods and locations would be historically unprecedented.

Conjectural History in Action

So, my conclusion is that Menger and Mises resorted to conjectural history. Conjectural history operates in the unexplored nether region between historical documentation and apodictic certainty, between Heraclitus's flowing stream and Parmenides's logical order. It is more like common sense than anything else. The problem, as always, is that common sense is not all that common.

---

12   That was the estimate of David Noel Freedman. He offered it in a 1978 speech at Duke University on the Ebla tablets. He served as the Albright Institute of Archaeological Research (American Schools of Oriental Research, Jerusalem), Annual Director, 1969–70, 1976–77.

Some critics have rejected such exercises in common sense as *just-so stories*: fantastic explanations of origins. Others have substituted their own conjectural histories. We find this in rival stories concerning the origin of civil government. Thomas Hobbes, John Locke, and Jean-Jacques Rousseau all offered conjectural histories of the social contract. They all offered a version of how men must have gotten together once upon a time before there was writing to make documentary records. Men agreed to surrender sovereignty to the state. There is no documentary record of such a meeting. So, each of these scholars felt free to describe the event. The classic statement of all time regarding conjectural history is Rousseau's, which he wrote early in Chapter 1 of his *Discourse on the Origin and the Foundation of the Inequality Among Mankind* (1754). "Let us begin therefore, by laying aside facts, for they do not affect the question." The statement has generated its share of ridicule. But the paragraph that preceded it is insightful.

> The philosophers, who have examined the foundations of society, have, every one of them, perceived the necessity of tracing it back to a state of nature, but not one of them has ever arrived there. Some of them have not scrupled to attribute to man in that state the ideas of justice and injustice, without troubling their heads to prove, that he really must have had such ideas, or even that such ideas were useful to him: others have spoken of the natural right of every man to keep what belongs to him, without letting us know what they meant by the word belong; others, without further ceremony ascribing to the strongest an authority over the weakest, have immediately struck out government, without thinking of the time requisite for men to form any notion of the things signified by the words authority and government. All of them, in fine, constantly harping on wants, avidity, oppression, desires and pride, have transferred to the state of nature ideas picked up in the bosom of society.[13]

It is not that Menger and Mises laid aside the facts. It is that there were no facts to lay aside. The explanation which they gave for the rise of the money economy is reasonable, in the sense that it is difficult for an Austrian School economist to reject. He does not believe that a fiat declaration by a political sovereign would have been capable of changing the self-interested behavior of individuals in a barter-based economy. Such a declaration would not have persuaded large numbers of people to substitute metals of

---

13   See http://www.bartleby.com/34/3/1002.html

ornamental value for goods valued in exchange for their immediate use. An expensive bar of metal is neither a tool nor a consumption good. It is safer to store up other goods to be used to exchange later. Salt could work. Arrowheads could work. But not bars of shiny metal. The Austrian School economist looks to the free market for creative solutions to widespread problems. But, for economists and non-economists who are prepared to accept the word of a political sovereign as both creative and authoritative, the story of the origin of money in the declaration of a monarch sounds plausible.

HISTORY VS. DEVELOPMENT

Robert Nisbet, in his book *Social Change and History* (1969), presented a detailed study of two approaches to studying the past. The one approach, which he called the historian's past, involves a study of dates, personalities, and events. The other approach takes a broader perspective. He called this developmentalism or evolutionism. In such an outlook, he wrote,

> the emphasis is not upon the past as conceived as a genealogy of happenings and persons, but upon more or less timeless sequences of emergent *changes*. If *event* is the key to the historiographic perspective, *change* is the key concept in the developmental perspective. Time in the very broad sense matters, of course, but the developmentalist, whether social or biological, is far more interested in arriving at correct before-and-after relationships in his changes and types than in the probably futile search for dates as to when exactly a certain change occurred.[14]

Given this analysis, Menger and Mises were more developmentalists than historians when they discussed the origin of money. Their joint attempt to explain the origin of money in terms of individual human action, governed by subjective value, has the characteristic features of developmentalism. They did not search for documents in a dozen archives or museums relating to the use of gold and silver in ornaments, determining when and under what circumstances the transition to money occurred. They offered a theory of how it could have happened, and more than this, how it must have happened, given the goal of individuals to improve their circumstances. Yet they stopped short of identifying their account as

---

14   Robert A. Nisbet, *Social Change and History: Aspects of the Western Theory of Development* (New York: Oxford University Press, 1969), p. 31.

inherent in human action in the way that higher prices reduce the quantity demanded. So, in a peculiar development, which we can in fact date historically, Menger and Mises invoked a form of developmentalism in order to explain individual action. The origin of money must have happened this way every time.

CONCLUSION

The Menger-Mises regression theorem is not historical. It is developmental. It is an example of conjectural history. It seems more consistent with known human behavior than the theory of state-created money. But I speak as someone persuaded of most of the categories of Austrian School economics, especially in monetary affairs.

I have devoted more time and space to Greenback monetary theory than any living Austrian School economist.[15] The Greenbackers are persuaded that fiat money is a category of human action. They regard money as inherently statist. In contrast, I see no way that sovereigns declared money into existence: i.e., speaking something into existence. The state is not God. But I find it odd that I would accept as a substitute a conjectural theory of the origin of money. It would be nice to have some case studies.

Mises did not approve the use of historical examples to prove economic theory, but unless he regarded the origin of money as an inescapable historical corollary of the timeless axioms of human action, which he never asserted for his regression theory, then I find myself knee-deep in developmentalism. This is not where I planned to be when I first read *The Theory of Money and Credit* in 1963.

---

15   Gary North, *Gertrude Coogan's Bluff: Greenback Populism as Conservative Economics* (Auburn, Ala.: Mises Institute, 2010). Gary North, "Ellen Brown: Critique," http://bit.ly/BrownCritique

8

DAVID HOWDEN

Expansionist Monetary Policies and the Trade Balance

MUCH CONVENTIONAL WISDOM of modern international economics can be condensed into two statements:

1. currency depreciations improve a country's trade balance, and
2. trade deficits cause currency depreciations.

Historians of economic thought will notice that the first claim is not confined to "modern" economics. The sixteenth century advocates of mercantilism argued for similar policies.[1] In the mercantilist view, international trade is a zero-sum game, and the winning side will be the one with a trade surplus. A country can achieve a trade surplus via specific policy prescriptions, among them controlling imports, promoting exports, or depreciating one's currency.

Ludwig von Mises devoted one section of his *Theory of Money and Credit* to questioning the claim that exports can be stimulated through currency

DAVID HOWDEN is chair of the department of business and social sciences, and associate professor of economics at St. Louis University, at its Madrid Campus.
1   Murray N. Rothbard, *Economic Thought Before Adam Amith: An Austrian Perspective on the History of Economic Thought*, Volume I (Auburn, Ala.: Ludwig von Mises Institute, [1995] 2006), chaps. 7 and 8.

depreciation.[2] Mises's approach mostly rests on a long-run neoclassical analysis in which price level rigidity is largely excluded from the analysis. In this chapter we will first summarize Mises's core argument. We will then consider objections to it, largely based on price-level considerations. Finally we will note that Mises's original claims against policies aimed at depreciating the currency and promoting exports are actually stronger than he made in 1912, though never stated in a cohesive and complete manner.

Exchange Rates and the Trade Balance: The Conventional View

The conventional analysis of the trade balance starts with David Hume's price-specie-flow mechanism to draw conclusions for exchange rate movements. Start with two countries with their trade balances in equilibrium, and using the same currency (in this example we will use gold, though this is not essential to the argument). Country A reduces its demand for, and hence imports of, country B's goods. Immediately country A will reduce its gold transfers to B, thus increasing the money supply in A relative to B. This relative contraction of the money supply in B coupled with the increase in the money supply of A makes prices rise, on average, more quickly in country A than B. This incentivizes citizens from A to increase their purchases from B. The increased demand thus stops the gold outflow from B, stabilizing the trade balance.

Several immediate effects can be discerned. First, the contraction in the money supply in country B caused a deflation in the price level. This deflation allowed for an increase in competitiveness relative to country A, and stimulated B's exports. On the other hand, the expansion of the money supply in country A reduced its own competitiveness, and halted its exports to country B. Under the neoclassical view of perfectly flexible prices, this money outflow gave rise to price deflation, allowing for the balance of payments to remain equilibrated.

Once we move away from an international commodity standard, the situation depends on the exchange rate regime, whether flexible or fixed.[3]

---

2   Ludwig von Mises, *The Theory of Money and Credit*, H.E. Batson, trans. (Irvington-on-Hudson, N.Y.: The Foundation for Economic Education, [1912] 1971), chap. 8, sect. 4.

3   We will not consider the case for fixed exchange rates here.

Trade imbalances are self-correcting under flexible exchange rates. Assume that country *A* runs a trade deficit against *B*. Citizens in *A* must be selling their currency to purchase *B*'s currency, in order to purchase that country's goods. The increased buying pressure in country *B* increases the price of its goods, disincentivizing *A*'s citizens from continuing to import from it. An equilibrium obtains where trade is balanced again, but at an exchange rate that has appreciated for *B* relative to before.[4]

This example illustrates the two statements concerning international economics that we opened with. The currency depreciation in country *A* improved its trade balance (by decreasing its imports). This currency depreciation was itself originally caused by the trade deficit against *B*, whereby *A*'s citizens needed to sell *A*'s currency to purchase *B*'s.

From this example also comes an assumingly simple corollary. A country running a trade deficit can easily cure this through policy. A monetary policy that results in a depreciated exchange rate will increase foreign demand for a country's goods, while simultaneously reducing domestic demand for foreign goods. The net result is a trade deficit improvement.

Currency depreciation as a policy tool to combat a trade deficit is increasingly favored by economists as a substitute for other measures. As monetary responses, exchange rate depreciations are only one of three measures that can be used, alongside domestic price level deflation and capital controls. The mainstream view today is that capital controls interfere with important trade flows and should be used only as a last resort, while price level deflation may only be reasonable in the long run (and may not even then be desirable). On the nonmonetary side of policies, tariffs and quotas, export promotion (through subsidies) and import substitution (through targeting domestic producers) can all limit a trade imbalance. They also come with the baggage of deadweight losses or rent-seeking questions surrounding what industries to specifically target. Manipulation

---

4   If price inflation is higher in *A* relative to *B*, country *A*'s currency will depreciate relative to *B*'s. In *The Theory of Money and Credit* Mises developed this conclusion based upon purchasing power parity four years prior to Gustav Cassel, although the latter is more often given credit for the development (Joseph T. Salerno, "International Monetary Theory," reprinted in *Money, Sound and Unsound* [Auburn, Ala.: Ludwig von Mises Institute, [1994] 2010, pp. 165–66). Importantly, Mises did not couch his analysis in terms of the quotient of general price levels, but instead treated PPP as holding true in specific applications of goods (Joseph T. Salerno, "Ludwig von Mises's Monetary Theory in Light of Modern Monetary Thoughts," reprinted in ibid, p. 108). Compare with Ludwig von Mises, *Human Action: A Treatise on Economics* (Auburn, Ala.: Ludwig von Mises Institute, [1949] 2010), p. 455.

of the exchange rate has come to be seen as one option that evades these problems, and is straightforward to implement via a central bank.

MISES'S ARGUMENT REVISITED

In chapter eight of the *Theory of Money and Credit*, Mises takes the conventional balance-of-payments analysis and augments it to account for the process through which international competitiveness can be regained. Along the way, he also foreshadowed the Lucas Critique by over six decades.[5]

Mises is keen to note that any policy aimed at depreciating the exchange value of a currency to stimulate exports will likely be self-defeating.[6] His rationale invokes real exchange rates—nominal rates adjusted for changes in money's purchasing power—to make the point.

Depreciating the exchange rate on the foreign exchange market can only be achieved by reducing its purchasing power domestically relative to a foreign currency. Such an inflationary monetary policy thus has a two-pronged effect. On the one hand it increases the price of the good in question in nominal domestic currency terms through price inflation. On the other hand it decreases the number of foreign currency units necessary to purchase a unit of domestic currency. In equilibrium the effect would be a draw, as the effects of one cancel against the other.

As Mises notes, the "beneficial effects" on trade that a depreciated currency provides last only so long as the domestic price inflation comes either, (1) later than the depreciation on the foreign exchange market, or (2) at a slower rate than the depreciation of the currency. Inflationists aiming to increase international competitiveness through this depreciation could only see their policy maintained through continual diminutions of the currency's purchasing power. It is doubtful that lenders would continually lend money in this currency while cognizant of their ensuing purchasing power loss—it may be possible to fool some of the people some of the time, but eventually expectations will catch up and make the real price of the country's goods more expensive than before the policy was enacted.

If the effects of an export-promoting monetary policy are null in the long run, Mises raises another complication—the policy itself must be kept

---

5   Robert E. Lucas, "Econometric Policy Evaluation: A Critique," *Carnegie-Rochester Conference Series on Public Policy* 1, no. 1 (1976): 19–46.

6   Mises, *The Theory of Money and Credit*, p. 224.

unapparent from the market for its effectiveness, by its purveyors' own reckoning, to even be possible.

That this depreciation in the value of money must be unforeseen by individuals for the policy's effectiveness is now apparent. Mises builds on the still relatively recent work of Irving Fisher[7] to explain why it is that any inflationary measure aimed at reducing the value of money must be shrouded from the market.[8] Specifically, Mises[9] cites and builds upon the Fisher effect whereby any expected loss in purchasing power by a creditor will be compensated by an *ex ante* higher requested interest rate.[10] The extension is that one can never know in advance the exact position of the creditor and debtor—who it is that gains at the expense of the other—because one can never know in advance the path that price inflation will take. Hence, it is possible that inflation possibly can benefit a debtor, if the *ex ante* interest rate was not increased sufficiently to cover the creditor's loss of purchasing power.

Short- and the Long-run Considerations

While Mises invokes a long-run flexible price stance in his treatment of the balance of trade, we may now relax this assumption. The neoclassical tradition that Mises worked within assumed prices to be fully flexible, or at least did not focus on short-run phenomena during which prices could be "stuck" in place.

The modern view holds that currency depreciations can improve the trade balance in the short run, as prices adjust slower than exchange rates. Any increase in the money supply will affect the exchange rate instantly, based upon the expectation that future prices will increase. In the present, however, prices will require some time to adjust, typically as the new

---

7   Irving Fisher, *The Rate of Interest* (New York: MacMillan, 1907), p. 356.

8   While today we refer to the price inflation component of interest rates as the "Fisher effect," while writing *Man, Economy, and State*, Rothbard would refer to it more correctly as the "Fisher-Mises effect" (Murray Rothbard, *Man, Economy and State* [Auburn, Ala.: Ludwig von Mises Institute, 2004], p. lv).

9   Mises, *Theory of Money and Credit*, p. 200.

10   Rothbard (*Man, Economy, and State*, chap. 11, sect. 5G) takes a different approach, negating the usefulness of the Fisher effect. Rothbard takes the interest rate as being determined on the goods market, and finds that instead of demanding to be compensated for price inflation by a higher interest rate today, borrowers would pay more today for the goods that they are purchasing with the borrowed funds in expectation of the future price increase. While the analytical distinction is useful to the extent that the interest rate originates on the goods market, the distinction is not important for this chapter.

money will take time to work its way through the economy to affect prices.[11] As a consequence, the real exchange rate will depreciate in the short
run to provide an advantage for export industries, but in the long run this
advantage will be slowly removed as the price level catches up.[12]

Such thinking is spurious for two primary reasons.

The first issue is one of over-aggregation. Depreciations of the real exchange rate are enacted by increasing the money supply, thus placing upward pressure on all prices. As the real exchange rate (q) is given as

$$q = E\left(\frac{P}{P^*}\right),$$

where E is the nominal rate, P the domestic price level and P^* the foreign
price level, any alteration to the money supply is aimed at affecting the
general price level to promote a real depreciation.[13]

The first issue that we may raise is the overly aggregative nature of the
variables at hand. What matters is not the respective general price levels
of two countries, but rather the specific prices for the goods being pur-
chased. For example, the trade deficit in Spain today and the trade surplus

---

11   Alternatively, Mises (*Human Action*, pp. 455–56) viewed the exchange rate as
quicker adjusting because it is set on a more or less organized market with specialized deal-
ers anticipating its price. The price level, in distinction, is set by the diverse demands of
individuals with little knowledge of monetary matters.

12   Allowing for a contractionary money supply, despite appreciating the currency,
would in the long run allow for price level deflation and potentially promote exports in spite
of more highly valued currency. While not due to a contracting money supply (at least, not
in absolute terms but perhaps contracting relative to the increased demand to hold cash
balances), the Japanese economy throughout the 1990s to now has had a positive trade
balance despite a strengthening nominal yen due to a deflating price level (David Howden
and Brenna Kajikawa, "Japan's Blessing of a Strong Currency," Ludwig von Mises Institute
Daily Article, March 2, 2012; available at http://mises.org/daily/5928/The-Blessing-of-a-
Strong-Currency). In a counterexample, when Iceland's króna started depreciating in 2007
its central bank simultaneously embarked on an expansionary monetary policy. The ensuing inflation and purchasing power loss made imports all but impossible to the small island
nation, while exports were not stimulated as much as one might have thought due to the
counteracting effects (Philipp Bagus and David Howden, *Deep Freeze: Iceland's Economic
Collapse* [Auburn, Ala.: Ludwig von Mises Institute, 2011], pp. 66–67).

13   Taking the log of both sides, the real appreciation/depreciation of q will be given
by, $\%\Delta q = \%\Delta E + \%\Delta P - \%\Delta P^*$. Provided that the domestic price level is sticky in the short
run, any increase in the money supply depreciating the nominal rate E will also depreciate
the real rate q. As the price level becomes flexible in the long run and the general domestic
price level increases, the real exchange rate will depreciate.

in Germany is not the result of all goods being x-percent more expensive in Spain than in Germany. Some goods in Germany will be less expensive (cars and elevators, for example) while others will be more expensive than in Spain (wine and olives, for example). The trade surplus that Germany has is not the result of being more cost effective in all goods, but is instead the aggregate result of some goods being in a trade surplus offsetting those that have a deficit position. In trade relations it is never the brute movements of aggregate numbers that define the important relations, but rather the "interrelated variations in the complex of individual cash balances, incomes, and prices."[14]

On the other hand, the effectiveness of a monetary expansion in depreciating the real exchange rate must also assume the long-run neutrality of money. In this way, any changes in the money supply affect the general price level, but not the individual array of prices. This is questionable for three reasons.

First, as the analysis is short-run given the assumption of sticky prices, any assumption of money's neutrality must also be short-run. While Austrian economists are unified in the belief that money is never neutral, most mainstream economists would also agree that it is only in the long run that this neutrality reigns.[15] A bifurcation occurs whereby the assumption

---

14   Salerno, "International Monetary Theory," p. 162; see also Friedrich A. Hayek, *Monetary Nationalism and International Stability* (New York: Augustus M. Kelley, [1937] 1971, pp. 19–24). To show how misleading aggregative balance of payments reasoning is, Rothbard (*Man, Economy, and State*, chap. 3) applies such an analysis to an individual. It is misleading in the sense that a trade balance in such an individual analysis is never a "problem" in the sense that a person's unfavorable balance will continue only so long as someone is willing to purchase his money for goods, and he is willing to keep drawing down his cash balance (*Man, Economy, and State*, p. 205). Hayek (*Denationalisation of Money—The Argument Refined*, 3rd ed. [London: The Institute of Economic Affairs, [1976] 1990), pp. 103–04) treats balance of payments crises as largely a figment of the statistics, as money flows are tracked across borders. The elimination of national currencies would eliminate these crises as trade flows between countries (with their corresponding currency flows) would be akin to those between regions of the same country today.

15   Outside of the mainstream and with the Austrian economists are the Post-Keynesians who, following Keynes, also question the neutrality of money (Paul Davidson, *Financial Markets, Money and the Real World* [Cheltenham, U.K.: Edward Elgar, 2002], pp. 7–8). Some others firmly within the mainstream, such as IMF chief economist Olivier Blanchard, also see the assumption of monetary neutrality as just that: "All the models we have seen impose the neutrality of money as a maintained assumption. This is very much a matter of faith, based on theoretical considerations rather than on empirical evidence" (Olivier Blanchard 1987, p. 70, "Why Does Money Affect Output? A Survey," *NBER Working Paper* No. 2285).

is that the way prices behave is short run as it concerns price inflation, yet long run in how the price vector is affected by monetary policy.

Second, the assumption that the effects of monetary policy are neutral is questionable.[16] The crux of the Austrian business cycle is based on the fact that monetary policy results in "Cantillon" effects. As money is necessarily injected "somewhere" in the economy, it is only through a time-consuming process that its effects (i.e., price inflation) alter prices. That it will affect prices asymmetrically arises as a physical result of the lengthy process for money to filter through different stages of production[17] and also because the further away from the source freshly injected money strays, the less knowledge entrepreneurs have of its nature, effects and sustainability.[18]

The third questionable aspect, and a consequence of the first two, is the question of what price is "stuck" in the short run. Not all prices are equally sticky, resulting in different price adjustments as new money works its way through the economy.[19] In this sense, claiming that an increase in the money supply will bring a real depreciation because the general price level is sticky in the short run misplaces a key aspect—as the general price level can only be comprised of its individual component prices. Any monetary policy will alter the individual constellation of prices, and while it is true that the general price level will also increase, not all individual prices will do so uniformly.

THE SECONDARY EFFECTS OF DEPRECIATION

The fact that not all prices will react uniformly to monetary policy is significant as it raises secondary considerations. Chief among these concerns the business cycle, while others concern the effect on the balance of trade if such a policy is undertaken.

---

16   Ludwig von Mises, "The Non-Neutrality of Money," in *Money, Method and the Market Process*, Richard M. Ebeling, ed. (Norwell, Mass.: Kluwer Academic Publishers, [1938] 1990), chap. 5

17   Ludwig von Mises, "Monetary Stabilization and Cyclical Policy," *On the Manipulation of Money And Credit*, Bettina Bien Greaves, Jr., and Percey L. Greaves, Jr., ed. and trans. (Auburn, Ala.: Ludwig von Mises Institute, [1928] 2002), pp. 100–03.

18   David Howden, "Knowledge Shifts and the Business Cycle: When Boom Turns to Bust." *Review of Austrian Economics* 23, no. 2 (2020): 165–82.

19   Philipp Bagus and David Howden, "Monetary Equilibrium and Price Stickiness: Causes, Consequences and Remedies," *Review of Austrian Economics* 24 no. 4 (2011): 396.

The traditional Austrian business cycle commences with new credit being injected into the economy for commercial purposes. As interest rates are depressed below their natural levels, long-term projects gain the appearance of profitability. Entrepreneurs are enticed to invest in longer-dated projects, thus causing prices to inflate at the higher orders of production relative to the lower orders (i.e., producers' prices increase faster than consumers' prices).[20] The result has one of two options, neither one conducive to growth.

On the one hand, if entrepreneurs have undertaken plans inconsistent with the amount of real savings (i.e., too many projects are undertaken relative to savings), as the boom culminates a rush to borrow the scarce savings will drive up interest rates. Short-term interest rates surge on the eve of the bust as borrowers scramble for the necessary but now recognizably scarce funds.[21] As interest rates increase, higher order goods' prices are negatively affected as they are capitalized at a higher interest rate.[22] Alternatively, if a continued loose monetary policy prohibits upward pressure on interest rates, producers' prices will surge as a scramble by entrepreneurs, not for scarce monetary funds, but for the scarce physical goods to complete projects.

The importance of this for the task at hand is the effect on trade flows from this policy. The expansionary monetary policy has been undertaken with the aim of depreciating the real exchange rate, in hopes of promoting the domestic country's export-based industries. Yet four detrimental side effects will result.

First, the reallocation of spending from the late to early stages of production when credit is directed to commercial borrowing implies that less

---

20   If consumers are also making use of fresh credit, as is the case in Mises's (*Human Action*, pp. 432, 470, 492, and *passim*) over-consumption theory of the business cycle, prices of consumers' goods will also be under upward pressure. In this way the structure of production is strained at both ends—at the higher orders through producers' demands and at the lower orders through the demands of consumers (Roger W. Garrison, *Time and Money: The Macroeconomics of Capital Structure* [London: Routledge, 2001], p. 72).

21   Paul F. Cwik, "The Inverted Yield Curve and the Economic Downturn," *New Perspectives on Political Economy* 1 no. 1 (2005): 21–33; and Philipp Bagus and David Howden, "The Term Structure of Savings, the Yield Curve and Maturity Mismatching," *Quarterly Journal of Austrian Economics* 13, no. 3 (2010): 64–85.

22   Fritz Machlup, "The Liquidity of Short-Term Capital," *Economica* 12, no. 37 (1932): 271–84; and Paul F. Cwik, "Austrian Business Cycle Theory: A Corporate Finance Point of View," *Quarterly Journal of Austrian Economics* 11, no. 1 (2008): 60–68.

domestic attention is given to producing consumers' goods. This shift can either occur with an increase in total expenditure directed at the higher stages, or with no aggregate increase and only a funding reallocation between stages. For countries lacking the input factors for higher-order production (natural resources, for example), imports can surge to meet the increased demand. Take the case of the United States since 1980 to 2000 (Figure 1). A continual monetary expansion and reduction in interest rates during the great moderation enticed entrepreneurs to move investment to higher stages of production. The increased demand this created on the country to import natural resources such as oil increased the trade deficit throughout the period culminating in the dot.com bust in 2000.

Second, a credit-induced boom increases the demand for all goods—imports as well as those domestically produced. If the goods demanded come from overseas, the result is a worsening trade balance. Since there is no reason to believe that an expansionist monetary policy will alter the demand foreigners have for the domestic country's goods, the trade balance will worsen. Moreover, if the goods demanded domestically are also sourced domestically, price pressure will build on these goods. As these prices increase, foreigners are disincentivized from purchasing them. In this case the trade balance worsens because exports are stifled. Alternatively, if nominal incomes are not increased through an inflationary monetary policy, individuals will have to restrict their consumption of both domestically produced and imported goods. In this first case exports would increase and in the second case imports would decline.[23] In both cases the non-expansionary monetary policy improves the balance of trade.

Third, as a credit-induced boom creates malinvestments along the domestic structure of production, the home country may find itself increasingly needing to turn to foreign markets to supply it with goods. Take the example of the United States during its recent housing boom from 2002–2007. As the structure of production became heavily skewed to producing higher order goods, mostly in industries related to housing, other common goods had to be sourced from foreign countries due to a lack of domestic productive capacity. The net result was a worsening trade balance, as imports increased while exports were unaffected.

The fourth and final point is that only the end of a credit-induced boom will turnaround a trade deficit set in motion by an expansionary monetary

---

23   Mises, *Human Action*, p. 456.

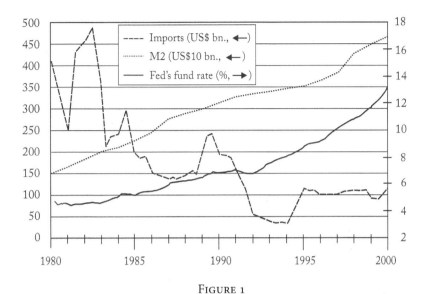

FIGURE 1
U.S. Imports, Money Supply and Federal Reserve Discount Rate
Source: Federal Reserve Bank of St. Louis, FRED

policy. As the boom created either the illusion of increased wealth or an actual increase in unsustainable credit-based wealth, the decrease in income during the ensuing bust will reverse this trend. The reason is that the decrease in income during the cleansing bust will reduce demand for all goods—both domestically and foreign produced. Yet provided that foreigners are not also undergoing a simultaneous recession, demand for the home country's exports will remain unaffected. The net result will be an improvement in the balance of trade.

CONCLUDING REMARKS

Mises's analysis in the *Theory of Money and Credit* of expansionist monetary policies to aid a country's trade position is lucid and ahead of its time in terms of the attention afforded to expectations, prices and exchange rates. I noted in the introduction, however, that Mises's[24] claims against such policies were less strong than is warranted given his other contributions. With the completion of his business cycle theory nearly four decades later, we can now integrate the analysis into a unified whole.

---

24   Mises, *Theory of Money and Credit*.

188 Theory of Money and Fiduciary Media: Essays in Celebration of the Centennial

The idea that an expansionary monetary policy can be beneficial in promoting exports must assume that the domestic price level increases slower under such a policy than the nominal exchange rate. As conventional wisdom ranks expectations and financial variables as faster adjusting to shocks than real variables in the short run, such a policy can only be effective in the short run. As prices adjust to the inflationary policy, any benefits accruing to the real exchange rate are reversed.

Mises latched onto this key insight and concluded that any expansionist policy aimed at improving a country's balance of trade would be self-defeating.

Yet there are secondary considerations that would not become apparent until he more thoroughly developed his business cycle theory. Any expansionary monetary policy also alters the base rate of interest permeating the economy, forcing it to diverge from the natural rate. The two consequences—malinvestment and over-consumption—affect the balance of trade in separate ways.

As entrepreneurs are deceived about true savings preferences they undertake projects of longer duration than would otherwise be the case. Economic activity shifts from the lower orders of production (those closer to consumption), to those at the higher orders. Note that this shift may occur with no change in the overall level of economic activity or aggregate spending. Countries that lack the necessary input factors to fuel this new production in the higher orders will see their trade account worsen as imports are necessary to make up the difference.

Consumers, for their part, are incentivized to save less and consume more as interest rates decline lower than would otherwise be the case. In this way, consumption increases relative to what it was before the boom and also relative to what is sustainable given the production plans of producers. If the productive shift moves to sufficiently high orders there will be a relative dearth of consumers' goods available to meet consumers' needs. In the most recent boom in the United States from 2002–2007 we could see this was apparent as producers moved to the higher order production good of housing, along with research and development (in lieu of the "middle" order production of basic capital goods, such as infrastructure). As a consequence American consumers imported the goods that were necessary to meet their over-consumptive patterns. A sharp trade deficit developed.

Perhaps the most important conclusion is that the necessary bust following the credit-induced boom will move the balance of trade to a more sustainable position. As the production and consumption patterns during the boom are unsustainable, they will eventually be reversed. This reversal will be accompanied by either: (1) increasing interest rates in a scramble for funding now realized to be scarce, or (2) an increase in factor prices, particularly commodity or basic input prices. Either of these events will have the effect of reducing the trade deficit sustained by the expansionary monetary policy.

As interest rates increase, longer-dated investment projects are divested from in favor of shorter-term projects. This shift favors expenditure on domestically produced goods—infrastructure projects, for example—at the expense of imports. As factor prices increase, projects dependent on imported goods will also increase, disincentivizing consumption of them. As consumption of imported goods decreases the trade deficit will gradually improve.

The effects of an expansionary monetary policy on the trade balance of a country are not only counter to what the advocates state, they are also detrimental in the sense that they will set in motion a credit-induced boom. This boom has the unfortunate side effect that it is unsustainable, and also that it actually worsens the balance of trade by the production and consumption patterns it incentivizes. A cleansing recession will not only undo the malinvestments of the previous boom and return consumption patterns to sustainability, but will also rectify an unsustainable trade deficit.

REFERENCES

Bagus, Philipp, and David Howden. 2010. "The Term Structure of Savings, the Yield Curve and Maturity Mismatching." *Quarterly Journal of Austrian Economics* 13, no. 3: 64–85.

———. 2011a. *Deep Freeze: Iceland's Economic Collapse*. Auburn, Ala.: Ludwig von Mises Institute.

———. 2011b. "Monetary equilibrium and price stickiness: Causes, consequences and remedies." *Review of Austrian Economics* 24, no. 4: 383–402.

Blanchard, Olivier. 1990. "Why Does Money Affect Output? A Survey." *NBER Working Paper* No. 2285.

Cwik, Paul F. 2005. "The Inverted Yield Curve and the Economic Downturn." *New Perspectives on Political Economy* 1(1): 1–37.

——. 2008. "Austrian Business Cycle Theory: A Corporate Finance Point of View." *Quarterly Journal of Austrian Economics* 11, no. 1: 60–68.

Davidson, Paul. 2002. *Financial Markets, Money and the Real World*. Cheltenham, U.K.: Edward Elgar.

Fisher, Irving. 1907. *The Rate of Interest*. New York: MacMillan.

Garrison, Roger W. 2001. *Time and Money: The Macroeconomics of Capital Structure*. London: Routledge.

Hayek, Friedrich A. [1937] 1971. *Monetary Nationalism and International Stability*. New York: Augustus M. Kelley.

——. [1976] 1990. *Denationalisation of Money—The Argument Refined: An Analysis of the Theory and Practice of Concurrent Currencies*. 3rd ed. London: The Institute of Economic Affairs.

Howden, David. 2010. "Knowledge Shifts and the Business Cycle: When Boom Turns to Bust." *Review of Austrian Economics* 23, no. 2: 165–82.

Howden, David, and Brenna Kajikawa. 2012. "Japan's Blessing of a Strong Currency." Ludwig vonMises Institute Daily Article, March 2nd. [Available] http://mises.org/daily/5928/The-Blessing-of-a-Strong-Currency

Lucas, Robert E. 1976. *Econometric Policy Evaluation: A Critique*. Carnegie-Rochester Conference Series on Public Policy 1, no. 1: 19–46.

Machlup, Fritz. 1932. "The Liquidity of Short-Term Capital." *Economica* 12, no. 37: 271–84.

Mises, Ludwig von. [1912] 1971. *The Theory of Money and Credit*. H.E. Batson, trans. Irvington-on-Hudson, N.Y.: The Foundation for Economic Education.

——. [1928] 2002. "Monetary Stabilization and Cyclical Policy." In *On the Manipulation of Money And Credit*. Bettina Bien Greaves, Jr., and Percey L. Greaves, Jr., ed. and trans. Auburn, Ala.: Ludwig von Mises Institute. Pp 63–179.

——. [1938] 1990. "The Non-Neutrality of Money." In *Money, Method and the Market Process*. Richard M. Ebeling, ed. Norwell, Mass.: Kluwer Academic Publishers.

——. [1949] 1998. *Human Action: A Treatise on Economics*. Auburn, Ala.: Ludwig von Mises Institute.

Rothbard, Murray N. [1962] 2004. *Man, Economy and State*. Auburn, Ala.: Ludwig von Mises Institute.

——. [1995] 2006. *Economic Thought Before Adam Smith: An Austrian Perspective on the History of Economic Thought*, Volume I. Auburn, Ala.: Ludwig von Mises Institute.

Salerno, Joseph T. [1982] 2010. "Ludwig von Mises's Monetary Theory in Light of Modern Monetary Thoughts." Reprinted in *Money, Sound and Unsound*. Auburn, Ala.: Ludwig von Mises Institute. Pp. 63–118.

——. [1994] 2010. "International Monetary Theory. Reprinted in *Money, Sound and Unsound*. Auburn, Ala.: Ludwig von Mises Institute. Pp. 63–118.

9

E D U A R D   B R A U N

The Subsistence Fund
in Ludwig von Mises's
Explanation of the Business Cycle

IN 1974 FRIEDRICH VON HAYEK was awarded the Nobel Prize in Economics for his contributions to the circulation credit theory of the trade cycle. The first exposition of this theory goes back to the year 1912. Ludwig von Mises expounded on it briefly in his habilitation treatise entitled *Theorie des Geldes und der Umlaufsmittel* [Theory of Money and Fiduciary Media].[1] Today this theory is one of the central themes in Austrian economics. For this reason, it is very often called the "Austrian" theory of the business cycle (ABCT). It is mainly concerned with the effect that the financial sector—especially the monetary policy of the central bank or the banking system—has on the "real" sector. Its principle examination object is the artificial expansion of *circulation credit* and the influence the latter has on the economic system. Although circulation credit originates in the *financial* market, ABCT maintains that it has devastating effects on the *real* economy. In short, an expansion of circulation credit is supposed to cause

---

EDUARD BRAUN holds a Ph.D and is a research assistant at Clausthal University of Technology in Clausthal -Zellerfeld, Germany. An earlier version of this paper appeared in the December 2012 issue of *Procesos de Mercado: Revista Europea de Economía Política*.

1   Translated as *The Theory of Money and Credit* (New Haven, Conn.: Yale University Press, [1912] 1953). Page references are to the 1953 edition unless otherwise noted.

an artificial lowering of the interest rate which provokes entrepreneurial malinvestments that, sooner or later, will lead to an economic crisis as the malinvestments will have to be liquidated.

In this paper it is argued that Ludwig von Mises, the originator of this theory, did not expound his theory homogenously. During his career, he changed the way he explained the feedback between the financial and the real sector rather substantially. Whereas he stressed the role of the subsistence fund in the original version, he substituted it by other concepts in later publications. It will be shown that, at least in this respect, the original version in *Theorie des Geldes und der Umlaufsmittel* is more consistent than the later ones, even the elaborated exposition that can be found in Mises's most important work, *Human Action*.

COMMODITY CREDIT AND CIRCULATION CREDIT

In order to understand the ABCT it is necessary to grasp a distinction between two different kinds of credit first introduced by Ludwig von Mises himself.[2] The first one, *commodity credit*, is, in Mises's opinion, the healthy kind of credit. Somebody saves out of his income and transfers the savings to somebody else, mainly by means of financial intermediaries. As this kind of credit necessitates savings, it involves an exchange of present goods for future goods.[3] In the words of Mises, credits of this kind are

> characterized by the fact that they impose a sacrifice on that party who performs his part of the bargain before the other does—the foregoing of immediate power of disposal over the exchanged good.[4]

In short, before commodity credit can be granted, somebody must have saved up goods or money that can now be lent to the debtors. The sacrifice of the savers is the necessary condition for this kind of credit.

The second kind of credit Mises calls *circulation credit*. In his opinion, it constitutes the unhealthy kind of credit. It does not stem from anybody's savings, but from the power of banks to lend additional money into existence. It is not necessary to go into the details of fractional reserve banking

---

2   Antoine Gentier, *Economie Bancaire. Essai sur les effets de la concurrence et la réglementation sur le financement du crédit* (Paris: Publibook, 2003), p. 46.

3   Mises, *Theory of Money and Credit*, p. 264.

4   Ibid., p. 264

here. That this kind of banking is able to create additional credit via lending out its own banknotes (in earlier times) or demand deposits that are at any time convertible into money is generally accepted by economists.[5] The phenomenon is called the money multiplier. Mises's point is that this kind of credit creation does not presuppose savings and therefore causes nearly no costs to either the issuing bank or anybody else. This

> group of credit transactions is characterized by the fact that in them the gain of the party who receives before he pays is balanced by no sacrifice on the part of the other party.[6]

According to Mises's definition, what he calls circulation credit is not a proper credit transaction from an economic point of view. "[T]he essential element, the exchange of present goods for future goods, is absent."[7] No savings and no sacrifices are necessary:

> If a creditor is able to confer a loan by issuing claims which are payable on demand, then the granting of the credit is bound up with no economic sacrifice for him.[8]

Now, in all of his versions of the ABCT, Mises maintains that an expansion of circulation credit, as distinguished from an increase of commodity credit, causes a boom that must ultimately result in a bust. So far, the earlier and the later versions are homogeneous. However, they differ in the way that Mises explains the effect that an expansion of circulation credit has on the economy. It will be shown that it is on this point that Mises's first theoretical book, *The Theory of Money and Credit*, has to be preferred to all of his later writings.

---

5   See Jesús Huerta de Soto, *Money, Bank Credit, and Economic Cycles*, 2nd ed. (Auburn, Ala.: Ludwig von Mises Institute, 2009), pp. 182 ff.; Ansgar Belke and Thorsten Polleit, *Monetary Economics in Globalized Financial Markets* (Berlin and Heidelberg: Springer Verlag, 2009), pp. 29 ff.; Rudiger Dornbusch, Stanley Fisher, and Richard Startz, *Macroeconomics*, 10th ed. (Boston: McGraw-Hill, 2008), pp. 395 ff.

6   Mises, *Theory of Money and Credit*, p. 264.

7   Ibid., p. 269

8   Ibid., p. 265

THE EXPOSITION IN MISES'S *THEORY OF MONEY AND CREDIT*

The Role of the Subsistence Fund in the Exposition of the ABCT

In *Theorie des Geldes und der Umlaufsmittel,* Mises explains the influence of circulation credit on the economy in terms of the so-called *subsistence fund.* This fund—which consists of saved-up consumers' goods—looms large in his then exposition of the production process. To explain the subsistence fund theory in a few words: Consumers' goods are a necessary pre-condition of every production process. Without something to eat, something to drink, clothes, and so forth, nobody will participate in production. The owners of the originary factors of production, most notably workers, need to be furnished with consumers' goods during the production process. The subsistence fund is especially important when it comes to determing the possible length of the production processes. It is this point which Mises stresses in his 1912 book:

> The period of production . . . must be of such a length that exactly the whole available subsistence fund is necessary on the one hand and sufficient on the other for paying the wages of the laborers throughout the duration of the productive process. For if it were [longer],[9] all the workers could no longer be provided for throughout its whole course, and the consequence would be an urgent offer of the unemployed economic factors which could not fail to bring about a transformation of the existing arrangement.[10]

He further states that the "national subsistence fund is necessarily altered by the increase of savings."[11] Thus savings, in influencing the size of the subsistence fund, determine the way production is organised in the economy:

> A lengthening of the period of production is only practicable . . . when either the means of subsistence have increased sufficiently to support the laborers and entrepreneurs during the longer period or when the wants of producers have decreased sufficiently to enable them to make the same means of subsistence do for the longer period.[12]

---

9   Mises here says "shorter" which must be a typo.

10   Mises, *Theory of Money and Credit,* p. 360 and (1912), p. 428

11   Mises, *Theory of Money and Credit,* p. 347

12   Ibid., p. 361

So in the *Theory of Money and Credit*, it is the subsistence fund, the fund of saved-up consumers' goods that determines the length of the period of production.

Entrepreneurs, when they evaluate the profitability of the different investments and decide about the production processes they want to implement, do not, of course, orientate themselves by the size of the national subsistence fund. They have probably never heard of such a thing, and even if they had, they surely could not determine its size. Instead, they are guided by the *interest rate*. Yet, in the *Theory of Money and Credit*, the interest rate bears a close relationship to the subsistence fund. It provides the entrepreneurs with the information as to how lengthy the production processes can reasonably become, that is, it informs them about the size of the subsistence fund. This can be seen especially in Mises's exposition of the ABCT.

As was already indicated, in 1912 Mises expounds the ABCT in terms of the subsistence fund. In expanding the amount of circulation credit, the banking system decreases interest below the rate that is indicated by the amount of savings.[13] So despite the fact that the subsistence fund has not increased, i.e., that "there is no possibility of lengthening the average period of production," nonetheless "a rate of interest is established in the loan market which corresponds to a longer period of production."[14] As a consequence, in creating the illusion of the profitability of new investment possibilities—the longer production processes—"[c]redit expansion initially can produce a boom."[15] However, as the subsistence fund has not increased at all, "there cannot be the slightest doubt as to where this will lead."[16]

> A time must necessarily come when the means of subsistence available for consumption are all used up although the capital goods employed in production have not yet been transformed into consumption goods. . . . The means of subsistence will prove insufficient to maintain the laborers during the whole period of the process of production that has been entered upon. Since production and consumption are continuous, so that every day new processes of production are started upon and others completed, this situation does not imperil human existence

---

13   See ibid., pp. 361 ff.

14   Both quotes from ibid., p. 362

15   Ibid., p. 422

16   Ibid., p. 362

by suddenly manifesting itself as a complete lack of consumption goods; it is merely expressed in a reduction of the quantity of goods available for consumption and a consequent restriction of consumption. The market prices of consumption goods rise and those of production goods fall.[17]

As can be seen in the preceding quotes, in the *Theory of Money and Credit* the subsistence fund plays a prominent role. Its size has a crucial effect on the production process as it limits the length of the production period. The entrepreneurs are informed about the size of the subsistence fund by means of the interest rate. In expanding circulation credit, the banking system artificially lowers the interest rate and thusly creates the illusion of an increased subsistence fund. Subsequently, entrepreneurs behave as if the subsistence fund has increased, i.e., they embark upon long-term investment projects. Ultimately, these projects turn out to be malinvestments as they require an amount of the subsistence fund that is not available. So after the rate of interest has fallen because of the additional circulation credit and has caused a boom, at last a counter-movement sets in. With higher consumers' goods prices and lower producers' goods prices, the interest rate rises again.[18] It turns out that the increase of the subsistence fund has been an illusion. The consequence will be an economic crisis. Some of the longer processes of production have to be abandoned; with the higher rate of interest they cease to be profitable. A part of the new production goods "cannot be withdrawn and must therefore either be left entirely unused or at least be used less economically."[19] So, to quote Mises once more,

> there has been a loss of value. Economic goods which could have satisfied more important wants have been employed for the satisfaction of less important; only in so far as the mistake that has been made can be rectified by diversion into another channel can loss be prevented.[20]

To sum up, according to the theory as contained in The Theory of Money and Credit, *additional circulation credit creates the illusion of an increase of the subsistence fund. This way, entrepreneurs are trapped into malinvestments.*

---

17   Ibid.

18   See ibid., p. 363

19   See ibid., p. 364

20   Ibid.

Some Smaller Inconsistencies in the Exposition

It must be pointed out that even the 1912 version is not formulated unambiguously. As long as Mises employs the term "means of subsistence," it is clear what he is talking about. These means are definitely "available for consumption" and he contrasts them with capital goods.[21] But Mises is not totally clear when it comes to defining and employing the term "subsistence fund." On the one hand, he employs it synonymously to the "means of subsistence." As was shown above, what he says about the subsistence fund and its role in the business cycle is consistent with this interpretation. On the other hand, he takes the term from Böhm-Bawerk, who wants it to include all kinds of goods, not only consumers' goods.[22] A point which indicates that Mises, at least sometimes, endorses this interpretation is that, in his opinion, the "quantity of metal available for industrial purposes,"[23] which definitely is no consumers' good, is part of the subsistence fund. Furthermore, at one point he even formulates his theory not in relation to either the subsistence fund or the means of subsistence, but to intermediate products:

> [D]espite the fact that there has been no increase of *intermediate products* and there is no possibility of lengthening the average period of production, a rate of interest is established in the loan market which corresponds to a longer period of production;[24]

To be sure, shortly after he had written this sentence he again spoke of the *means of subsistence* that were missing. Yet, it can be seen from the quotes given that, even in the *Theory of Money and Credit*, his theory is not always and consistently formulated in terms of the subsistence fund as a fund of consumers' goods. At some places, a different interpretation seems permissible.

---

21   See ibid., p. 363

22   Eugen von Böhm-Bawerk, *Positive Theorie des Kapitals, Band I*, no. 4. (Jena: Fischer, 1921), pp. 391 f.

23   Mises, *Theory of Money and Credit*, p. 346.

24   Ibid., p. 362

Further Development of the ABCT by Mises

The Evolution of the Theory Up to 1936

It has been shown that even the 1912 version is not formulated unambiguously. Over the following decades, Mises changed the exposition of the ABCT. In 1928, Mises further developed it in his *Geldwertstabilisierung und Konjunkturpolitik*. At this point, he still uses the terms "subsistence fund" and "means of subsistence" as part of his explanation. He describes their role in the same way as in 1912:

> Roundabout methods of production can be adopted only so far as the *means for subsistence* exist to maintain the workers during the entire period of the expanded process. All those projects, for the completion of which means are not available, must be left uncompleted, even though they may appear technically feasible—that is, if one disregards the *supply of capital*.[25]

From this quote, one could imagine that he uses "means of subsistence" and "capital" synonymously. And indeed, he even writes that

> [i]n a given economic situation, the opportunities for production, which may actually be carried out, *are limited by the supply of capital goods* available.[26]

Shortly afterward, he employs the terms "existing resources,"[27] "subsistence fund,"[28] and "funds"[29] to express the same idea. It is not clear what exactly, in his opinion, limits the length of the production period. In some places, it is still the subsistence fund, but as the quotes show, sometimes he refers to other entities like capital goods and resources. Unfortunately, he does not clarify the relationship between these entities.

Although there are some terminological inaccuracies, Mises's 1928 explanation of the business cycle still runs in terms of a "subsistence fund,"

---

25   Ludwig von Mises, "Monetary Stabilization and Cyclical Policy," (1928) reprinted in Percy L. Greaves, Jr., ed., *The Causes of the Economic Crisis and other Essays Before and After the Great Depression* (Auburn, Ala.: Ludwig von Mises Institute, 2006), pp. 110 f., emphasis added.

26   Ibid., p. 110, emphasis added

27   Ibid., p. 111

28   Ibid.

29   Ibid., p. 112

however defined, that does not suffice in case of projects that only seem profitable because of credit-expansion. In the following years, Mises changes his formulation of the theory and abandons the term "subsistence fund" altogether in connection with capital or business cycle theory. In 1931, in an admittedly very short formulation of the theory, he only mentions "resources" as the decisive factor without any detailed explanation of the term.[30] In 1936, it is neither the subsistence fund, nor the means of subsistence, that limit the length of the production period. Instead,

> [t]he *material means of production and the labor* available have not increased; all that has increased is the quantity of the fiduciary media which can play the same role as money in the circulation of goods. The means of production and labor which have been diverted to the new enterprises have had to be taken away from other enterprises. Society is not sufficiently rich to permit the creation of new enterprises without taking anything away from other enterprises. As long as the expansion of credit is continued this will not be noticed, but this extension cannot be pushed indefinitely.[31]

Here, it is the means of production and labor that are not available in sufficient quantities. He also states that society is not "rich" enough, not specifying if this expression is supposed to correspond to the "material means of production and the labor available," or to something else. It has to be said that this quotation is also taken from a minor publication, but still it shows that something has changed. The subsistence fund is not mentioned here at all.

The Exposition of the Business Cycle Theory in Human Action

The important question is how Mises formulates his theory in his *magnum opus Human Action* of 1949. There he further develops his capital theory, and so it suggests itself that an analysis of this book will help to clarify the interrelation between the terms in question. In earlier publications Mises treated the issues of capital theory only randomly.

---

30   Ludwig von Mises, "The Causes of the Economic Crisis: An Address," (1931) reprinted in ibid., p. 162, emphasis added.

31   Ludwig von Mises, "The 'Austrian' Theory of the Trade Cycle," in *The Austrian Theory of the Trade Cycle and other Essays*, compiled by Richard M. Ebeling (Auburn, Ala.: Ludwig von Mises Institute, 1996), p. 29, emphasis added.

Although, as will be shown below, Mises significantly alters the exposition of the circulation credit theory and although he does not use the term "subsistence fund" in his explanation of the ABCT, he does not forget about the "means of subsistence" altogether.

> People eager to embark upon processes with a longer period of production must first accumulate, by means of saving, that quantity of *consumers' goods* which is needed to satisfy, during the waiting time, all those wants the satisfaction of which they consider more urgent than the increment in well-being expected from the more time-consuming process.[32]

On the same page he explicitly calls these consumers' goods "means of subsistence," so-far-as they are used to pay labor. So, in a nutshell, he still says that the means of subsistence are the prerequisite for a lengthening of the period of production. In his *Nationalökonomie*, the German-language predecessor of *Human Action*, he specifies this thought in saying that these means serve to free [*freimachen*] original and produced means of production from being employed in shorter ways of production.[33]

It might be inferred from this quote that Mises still argues in the same vein as 1912. Yet, he does not use this concept continuously when he comes to explain the business cycle. In his earlier works, as we have seen, it was the "subsistence fund" that limited the length of the production processes. An artificial lowering of the interest rate induced the entrepreneurs to embark upon unsustainable ("too long") production processes. In *Human Action*,

> the drop in interest rates falsifies the businessman's calculation. Although the amount of *capital goods* available did not increase, the calculation employs figures which would be utilizable only if such an increase had taken place.[34]

So the entrepreneurs do not act as if the subsistence fund had increased, but as if the amount of capital goods had increased. He restates this point a few pages later:

> A further expansion of production is possible only if *the amount of capital goods* is increased by additional saving, i.e., by

---

32   Ludwig von Mises, *Human Action: A Treatise on Economics*, 3rd ed. (New Haven, Conn.: Yale University Press, 1949), p. 488, emphasis added.

33   See Ludwig von Mises, *Nationalökonomie—Theorie des Handelns und Wirtschaftens* (Geneva: Editions Union, 1940), p. 450.

34   Mises, *Human Action*, p. 550, emphasis added.

surpluses produced and not consumed. *The characteristic mark of the credit-expansion boom is that such additional capital goods have not been made available.* The capital goods required for the expansion of business activities must be withdrawn from other lines of production.[35]

Obviously, the limiting factor here is the capital goods. In this point, Mises differs from his earlier expositions. However, he tries to integrate both phenomena, scarce means of subsistence and scarce capital goods, in his explanation. He also echoes his earlier formulations by saying:

Production has been altered in such a way that the length of waiting time has been extended. But the demand for consumers' goods has not dropped so as to make the available supply last for a longer period.[36]

With this integration of capital goods and consumers' goods Mises simply employs Böhm-Bawerk's concept of the subsistence fund that consists of both capital goods and consumers' goods. Anyway, the *decisive* factor that marks the turning point of the business cycle is the scarcity of capital goods, not of consumers' goods:

[The entrepreneurs] embark upon an expansion of investment on a scale for which the *capital goods* available do not suffice. Their projects are unrealizable on account of the *insufficient supply of capital goods.* They must fail sooner or later.[37]

To sum up our findings so far: In his earlier works Mises stresses the importance of the subsistence fund, though not clearly defining it. Later on, roughly since the 1930s, he starts to stress different ideas more strongly. Though he still recognizes the importance of the means of subsistence, he doesn't think these to be the central limiting factor for an expansion of production. Rather that capital goods gain prominence.

Now, to derive an exact notion of how he thinks the business cycle will elapse in his later writings, it is necessary to understand what he means exactly by capital goods. On one occasion in the third edition of *Human Action*, Mises defines capital goods as

---

35   Ibid., p. 554, emphasis added.

36   Ibid., p. 553.

37   Ibid., p. 556, emphasis added.

either intermediary stages in the technological process, i.e. tools and half-finished products, or goods ready for consumption that make it possible for man to substitute, without suffering want during the waiting period, a more time-absorbing process for another absorbing a shorter time.[38]

But, as shown by the following quote taken from the same edition, capital goods as just defined are not scarce at all at the onset of the crisis:

However, raw materials, primary commodities, half-finished manufactures and foodstuffs *are not lacking* at the turning point at which the upswing turns into the depression. On the contrary, the crisis is precisely characterized by the fact that these goods are offered in such quantities as to make their prices drop sharply.[39]

This is exactly the opposite of what he says in the passages quoted before where he maintains that capital goods are the bottleneck at the turning point of the business cycle. However, we will not evaluate Mises's business cycle theory on the basis of the definition just quoted. It does not appear in the first and apparently most stringent[40] edition of *Human Action*. And there he has a different concept in mind when he states that the supply of capital goods is insufficient in the crisis, namely the following: "We may acquiesce in the terminological usage of calling the produced factors of production *capital goods*."[41]

CAPITAL GOODS OR THE SUBSISTENCE FUND AS THE LIMITING FACTOR?

Unfortunately, Mises does not explain why he thinks that the business cycle is caused by the fact that entrepreneurs, as a reaction on credit expansion, calculate as if the *amount of capital goods* had increased. It is the purpose of this chapter to demonstrate that this point could not be upheld, anyway. It is not the supply of capital goods that limits the length of the

---

38   Mises, "The 'Austrian' Theory of the Trade Cycle," p. 260.

39   Ibid., p. 560, emphasis added.

40   See Jeffrey M. Herbener, Hans-Hermann Hoppe, and Joseph T. Salerno, "Introduction to the Scholar's Edition," in Mises: *Human Action: A Treatise on Economics*. The Scholar's Edition (Auburn, Ala.: Institute, 1998), pp. xx ff.

41   Mises *Human Action*, p. 263, emphasis by Mises.

production period, and also, an expansion of circulation credit does not create the illusion of an increased supply of capital goods. *The scarcity of capital goods cannot produce a bust.*

Let us assume that the entrepreneurs have indeed been counting on a large supply of capital goods because of an artificially lowered interest rate. At some point, they realize that their expectations have been flawed. The price of capital goods rises. Now, it is true, this development would increase the costs to those entrepreneurs who need these goods as input. Those entrepreneurs might indeed have to stop or closes their businesses.

However, it must be remembered that capital goods, in the definition given by Mises himself, are *produced means of production. If they become scarce, their supply can be increased simply by producing them.* The rise of capital goods prices will establish new profit opportunities. Entrepreneurs will be eager to produce capital goods. Their supply should, therefore, increase and their prices decrease again. *So the bottleneck that Mises thinks will trigger an economic crisis can easily be overcome.* There is no problem with this solution unless something might hinder the production of capital goods, that is, unless another bottleneck should hinder this adjustment of the production process. If this occurred, the described solution would become unprofitable for the entrepreneurs. But then the fact that it is unprofitable to produce capital goods cannot signify their "insufficient supply." Rather the opposite is true. Apparently, there are enough capital goods available when their production is unprofitable. To sum up, *the scarcity of capital goods can be healed by producing them. When it is unprofitable to produce them they are not scarce and do not constitute a bottleneck that triggers an economic crisis.*

It is different with the version that can be found in the *Theory of Money and Credit.* There, it was the scarcity of the subsistence fund that triggered the bust. Concerning the subsistence fund it cannot be said what was just said about capital goods. When the means of subsistence become scarce, it cannot be argued that this does not constitute problems because they can easily be produced—like capital goods. The subsistence fund comes into being by people who *save* parts of their income. It is necessary that some people abstain from consumption, i.e., incur a sacrifice of potential consumption. This way, consumers' goods are made free that can now be bought by workers who do not themselves produce consumers' goods, but work in roundabout production processes. *Without savings, these workers cannot be provided with means of subsistence; no subsistence fund can be built up, and roundabout ways of production become unfeasible.*

So one cannot argue that the scarcity of consumers' goods can be overcome by producing them. The fund of consumers' goods can only be increased by *saving*. And if the savings are not enough to finance the actual production processes, the interest rate will rise and many projects will become unprofitable. Businessmen themselves can do nothing to prevent this consequence as long as people do not save more. *This* is the problem that causes the crisis. *This* indeed is a bottleneck. Given the unjustifiably long production period—the result of the artificially lowered interest rate—people do not save enough, the subsistence fund shrinks, and many investment projects cannot be finished and turn out to be malinvestments. This problem cannot be healed by production, but only by saving. If people do not save more, the crisis cannot be avoided.

CONCLUSION

We find that the limiting factor at the turning point of the business cycle must be the available subsistence fund. This point was stressed by Ludwig von Mises in his *Theory of Money and Credit*. Later on, he more and more abandoned this line of reasoning and substituted the concept of capital goods. It has been shown that this change was for the worse. Capital goods—produced means of production—can never be a bottleneck in the production process as their supply can easily be increased by merely producing them. The same argument cannot be employed to refute the original version that runs in terms of the subsistence fund. The latter can only be increased by saving, not merely by production. Thus, in case savings should not increase at the turning point of the business cycle, the crisis sets in as described by Mises in his 1912 *Theorie des Geldes und der Umlaufsmittel.* Consumers' goods prices rise and producers' goods prices fall, making necessary a painful adaptation of production. As a final point, it might be interesting to note that it was Richard von Strigl who, in his book, *Kapital und Produktion*, elaborated on Mises's original formulation and expounded his version of the ABCT solely in terms of the subsistence fund.[42]

---

42   See Richard von Strigl, *Capital and Production*, trans. Margaret R. Hoppe and Hans-Herman Hoppe, edited with an Introduction by Jörg Guido Hülsmann (Auburn, Ala.: Ludwig von Mises Institute, 2000).

REFERENCES

Belke, Ansgar, and Thorsten Polleit 2009. *Monetary Economics in Globalised Financial Markets*. Berlin and Heidelberg, Springer.

Böhm-Bawerk, Eugen von. 1921. *Positive Theorie des Kapitals*, Band I, 4. Auflage. Jena, Fischer.

Dornbusch, Rudiger, Stanley Fischer, and Richard Startz. (2008): *Macroeconomics*. 10th edition, Boston: McGraw-Hill/Irwin.

Gentier, Antoine. (2003). *Economie Bancaire. Essai sur les effets de la concurrence et la réglementation sur le financement du crédit*. Paris: Publibook.

Herbener, Jeffrey M., Hans-Hermann Hoppe, and Joseph T. Salerno. 1998. Introduction to the Scholar's Edition. In: Ludwig von Mises, *Human Action: A Treatise on Economics*. The Scholar's Edition, Auburn, Ala.: Ludwig von Mises Institute. Pp. v–xxiv.

Huerta de Soto, Jesús. 2009. *Money, Bank Credit, and Economic Cycles*. 2nd ed. M.A. Stroup, trans. Auburn, Ala.: Ludwig von Mises Institute.

Mises, Ludwig von. 1912. *Theorie des Geldes und der Umlaufsmittel*. Munich and Leipzig: Duncker & Humblot.

——. 1940: *Nationalökonomie: Theorie des Handelns und Wirtschaftens*. Genf, ed. Union.

——. 1949. *Human Action: A Treatise on Economics*. New Haven, Conn.: Yale University Press.

——. [1912] 1953. *The Theory of Money and Credit*. New Haven, Conn.: Yale University Press.

——. 1966. *Human Action: A Treatise on Economics*. 3rd rev. ed. Chicago, Regnery.

——. [1936] 1996. "The 'Austrian' Theory of the Trade Cycle." In *The Austrian Theory of the Trade Cycle and other Essays*. Compiled by Richard M. Ebeling. Auburn, Ala.: Ludwig von Mises Institute. Pp. 25–35.

——. [1928] 2006. "Monetary Stabilization and Cyclical Policy." In *The Causes of the Economic Crisis and other Essays Before and After the Great Depression*. Percy L. Greaves, Jr. Auburn, Ala.: Ludwig von Mises Institute. Pp. 53–153.

——. [1931] 2006. "The Causes of the Economic Crisis: An Address." In *The Causes of the Economic Crisis and other Essays Before and After the Great Depression*. Percy L. Greaves, Jr. Auburn, Ala.: Ludwig von Mises Institute. Pp. 155–81.

Strigl, Richard von. 2000. *Capital and Production*. Margaret R. Hoppe and Hans-Hermann Hoppe, trans. Edited with an Introduction by J. G. Hülsmann. Auburn, Ala.: Ludwig von Mises Institute.

10

Nikolay Gertchev

The Inter-Bank Market
in the Perspective of
Fractional Reserve Banking

IN VIEW OF THE DIVERSITY and depth of the analytical contributions of
the *Theory of Money and Credit*, modern Austrians rightly consider Ludwig von Mises as the monetary theorist of the twentieth century. However,
Mises's monetary doctrine did not reach full completion until the publication of his broader treatise *Human Action*, which clarifies or even amends,
sometimes in a substantial manner, his earlier views on important monetary issues (Gertchev 2004). One question that is further elaborated in
Human Action is that of the existence of natural limits to the amount of
fiduciary media of exchange that freely competing fractional reserve (FR)
banks would be able to issue. In the *Theory of Money and Credit*, while
pointing out that there are no natural limits to the creation of fiduciary media of exchange, Mises adds repeatedly that a single bank could not expand
its circulation credit unlimitedly if its competitors decided to act otherwise. In *Human Action*, Mises strengthens his earlier position by asserting
painstakingly that a competitive FR banking system, i.e., one that is free
from government intervention and is only subject to private business law,
would be very efficient in restricting bank credit expansion, and hence in

NIKOLAY GERTCHEV holds a Ph.D. in economics from the University of Paris II Panthéon-
Assas and is currently based in Brussels, Belgium where he works for an international organization.

preventing inflation. Mises's completed argument, which was adopted and further expounded by Murray Rothbard, has become a building block of the standard Austrian banking theory.

One of the goals of this paper is to revisit the foundation of this building block. We try to show that the self-limitation of bank credit expansion, which Mises considers to be inherent to FR free banking, is not apodictic, but rather dependable on specific actions being undertaken by the banks. This allows us to present the inter-bank loan market as an alternative pattern of bankers' actions, namely a pattern that results in the removal of these so-called natural limits. The first section presents and critically analyzes the case for the existence of the natural limits. The second section offers an Austrian approach to the inter-bank market.[1] The third and last section contains an empirical illustration of the formal analysis based on recent developments in the euro area.

I. The Case for Natural Limits on Expansion in a Fractional Reserve Free Banking System

In *Human Action*, Mises goes to great lengths to show how the coexistence of multiple FR banks implies strong restraints on the capacity of the banking system to expand.[2] The argument first establishes the individual constraints for a single institution that would engage in credit expansion alone before drawing a generalization at the system's level.

Liquidity Outflows from Inter-Bank Settlement

At the level of the individual analysis, Mises makes a crucial distinction between the clients and the non-clients of the expanding bank. The clients are those who express a demand to hold the fiduciary media issued by that specific institution. To the contrary, non-clients are these individuals who do not have a demand to hold the bank's fiduciary media, and who

---

1   Throughout this paper, the notion of inter-bank market refers exclusively to loan transactions between banks, independently of their legal characteristics (secured by the pledge of collateral or unsecured). Thus, the inter-bank market is understood to be part of the so-called money market, which typically refers to all short-term financial investment instruments. For a comprehensive review of the money market, see Cook and Laroche (1993).

2   Chapter XVII, which deals exclusively with money and banking, dedicates to this specific question some 13 pages out of a total of 80 pages.

then present them for redemption in money, should they happen to receive them in exchange of goods and services. As a consequence, an expanding bank will soon be brought to contract by the amount which would be needed to redeem that portion of the additional media of exchange that would have fallen in the hands of non-clients. Otherwise, the bank would not have sufficient money reserves to pay out, and would have to acknowledge its insolvency. In Mises's own terms:

> But now, we assume further, one bank alone embarks upon an additional issue of fiduciary media while the other banks do not follow suit. . . . In order to settle the payments due to nonclients, the clients must first exchange the money-substitutes issued by their own—viz., the expanding bank—against money. The expanding bank must redeem its banknotes and pay out its deposits. Its reserve . . . dwindles. The instant approaches in which the bank will—after the exhaustion of its money reserve—no longer be in a position to redeem the money-substitutes still current. In order to avoid insolvency it must as soon as possible return to a policy of strengthening its money reserve. It must abandon its expansionist methods. (Mises 1998, p. 434)

Mises further notes that, even if everybody was accepting the new fiduciary media without discrimination for their issuer, some of them would have been deposited at competing banks, which in turn would have asked for redemption according to the same principle (ibid., p. 435). The process of inter-bank settlement would then act as a check on each bank's capacity to inflate alone. In both cases, the fundamental principle at action is rooted in the incapacity of a bank to expand its own clientele, i.e., the demand to hold its fiduciary media, by an expansion of its supply of bank credit:

> The concatenation which sets a limit to credit expansion under a system of free banking . . . is brought about by the fact that credit expansion in itself does not expand a bank's clientele, viz., the number of people who assign to the demand-claims against this bank the character of money-substitutes. Since the over-issuance of fiduciary media on the part of one bank, as has been shown above, increases the amount to be paid by the expanding banks' clients to other people, it increases concomitantly the demand for the redemption of its money-substitutes. (ibid., p. 441)

Mises generalizes his conclusion to the level of the system on the ground of competing banks' unwillingness to collude lest they should lose their good reputation. He calls "preposterous" the idea that free banks would form a cartel in order to expand together and thus remove the limits upon individual attempts at expansion. Mises concludes:

> It would be suicidal for a bank of good standing to link its name with that of other banks with a poorer good will. Under free banking a cartel of the banks would destroy the country's whole banking system. It would not serve the interests of any bank. (ibid., p. 444)

From this, Mises implies that any generalized expansion of credit is due to government intervention in the sector, which alone prevents the operation of the efficient natural check. Such is his confidence in the efficiency of a free FR banking system for averting credit expansion that he declares:

> What is needed to prevent any further credit expansion is to place the banking business under the general rules of commercial and civil laws compelling every individual and firm to fulfill all obligations in full compliance with the terms of the contract. ... Free banking is the only method available for the prevention of the dangers inherent in credit expansion. ... Only free banking would have rendered the market economy secure against crises and depressions. (ibid., p. 440)

Rothbard reiterates Mises's argument, while providing one additional point and one clarification. He justifies banks' unwillingness to collude on profitability grounds: "The banks are competitors, not allies. ... The longer the Boonville Bank holds off on redemption the more money it loses. Banks therefore have everything to lose and nothing to gain by holding up on redeeming notes or demand deposits from other banks" (Rothbard 2008, p. 118). While Rothbard acknowledges that a bank cartel is logically possible, considerations about tarnishing one's reputation lead him to conclude that *cartelization is highly unlikely* in a free banking system. One cannot avoid noticing that Rothbard's argument is not built upon a priori foundations, but upon contingent considerations about the most plausible course of action being undertaken by free FR bankers. On these fundamentally empirical grounds, he sides with Mises and reaffirms that credit expansion and inflation are not embedded in FR banking per se, but in a FR banking system that is protected by a central bank: "Free banking, then, will inevitably be a regime of hard money and virtually no inflation" (ibid., p. 125).[3]

---

3   Consider also the following statements: "Free banking, even where fractional reserve banking is legal and not punished as fraud, will scarcely permit fractional reserve inflation to exist, much less to flourish and proliferate. Free banking, far from leading to

Rothbard also clarifies that the drain on the expanding bank's reserves is but a specific case of the more general Hume-Ricardo specie outflow mechanism that explains the equilibration of the balance of payments between nations on the ground of international money transfers: ". . . we should now be able to see that the Ricardian specie flow price process is one and the same mechanism by which one bank is unable to inflate much if at all in a free banking system" (ibid., p. 122). This is indeed a valuable clarification. Even though Mises casts his account of the inter-bank settlement process in terms general enough to cover the case of the inter-nation settlements too, he does not explicitly state that it is but an application of the classical economists' specie flow price process.

By emphasizing so much the case for the existence of a natural check on credit expansion, Mises and Rothbard revive an old dispute from the beginning of the nineteenth century between advocates of free banking and proponents of the central banking system. Henry Parnell is the first to present the restrictive impact of the inter-bank clearing system (Parnell 1827, pp. 86–87).[4] Rothbard refers to Parnell very favorably as to one of the hard money advocates of the free banking school (Rothbard 1988, p. 237). Parnell's argument was already challenged at his time, and a critical assessment of Mises's strong faith in the non-inflationary virtues of a free FR banking system should start from the objections raised by McCulloch and Longfield.

The Critique: How Are Competitors Reacting?

McCulloch pointed out that non-expanding banks are equally impacted by the liquidity drain, because banknote users do not discriminate between banknotes issued by the expanding bank and those issued by others.[5] Non-expanding banks will then have to redeem part of their notes too, and at the end will lose market shares. The only means for them to avoid

---

inflationary chaos, will insure almost as hard and noninflationary a money as 100 percent reserve banking itself" (Rothbard 2008, p. 117).

4   Jacob Viner asserts: "That the power to over-issue of a single bank, operating in competition with other banks, was closely limited, had long been known" (Viner 1965, p. 238). He dates Parnell's mechanism back to an essay by Adam Dickens from 1773, as well as to a book by Lord King from 1804.

5   After providing a numerical example, McChulloch concludes: "And as all notes are, under the circumstances supposed, equally good in his estimation, he sends those in for payment that comes first to hand. . . . So long as he believes the different notes to be alike good, he will shew no preference to one more than to another, but will return them indiscriminately upon their issuers, while he can make a profit by doing so" (McCulloch 1831, p. 48).

such an outcome would be to follow suit, lower their own discount rate, and expand their issuance: "The over-issuing bank must necessarily deal with the public on terms more advantageous to them than her rivals; and this circumstance would effectually disable the latter from counteracting her operations, *except by following a similar line of conduct*" (McCulloch 1831, p. 50; original emphasis). However, McCulloch's criticism of Parnell misses the point. It refers only to that check on credit expansion which derives from the redemption of that part of banknotes that individuals consider excessive in their total money holdings. As a matter of fact, Parnell's specific point, namely the redemption demands which come out of the very spending process of the new fiduciary media of exchange, remains unaddressed.[6]

As a matter of fact, Parnell admits that the non-expanding banks will suffer from a liquidity drain, but suggests another final outcome:

> The principle of private interest, when the trade of banking is free, provides a complete protection against the interference of weak banks. For if a bank force a larger quantity of its notes into circulation than its capital and fair dealings justify, as the circulation will admit of only a certain amount in the whole, this bank will diminish the quantity of paper in circulation of the other banks, and injure their interest: *to this they will not submit, but they will combine together to collect the paper of the offending bank, in order to make a run upon it.* (Parnell 1827, p. 89; emphasis added)

This line of defense implies that cartelization of the banking sector is possible, but only among banks of good standing. However, what Parnell omits to clarify is how the collection of the expanding bank's notes will be funded. The non-expanding banks must acquire the banknotes in exchange of either money reserves or of an additional issue of their own notes. In the latter case, they follow suit and confirm McCulloch's point. In the former case, they lose an increasing portion of reserves, which makes them objectively weaker.

---

6   Jacob Viner makes this very clear: "McCulloch failed to point out that a single bank which expanded its note issue while other banks remained passive or contracted would suffer a drastic impairment of its reserves" (Viner 1965, p. 241). However, Viner does not notice that Parnell has foreseen McCulloch's main point and that he diverges in his assessment of the outcome of banks' interactions.

Longfield builds upon McCulloch's main observation and further notes the strong negative impact of credit expansion by a single institution on the reserve ratio of the non-expanding banks. The latter's attempt to come back to the previous higher reserve ratio would impose a contraction upon their banknote issuance, i.e., a further decline in their market shares. If the expanding institution is strong enough and continues its expansion, it could then drive its competitors out of business. Longfield suggests that, acting in self-defense and to avoid this outcome, all banks will follow the first-mover, thereby generalizing the expansionary process and forcing the economy into a boom-bust cycle (Viner 1960, p. 242).[7]

Our short account of this fascinating debate suggests that both camps hold a piece of the truth. On the one hand, Parnell is right in emphasizing that the inter-bank clearing mechanism is draining liquidity out of the expanding bank. On the other hand, McCulloch and Longfield are right in responding that the aggregate impact depends much on the way other banks will react, and they make a compelling case for the choice to follow the expansionary policy. Among the modern Austrians, Jesús Huerta de Soto is an advocate of this middle-way synthesis. He acknowledges that "the first bank to launch an expansionary policy derives the most profit and eventually establishes a position of advantage over its competitors" (Huerta de Soto 2006, p. 634). As a result, free FR banking is "incapable of avoiding credit expansion and the appearance of cycles," and it "invariably leads to the emergence of a central bank as a lender of last resort" (ibid., p. 666 and p. 638). While recognizing together with Mises and Rothbard the technical aspects of Parnell's mechanism, Huerta de Soto arrives at a diametrically opposed aggregate conclusion—free FR banking would be naturally inflationary.

This conclusion begs the question whether Rothbard's overall positive assessment of Parnell as one of the hard money free bankers is not exaggerated. A careful reading of Parnell's essay reveals that he is a follower of the Ricardo-Smith doctrine according to which paper currency, by substituting itself to gold and silver, increases the productive stock of capital in the economy (Parnell 1828, p. 2). Parnell goes as far as stating that a credit economy requires a transition to paper currency first: "A metallic currency not only deprives a country of one of the best supporters of industry, namely, the assistance of the discounts and loans of bankers, but it occasions a great loss

---

7   A lengthy discussion of this argument, together with a numerical annex and additional considerations as to the impact of the loan maturity on the liquidity drain experienced by the expanding bank, is to be found in Vera Smith (1990, pp. 177–85 and 197–200).

to the public in maintaining it" (ibid., p. 72). As a matter of fact, Parnell is a clear proponent of paper currency, i.e., of convertible fiduciary media of exchange, and an enthusiastic opponent of the monopolization of the issue of fiduciary media by a single bank: "The real evil is not paper money, but the system of banking which has the management of it" (ibid., p. 30). His essay must be seen as a blueprint for monetary reform in England that would be based on freedom from legislative interference, strong capitalization of banks by means of allowing the formation of joint stock companies and accepting the principles of rivalship and competition, thereby "preventing each other from abusing the power of issuing paper money, by forcing too much of it into circulation" (ibid., p. 37). The demonstration that inter-bank clearing will limit credit expansion in free banking is only meant to gain support for the suggested monetary reform by dissipating worries about its possible inflationary impact. The core of the plan, however, is to allow all banks, and not only the Bank of England, to collect the profits from issuing fiduciary media, by stretching their reserve ratios as much as possible: "On the whole, sufficient has been said to show that it is in the interest of every commercial country to introduce a free system of banking, *and the most extensive use of paper money*, consistent with its convertibility into coin" (ibid., pp. 91–92; our emphasis). Statements like this one would hardly qualify anyone as a hard money free banker.

The criticisms which were addressed to Parnell, and which Huerta de Soto has already integrated in the Austrian model, refer exclusively to the second part of Parnell's argument, namely the generalization of the individual liquidity outflows at the aggregate level. What we would like to show now is that the presumably unavoidable nature of even the individual liquidity outflows is equally subject to criticism.

II. The Case for an Inter-bank Market in a Fractional Reserve Banking System

An inter-bank market between 100-percent reserve banks would have no special features to analyze. The very fact of keeping an integral reserve implies that any transfer of bank-issued media of exchange, i.e., of monetary certificates in this case, from one bank to another must be accompanied by an immediate inter-bank settlement through an effective exchange of reserves. Otherwise, the 100-percent reserve ratio would be violated. Banks could still lend to each other, but only to the extent that they would engage in the additional, and analytically distinct, activity of financial intermediation, i.e., of borrowing and lending money. If such were the case, an inter-bank market would be limited in size, given the limited scope for a financial sector intermediary to borrow from competitors rather than from capitalist-savers. An inter-bank market related to the specific banking activity is conceivable only in the case of FR banking.

The Inter-Bank Market as an Indispensable Financial Institution

FR banks can operate in a commodity (gold, silver) money regime, without an explicit minimum reserve requirement, and keep their reserves separately from each other. Or they may also function in a fiat paper money system, be subject to a minimum reserve requirement, and pool all their reserves at a single central bank, which is in charge of controlling the quantity of reserve (base) money. While the latter case alone corresponds to present-day reality, there are economic incentives for FR banks to lend to each other under all circumstances.

Let us assume that two FR banks A and B issue fiduciary media of exchange, and that they are fully loaned up to the maximum allowed by their respective targeted reserve ratios. Any payment that a customer of bank A would make to a customer of the bank B would imply a liquidity outflow from A to B. Let us further assume that over the reference time period, after netting out all payments between customers of A and B, bank A has a negative net balance against B. Bank A must then find a solution to the problem of financing this negative balance.

An outright payment, i.e., an immediate settlement of the net balance by a transfer of reserve money, is the only case analyzed by Parnell. The point, however, is that this case is specific to FR banks that keep reserves in excess of their targeted ratio. A fully loaned-up FR bank can fund on the spot, i.e., by an outright money payment, only that fraction r $(0 < r < 1)$ of its net negative balance that corresponds to its reserve ratio. Should the FR bank go beyond this fraction, it would breach its targeted reserve ratio on the remaining fiduciary media of exchange it has issued. Hence, in order to keep the required reserve ratio, bank A *must* borrow money in order to finance that portion $(1-r)$ of the net negative balance that goes beyond the fraction r covered by reserves. This, in a nutshell, is the fundamental rationale for the existence of an inter-bank market. The periodic net negative balances between banks, related to and implied by their customers' usage of fiduciary media of exchange, necessarily imply that FR banks have to borrow money.

If bank A borrows from a third party, for instance by seeking re-financing from the bank C, then bank B receives as much reserves as is the net positive balance in its favor, i.e., the increase in the deposits it has issued. It ends up holding reserves above the targeted reserve ratio. It is then in the position to lend out these excess reserves or to expand its bank credit until it is again fully loaned up. Bank B could even consider lending these reserves to A, in which case A would not have to seek re-financing from C. In other words, B could accept delayed payment from A for that portion of A's negative net balance which physically cannot be financed by A's corresponding reserves. In addition to the interest gain that B would collect from this operation, there is a longer-term interest in accepting to grant A re-financing. In particular, the net balance of the next reference period could be to the advantage of A, in which case it would be B's turn to seek re-financing. Having already re-financed A in the first period, B could reasonably expect, and act accordingly, that A will be willing to grant it re-financing in the second period, as well as later on.

The inter-bank market appears as an efficient tool that FR banks can use to deal with the unpredictable effect that customers' economic transactions exert on banks' stock of reserves. By granting themselves mutual loans, FR banks can de facto re-finance themselves and remain in control of their targeted reserve ratios. The inter-bank market is the mechanism by which FR banks dissociate their individual holdings of reserves from the liquidity implications of customers' economic transactions. Hence, banks avoid the necessary swings in their credit granting activity, according to whether they need to replenish their targeted reserves by contracting credit or to use up their excess reserves by expanding credit. In the special case of a commodity money system with decentralized reserves, the inter-bank market also saves the cost of continuously shipping money between banks.

A comparison with the financing of a negative current account balance in international transactions would be highly instructive at this point. The Parnell-Mises-Rothbard model of how a FR banking system operates assumes that any negative balance between banks is financed on the spot through a money transfer. The fact is, however, that this needs not be the case, and that such a negative balance can be financed through a short-term loan, very much like the way in which negative current account balances are not always financed through a transfer of international reserves, but through an inflow of foreign capital by means of short or longer-term loans. Jacob Viner rightly points out that "Such movements of short-term funds in a reverse direction from the actual or incipient movement of specie are helpful to the international mechanism of adjustment in two main ways" (Viner 1965, p. 403). First, they smooth the movements of gold between countries. Second, they avoid a sudden contraction in bank credit, and subsequently in the money supply and in domestic prices. The analogy with the inter-bank market is straightforward.

More importantly, the inter-bank market also makes it possible for all banks to benefit from the expansionary policy of a single credit institution. Let us assume that bank A has noticed a permanent increase in its reserves above its targeted ratio and hence decides to expand its credit. By re-financing the subsequent net negative balance with other banks on the inter-bank market, the expanding bank de facto shares, with its new creditors, its credit expansion-induced profits. Hence, the inter-bank market effectively collectivizes the profits that an over-expanding bank might have tried to collect. This latter conclusion is of particular interest, as it puts into perspective the very notion of an over-expanding FR bank. Thanks to the inter-bank market, every bank can expand its credit by a multiple of its net increase in reserves, as long as it finds refinancing from other banks.[8] The latter have a financial incentive to grant this re-financing, as this is an effective means for sharing into the higher profits derived from the credit expansion. In a sense, it becomes immaterial how new reserves are distributed among banks and which bank *starts* credit expansion, as

---

8   This conclusion relativizes the common text-book presentation, also followed by Austrian economists, of the so-called money multiplier. The theory of the money-multiplier states that, at the aggregate level, the banking system can issue fiduciary media of exchange by a multiple of the increase in banks' money reserves. The multiplier is equal to the inverse of the complementary to one of the percentage of banks' liquidity outflows. Typically, the aggregate money multiplier is derived from a sequential analysis of individual banks' credit expansion, whereby each bank expands credit by the exact amount of the increase in its reserves, then loses part of its reserves to other banks because of customers' transactions, then it is the other banks' turn to expand credit to the increase in their reserves, etc. The system's multiple increase in the fiduciary media of exchange is then presented as the limit to the sum of infinite rounds of ever-decreasing issuances by the individual banks. This standard presentation de facto assumes that banks must fund their liquidity outflows by spot transfers of money exclusively, and that accordingly each bank must limit its credit expansion to the amount of liquidity inflow. However, this needs not be the case, as the individual institution might rely on the inter-bank market to finance its un-funded liquidity outflow. When the inter-bank market is taken into consideration, the money multiplier needs not be derived as the sum of an infinite geometrical series. It can be reached in a one-go, as long as the expanding bank can obtain refinancing from its peers.

the inter-bank market redistributes the associated profits according to each one's market share in the issuance of fiduciary media of exchange.

This conclusion seriously questions the existence of natural limits on credit expansion in a free FR banking system. As we have shown, it is in the short and long-term interest of any FR bank to take part in the inter-bank market, which *de facto* prevents the operation of the strict clearing mechanism described by Parnell. By engaging into mutual loan transactions, FR banks can free themselves from the restraints of the immediate outright clearing. Furthermore, we have shown that the very existence of fiduciary media of exchange is preconditioned on banks' accepting to lend to each other, as the principle of the fractional reserve is incompatible with the capacity to fully fund inter-bank net negative balances with money.

The inter-bank market is indispensable for FR banks in an even more fundamental way. Each FR bank must solve the difficult problem of creating a demand to hold its fiduciary media of exchange. In Mises's terminology, it must create, maintain, and enlarge its clientele. Now, how plausible is it that the fiduciary media issued by bank A would be acceptable to money holders at large if they are not acceptable to other FR banks? As a matter of fact, another way to look at the inter-bank market is to consider it as the emanation of banks' mutual recognition of their fiduciary media of exchange. Indeed, a bank B that does not require a money transfer from bank A for spot settlement of their mutual net balance de facto accepts to hold bank A's fiduciary media of exchange for a more or less determined period of time.[9] The inter-bank acceptability of fiduciary media of exchange is definitely a precondition for their acceptability by banks' clients. This means that the inter-bank market is an indispensable financial institution of the fractional reserve banking system. But then, contra Parnell, Mises and Rothbard, a free FR banking system is no rampart against inflation and the boom-bust cycle.

Factors that Determine the Extent of the Inter-Bank Market

While FR banks cannot avoid undertaking mutual credit transactions, there are a number of factors that determine the latter's extent. The size of the inter-bank market depends on the degree of concentration in the banking sector, the level of targeted reserve ratio, the degree of trustworthiness

---

9   Even if the inter-bank loan has an initial maturity, nothing precludes it from being extended upon expiration.

between banks and, most crucially, upon the presence of an unlimited lender of last resort.

The more concentrated the banking sector is, the greater is the scope for netting out inter-bank liquidity outflows, and hence the smaller is the net inter-bank balance that requires financing. On the contrary, the higher the number of institutions, and the smaller any individual market share is, the more complex becomes the multilateral compensation between outflows and inflows of liquidity. It could then be expected that each institution's net financing needs would aggregate into a larger and more complex nexus of inter-bank credit transactions. A higher degree of rivalry,[10] to borrow Parnell's quite aptly chosen term, increases then banks' financing needs and contributes to a more dynamic inter-bank market.

Second, the size of the inter-bank market is inversely related to the targeted reserve ratio. In the extreme case where the reserve ratio is at 100 percent, there is no scope for the emergence of inter-bank credit related to the activity of issuing media of exchange. In the other extreme case of a zero reserve ratio, which is conceivable only in the framework of a fiat paper money, any inter-bank transaction can be but a credit transaction, as no bank has any reserves or aims at holding any of it. Generally speaking, the lower the targeted reserve ratio, the lesser is banks' capacity to finance their negative balances with other institutions by reserves. The higher must then be the portion of the negative balance financed by a credit transaction. As a result, the inter-bank market is growing in size when the required reserve ratio is declining.

The third key factor, which ultimately determines the size of the inter-bank market, at given composition of the sector and reserve ratio, is the degree of trustworthiness among banks. The stronger the confidence of banks in their respective financial strength and solvency, the more inclined they will be to become creditors to each other. Inversely, when doubts arise about the ultimate capacity of a bank to reimburse the loans it has contracted, its creditors may refuse to keep re-financing it and require payment at the maturity of the loan transaction. To the extent that maturing credit transactions are not rolled-over or renewed, the inter-bank market shrinks in size. Trustworthiness in banks' financial soundness, in a free

---

10   Indeed, the notion of competition is to be reserved for the interactions between owners of legitimately acquired private property. There are some doubts as to whether FR banks would fall into this category. On the latter point, see in particular Huerta de Soto (2006).

FR system, would depend crucially on the quality of debtor banks' investments as well as on the conservativeness and foresight of their creditors. In particular, inter-bank credit would be reserved for institutions of similar, not lower, standing with respect to financial soundness. This does not imply that free FR banks would all be conservative lenders and very cautious about their financial standing. Rather, this means that the sector will be characterized by a uniform credit policy, from which individual deviations could be quickly sanctioned.

The last factor, which exerts a crucial influence on the size of the interbank market, is the presence of an unlimited lender of last resort. Under a fiat paper money regime, which is the only case when a central bank can increase banks' reserves *ad infinitum*, any bank can be re-financed by the central bank. Should a bank fail to pay at the maturity of a credit transaction, it could always seek support from the central bank, and there is no technical impediment to such bail-out. In this institutional environment, which describes well present-day reality, liquidity risk practically vanishes away. More importantly, banks' assessment of their rivals' trustworthiness becomes strongly biased in favor of granting unconditional loans, as the risk of making losses on them is objectively reduced by the very presence of an unlimited lender of last resort. Banks' higher willingness to lend to each other translates into an increased size of the inter-bank market and, subsequently, stronger interdependencies between institutions.[11] A fiat paper money regime becomes then exposed to regular banking crises due to a sudden degradation of the trustworthiness among banks. A revaluation of a bank's risk profile by its creditors would imply requests for repaying the loans at maturity. A bank which has lost the confidence of its rivals is then excluded from the inter-bank market and must seek the assistance of the central bank. While the presence of an unlimited lender of last resort leads to an expansion of the inter-bank market beyond what its size would be under a commodity standard, it also contains the seeds for regular swings in inter-bank loan transactions.

---

11   The presence of an unlimited lender of last resort increases the size of the interbank market also through its impact on the required reserve ratio, which is typically very low, given the unlimited bail-out possibilities.

III. The Euro Area Inter-bank Market

The presentation of the euro area inter-bank market provides a useful and timely illustration of the theoretical insights that have been derived in the previous section. This section will draw on statistics gathered and published by the European Central Bank in its Statistical Data Warehouse.[12] To begin with, a few clarifications on terminology would be necessary.

The data on money, banking and financial markets does not refer to banks exclusively, but to the broader category of Monetary Financial Institutions (MFIs). The characteristic mark of MFIs is their ability to increase the money supply in the broader sense. In practice, MFIs include credit institutions (commercial and cooperative banks), money market funds and the Euro-system. The Euro-system, which includes the European Central Bank as well as the 17 National Central Banks of the euro area member countries, is better thought of as the consolidated central bank in the euro area. Hence, for most analytical purposes, one must distinguish between, on the one hand, the Euro-system and, on the other hand, the MFIs, excluding the Euro-system. This latter category corresponds, more or less, to the whole of FR banks in the euro area. Statistics from the ECB report the consolidated balance sheet of the Euro-system as well as the aggregated balance sheet of MFIs, excluding the Euro-system. When put together, these two sources of data provide some concrete figures about the euro area inter-bank market. In statistical terms, the euro-area inter-bank market is represented by the loans granted by MFIs, excluding the Euro-system, to other MFIs, excluding the Euro-system.[13]

---

12   The database is available at this web-address: http://sdw.ecb.europa.eu/

13   This statistical category is not readily available, however. The aggregated balance sheet of the MFIs, excluding the Euro-system, distinguishes only between loans to MFIs, i.e., including the Euro-system, and loans to non-MFIs, i.e., households, corporates, the government and non-monetary financial institutions, such as pension funds and insurance companies. When looking at the inter-bank market, one needs data for the loans granted from banks to other banks, i.e., for loans from MFIs, excluding the Euro-system, to other MFIs, excluding the Euro-system. This category can only be derived, namely by subtracting MFIs' deposits at the Euro-system from loans from MFIs, excluding the Euro-system, to MFIs. Indeed, MFIs' deposits at the Euro-system are classified as part of the broader category of loans to MFIs. These deposits happen to be published as an independent series from the consolidated balance sheet of the Euro-system. That is why one needs to combine information from different balance sheets in order to arrive at data about loans from MFIs, excluding the Euro-system, to other MFIs, excluding the Euro-system.

The first characteristic of the inter-bank market illustrated by the data is its impressive size. Inter-bank loans amounted to 5.2 trillion of euros in April 2012, which represented more than 15 percent of banks' total assets and almost 43 percent of banks' loans to the euro-area economy. Moreover, the significance of the inter-bank market has been even more impressive during the boom years, when for every two euros lent to the economy, banks lent more than 1 euro among themselves (see Chart 1).

CHART 1

THE RELATIVE SIZE OF THE EURO-AREA INTER-BANK MARKET

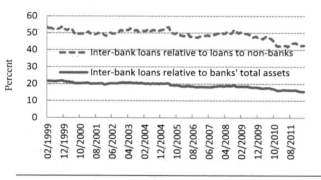

Source: BCB Statistical Data Warehouse

Second, the inter-bank market has grown in nominal terms, together with the expansion of bank credit to the non-monetary part of the economy. This illustrates our finding that the inter-bank market is the mechanism, by which banks refinance their liquidity needs on a daily basis, without having to borrow substantial amounts from the central bank. The substitutability between borrowing from others banks and refinancing at the central bank has become even more pronounced since the autumn of 2008, when the intensification of the world financial crisis resulted, inter alia, in an increased loss of confidence among European banks (see Chart 2). In order to repay their creditors, who refused to roll-over inter-bank loans, debtor banks had to borrow heavily from the Euro-system. This development has become even more pronounced in late 2011 and at the beginning of 2012. At the same time, the outstanding volumes in the inter-bank market have stabilized, although at levels which are some 15 percent below their peak in October 2008.

Third, the significance of the inter-bank market for accompanying credit expansion is clearly revealed when comparing the dynamics of loans

CHART 2

THE EURO-AREA INTER-BANK MARKET (LOANS TO MFIS, EXCLUDING THE
EURO-SYSTEM) AND REFINANCING AT THE CENTRAL BANK
(BORROWINGS FROM THE EURO-SYSTEM)

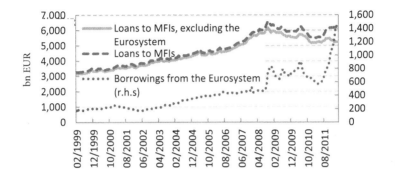

Source: BCB Statistical Data Warehouse

CHART 3

THE INTER-BANK MARKET AS A FOUNDATION FOR
BANK CREDIT EXPANSION

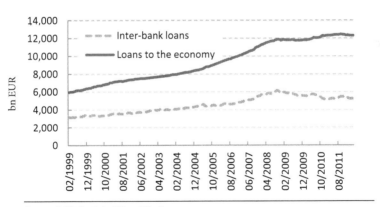

Source: BCB Statistical Data Warehouse

to the economy with loans among banks (see Chart 3). The stagnation of
loans to the economy in the aftermath of the Lehman bankruptcy goes hand
in hand with the contraction of inter-bank credit. The modest credit expansion since 2010 has occurred despite a further contraction in inter-bank

credit and thanks to the massive liquidity injections by the Euro-system.[14] Interestingly enough, there has been no significant recovery of credit to the economy, as there has been no recovery in the inter-bank lending.

Any of these three features of the euro area inter-bank market is fully consistent with our theoretical conclusions. In addition, they also portray the history of the single currency as a relatively long boom-bust cycle, with the crisis having emerged in late 2008. The shrinking of the inter-bank market since then is to be interpreted as the end of the acceptability of some banks' fiduciary media of exchange by other peer banks. The refusal to renew inter-bank loans at maturity is tantamount to a request for an outright settlement, i.e., for redemption of the fiduciary media of exchange. Put simply, this is a run on some banks by other banks. And because FR banks have no spare money available, such a bank run may result either in the banks' bankruptcy or in their refinancing by the central bank. While for now policy makers have taken the latter course of action, the fact that the euro area inter-bank market has not recovered four years after the outburst of the crisis suggests that the run on banks by other banks has not come to an end yet.

Conclusion

The inter-bank market, though impressive by its size and omnipresent in banks' daily business activity, has not received much attention in economic theory. The purpose of this paper has been to fill this gap from the point of view of Austrian economics. Two main conclusions have been reached.

First, an inter-bank loan market appears indispensable for the existence of fiduciary media of exchange in a decentralized banking system. It is an essential element of the fractional reserve system, in the sense that decentralized fractional reserve banks could not possibly exist without

---

14   In addition to the standard collateralized lending to banks, the Euro-system has increased banks' liquidity by measures that are non-orthodox for the euro area, such as 1) secondary market purchases of government bonds (Securities Market Program), 2) targeted purchases of banks' bonds (Covered bonds Programs I and II) and 3) dollar loans, after swapping euros for dollars from the FED. Hence, the increase in the amount of borrowings from the Euro-system is only a portion, albeit the largest, of all extra liquidity that has been injected since 2008.

accepting to engage in mutual loan transactions. The inter-bank market is foundational for bank credit expansion.

Second, the reality of the inter-bank market sheds a different light on the expected outcome of the so-called fractional reserve free banking system. In particular, the inter-bank market is incompatible with the view that banking freedom would put natural limits on the issuance of fiduciary media of exchange. This implies that banking freedom is not a guarantee against the inflation of the money supply in the broad sense. Hence, and despite Mises's and Rothbard's affirmations to the contrary, the policy of banking freedom could not be an element of a successful strategy for restraining credit expansion by fractional reserve banks. This finding rationalizes the widespread government-controlled policies of prudential regulation and supervision of banks. Whether these policies could be efficient for reining in inflation has been left outside the scope of this paper.

BIBLIOGRAPHY

Cook, Timothy, and Robert Laroche, ed. 1993. *Instruments of the Money Market.* Richmond: Federal Reserve Bank of Richmond.

Gertchev, Nikolay. 2004. "Dehomogenizing Mises's Monetary Theory." *Journal of Libertarian Studies* 18, no. 3: 57–90.

Huerta de Soto, Jesús. [1998] 2006. *Money, Bank Credit and Economic Cycles.* Auburn, Ala.: Ludwig von Mises Institute.

McCulloch, J.R. 1831. *Historical Sketch of the Bank of England: With an Examination of the Question as to the Prolongation of the Exclusive Privileges of that Establishment.* London: Longman, Rees, Orme, Brown and Green.

Mises, Ludwig von. [1949] 1998. *Human Action,* Auburn, Ala.: Ludwig von Mises Institute.

Parnell, Henry. 1828. *Paper Money, Banking and Overtrading, Including Those Part of the Evidence Taken Before the Committee of the House of Commons, which Explains the Scotch System of Banking.* London: Charles Wood and Son.

Rothbard, Murray N. [1983] 2008. *The Mystery of Banking,* Auburn, Ala.: Ludwig von Mises Institute.

——. 1988. "The Myth of Free Banking in Scotland. *Review of Austrian Economics* 2: 229–46.

Smith, Vera. [1936] 1990. *The Rationale of Central Banking and the Free Banking Alternative*. Indianapolis: Liberty Fund.

Viner, Jacob. [1937] 1960. *Studies in the Theory of International Trade*. London: Bradford and Dickens.

11

Modern Business Cycle Theories in Light of the ABCT

INTRODUCTION

IT WAS BEEN ONE HUNDRED years that Ludwig von Mises (1912) gave the world the first exposition of what has now come to be known as the Austrian business cycle theory (ABCT). Due to the recent financial and economic crisis dubbed as the Great Recession new interest in the ABCT from the media and the Internet has arisen (Masse 2008; Lawson 2008; Becker 2008). In this article we will evaluate alternative modern business cycles theories in the light of the already one hundred year old theory of Mises. After reviewing Mises's contribution we will compare the similarities and dissimilarities to modern business cycle theories and criticize them in the light of ABCT. We will then ask if these theories can enrich Mises's ABCT and modernize it.

THE AUSTRIAN BUSINESS CYCLE THEORY

Ludwig von Mises (1912) initially set out ABCT in his book *The Theory of Money and Credit*. ABCT was later elaborated by Mises (1928, 1998) himself, Friedrich A. von Hayek (1929, 1931) and Murray N. Rothbard

---

PHILIPP BAGUS is an associate professor of economics at Universidad Rey Juan Carlos, Madrid.

(2000). More recently, Jörg Guido Hülsmann (1998), Roger W. Garrison (2001) and Jesús Huerta de Soto (2009) have enriched ABCT with new details. In 1912 Mises did not start from scratch either but built on three main theoretical blocks combining them into something innovative and new.

First, Mises built on the Currency School which found the root of economic crisis in excessive credit expansion. The Currency School explained that when in a classical gold standard world banks of one country expand credits more than the banks of another country, there results an external drain of gold reserves in the country of higher credit expansion and consequently a recession (Mises 1953, p. 365). The Currency School remains, however, for Mises only a starting point. He considered its account unsatisfactory for several reasons. Mises points out that not only an internationally unequal credit expansion, but also a coordinated credit expansion (countries expanding credit at the same rhythm) triggers an artificial boom. Moreover, the Currency School analysis remains superficial as it does not explain the microeconomic discoordination caused by credit expansion.

As a second ingredient, Mises takes Wicksell's distinction between the money rate of interest and the natural rate of interest. He agrees with Wicksell that a divergence between the two leads to a natural reaction of the market (Mises 1953, p. 355). But Mises disagrees on the correction mechanism. Wicksell regarded banks raising interest rates in response to a falling reserve ratio in the wake of price inflation as the main correction mechanism.

The third and essential building block that Mises adds in is Böhm-Bawerkian capital theory, which allows him to describe the intertemporal distortions of the capital structure caused by credit expansion. Mises (1953, p. 360) cites Böhm-Bawerk when making reference to the subsistence fund; i.e., the fund that is necessary to sustain the factors of production during the productive process. The natural rate of interest indicates the sustainable length of the structure of production as determined by the subsistence fund.

Equipped with Böhm-Bawerkian capital theory Mises sets out the question of his research which had been only unsatisfactorily answered by Wicksell:

> We are conducting our investigation in order to . . . disclose the
> consequences that arise from the divergence (which we have

shown possible) between the money rate and the natural rate of interest. (Mises 1953, p. 359)[1]

Mises himself is surprised that this question has not been dealt with more extensively before:

> It is a striking thing that this problem, which even at the first glance cannot fail to appear extremely interesting, and which moreover under more detailed examination proves to be one of the greatest importance for comprehension of many of the processes of modern economic life, has until now hardly been dealt seriously at all. (Mises 1953, p. 360)

When banks lower the money interest rate by credit expansion (the production of additional fiduciary media), "below the natural rate of interest as established by the play of the forces operating in the market, then entrepreneurs are enabled and obliged to enter upon longer processes of production." Mises (1953, pp. 360–61). In this context, Mises defines the natural rate of interest as "[t]hat ratio between the prices of goods of the first order and of goods of higher orders which is determined by the state of the capital market" (p. 364).

Due to the reduction of the money interest rate new and more roundabout production processes are started. However, this lengthening of the structure of production will not be sustainable due to an insufficient amount of real savings. The subsistence fund will be used up before the additional projects are completed (Mises 1953, p. 361). A sustainable lengthening of the structure of production requires prior saving and an increase in the means of the subsistence fund (or reduced consumption during the longer production period). If savings do not increase—and they are likely to fall due to the lower interest rate that reduces the incentive to save—the new projects are bound to fail.

The recession comes as a correction of the distortions that "bank intervention" (p. 362) has caused in the loan market. Mises regards credit expansion or the production of fiduciary media as a violation of the free interaction in the market. The cause of the business cycle cannot be found

---

1   As Hülsmann (2007, p. 781) notes there is no natural rate of interest in the sense of an interest rate prevailing in a barter economy. Money is not just a veil over a barter economy, but it affects all economic variables. One cannot, therefore, compare the natural and money interest rates. Mises, himself, in his book *Nationalökonomie* established a new indicator for artificial low interest rates. The benchmark is no longer the interest rate of a barter economy but the monetary interest rate in the absence of credit expansion.

in the free market but rather in the intervention of a privileged banking system.

Mises explains the onset of the recession with the depletion of the subsistence fund. When the subsistence fund comes to an end, consumer good prices will increase relative to producer good prices. The interest rate, i.e., the spread between buying and selling prices, will increase again. In addition, the interest rate will also increase because a premium for price inflation is factored in.

Mises makes also clear that banks cannot prevent the bust by lowering monetary interest rates (1953, p. 363). Banks can via credit expansion only postpone the recession. The recession will set in irredeemably. The boundary set by real savings for the length of the production processes simply cannot be changed by the production of fiduciary media. After the bust society will be poorer. As capital goods are specific, some invested capital will be irredeemably lost or has to be used uneconomically.

In *The Theory of Money and Credit* Mises developed an endogenous monetary business cycle theory. The causes of the boom bust cycle are inherent in the institutional setup of the banking system: The "gratious nature of credit ... is the chief problem in the theory of banking" (Mises 1953, p. 352). Mises's analysis employs a developed capital theory, relies on the importance of time for production, and is based throughout on individual human action. Its reality and richness contrasts with the theories we are to examine in the following.[2]

MODERN BUSINESS CYCLE THEORIES

Monetarist Business Cycle Theories: Expectations-augmented Phillips Curve and Friedman's Plucking Model

Milton Friedman augmented the traditional Phillips curve analysis—that finds an inverse relationship between price inflation and unemployment—with adaptive expectations (Friedman 1968). Workers suffer a monetary illusion when prices start to rise offering more labor. However, sooner or later workers discover that prices rise faster than nominal wages and adapt their expectations negotiating for wages that permit them to

---

2   For comparisons of ABCT with other business cycle theories see also Garrison (1989), Bagus (2008a) and Alonso, Bagus and Rallo (2011). Maanen (2004) criticizes monetarist business cycle theories in detail.

maintain their purchasing power. Thus, in the long run the inverse relationship between inflation and unemployment breaks down. In a scenario of adaptive expectations, monetary authorities can only exploit in the long run the supposed tradeoff between inflation and unemployment when they continuously surprise workers with higher than expected inflation rates (Cagan 1956).

The inverse relation between inflation and unemployment is indeed consistent with ABCT. Credit expansion unbacked by real savings causes an artificial boom that reduces previously existing unemployment. The boom turns into bust and unemployment increases—not so much because workers start to anticipate inflation—but rather because malinvestments are liquidated. If credit expansion is continued at the moment of the bust, a reduction of unemployment will get ever more difficult. High price inflation and unemployment are the result.

In 1993 Friedman developed an alternative monetarist approach namely his "plucking model." Starting from an empirical analysis of the second half of the twentiethth century Friedman argues that economic growth rates remained below an upper boundary and tended toward it. In the plucking model an exogenous shock reduces economic growth below its potential provoking a recession. Exogenous shocks are caused by a monetary contraction or the failure to increase the money supply in response to an increase in the demand for money. The excess demand for money and price rigidities causes a recession.

The main problem of the plucking model is that it does not allow for artificial booms. Economic fluctuations are only negative deviations from and returns to the long term economic growth path. These fluctuations are caused by errors in monetary policy. The plucking model goes in hand with Friedman´s interpretation of the Great Depression. Friedman does not think that the artificial boom in the 1920s played an important role to explain the Great Depression. In his view the Great Depression was caused by a failure of the Federal Reserve who permitted a monetary contraction.

As for a more fundamental critique, Friedman just supposes an exogenous shock but does not ask if the structure of production is sustainable. He focuses on the monetary contraction, but does not discuss if the supply of money had been artificially inflated before. He fails to see that even though credit contraction coincides with the recession it is not its cause. The recession is caused by the artificial expansion of credit that led to an unsustainable structure of production. Friedman´s analysis neglects the effects of credit expansion on the structure of production completely. Unsustainable growth is ruled out in the plucking model by definition.

Friedman fails to understand the concept of unsustainable growth because he sees no connection between money and the real economy. Friedman, such as Keynes, believes in the short-term Phillips curve mechanism, namely that inflation can, at least temporarily, reduce unemployment. For him this reduction of unemployment is the only effect of inflation. For monetarists and Keynesians the interest rate and the money supply are merely monetary phenomena manipulable by the banking system without causing adjustments in the structure of production or the real economy.

Equilibrium Business Cycle Theory

The equilibrium business cycle theory is the business cycle theory of new classical macroeconomics. It assumes rational expectations, continuous market clearing and maximizing behavior of a representative agent. In a common metaphor the representative agent lives on an island knowing local prices but ignoring the global price level. When his local selling price starts rising, the agent will rationally increase his output as he does not know if he is dealing with a real increase in his relative prices or if just the general price level increases. When he finds out that the change implied only a nominal increase in prices, he will reduce his output again. As a consequence of unanticipated increases in the money supply we can then see fluctuations of real variables (Lucas (1975), Lucas (1977), and Snowson, Vane, and Wynarczyk (1994, pp. 188–235).

There are two main similarities of EBCT and ABCT. Both are monetary business cycle theories (Arena 1994, p. 214) and in both there are difficulties in interpreting price signals, as they do not contain all relevant information (Garrison 1991). Due to these similarities sometimes it is even maintained that EBCT is the intellectual heir of ABCT (Bordo 1986, p. 457). Lucas (1977, p. 8) himself regards Hayek as his intellectual ancestor and Laidler (1983, p. 72) regards Lucas, Barro, Sargent and Wallace as Neo-Austrians. However, historically EBCT evolved from monetarism and the formalization of Milton Friedman´s claim that the long term Phillips curve is vertical (Zijp 1993, p. 146).

More importantly, the theoretical differences between EBCT and ABCT are profound.

First, prices are distorted for different reasons in the respective theories (Clark and Keeler 1990, p. 210). In the ABCT it is the institutional setup of the banking system that distorts the interest rates as new fiduciary media are introduced through the credit market. In the EBCT an unanticipated money supply shock distorts output prices. While ECBT focuses on the general price level, ABCT focuses on relative prices of different order goods and especially interest rates as a coordinator of the structure of production. While Lucas develops a theory of overinvestment, Mises develops a theory of malinvestments.

Second, in the EBCT there prevails at all time an equilibrium as the proper name indicates. As such, bankruptcies and unemployment in a recession do not appear as an entrepreneurial error but rather as planned. The ABCT makes emphasis of an intertemporal disequilibrium caused by the distortion of the interest rate. The distortion of the interest rates induces entrepreneurs to commit investment errors that are corrected in a recession. The resulting unemployment had not been planned for.

Third, the EBCT claims that anticipated changes in monetary policy will not affect real variables. Money is neutral (Snowdon, Vane, and Wynarczyk 1994, p. 197) Yet, for Austrian theory and ABCT in particular money is never neutral (Mises 1998, pp. 413–16). It always leads to redistribution and affects the structure of production at the specific places it is injected (Garrison 1989).

A related question is if better information of entrepreneurs about credit expansion and its effects could cushion its effects. Mises (1998, p. 791) argues that entrepreneurs may in the future anticipate the effects of credit expansion and avoid using the easy credit. But would the Austrian business cycle disappear with rational expectations? For that to be the case, as Huerta de Soto (2009, pp. 423 and 535–42) argues all economic agents would have to agree that ABCT is the correct theory, and exactly know how much money is injected and where in the economy it is injected. They would have to have all the relevant information. And even if they had this information, the future would remain uncertain. Thus, economic agents would be tempted to participate in the boom trying to withdraw from the corresponding investment projects before the recession sets in (Garrison 1989). But they could not know how long the boom would last.

In an additional argument, Hülsmann (1998) asserts that there may exist a general illusion in the economy that the reduction of interest rates through monetary means would be beneficial to the economy. The illusion allows for the error cycle called ABCT.

Real Business Cycle Theory

RBCT evolved from new classical macroeconomics. Likewise it assumes continuous market clearing, a representative agent and in addition perfect information. According to RBCT money does not cause cycle fluctuations but there are only adjustments to real shocks such as technological progress. For instance, temporary technological innovation causes an increase in real wages which spurs employment. In contrast, technological progress interpreted as permanent reduces the supply of labor due to a wealth effect (Snowdon, Vane, and Wynarczyk 1994, pp. 248 and 281). Fluctuations are just optimizing reactions to market changes.

Similar to ABCT, the policy implication of RBCT (and of EBCT) is to flexibilize factor markets. In general RBCT has even less in common with ABCT than EBCT as monetary changes have no influence on the fluctuations of RBCT. Most importantly, RBCT neglects the interest rate as the price coordinating present and future behavior, i.e., consumption and investment plans.

The fluctuations stipulated by RBCT may or may not exist depending on the reaction of individuals to shocks such as technological progress. Individuals may react differently to these kinds of shocks. Of course, technological progress leads to adjustments in the structure of production. However, these fluctuations have no cyclical form of boom and bust. Some industries producing the old technology contract, others expand. In strict terms, RBCT is no cycle theory.

New Keynesian Business Cycle Theory

New Keynesian Business Cycle theory (NKBCT) focuses on rigidities in the price system.[3] Monetary shocks but also technological shocks can affect real variables due to nominal rigidities. These price rigidities may result from uncompetitive markets, menu costs or wage rigidities (caused by long term contracts, efficiency wages or insider-outsider problematic).[4] Similar to ABCT money in NKBCT is not neutral. As another similarity

---

3   Monetary disequilibrium theorists hold a similar theory in which price stickiness leads to fluctuations (Warburton 1966, or Yeager 1997). The reasons for necessary price adjustments are in contrast to NKBCT merely monetary. As price adjustments are sluggish, quantity adjustments follow upon monetary changes. Monetary disequilibrium theory may, therefore, be regarded as a subset of NKBCT.

4   For an account of NKBCT see Snowdon, Vane, and Wynarczyk (1994, pp. 292–318).

price rigidities may play a role in ABCT, namely in the context of a secondary depression. If factor markets, especially labor markets, are inflexible the recession will be prolonged. The readjustment of the structure of production is inhibited by these institutional price rigidities.

In contrast to NKBCT price rigidities are not the cause of the boom in ABCT. The boom is caused by credit expansion. Price rigidities caused by privileged labor unions, unemployment benefits, subsidies or labor market regulation merely delay the recovery. The rigidities´ origin is found in government interventions and not in the free market as by the New Keynesian theory.

Financial Instability Hypothesis

The financial instability hypothesis developed by Post-keynesian Hyman Minsky (1974, 1992) also received renewed attention in the wake of the recent financial crisis.[5]

According to Minsky´s descriptive hypothesis, during economic booms the accumulation of debts by economic agents makes the financial system ever more vulnerable. At some point the over-indebted financial structure falls apart. Overindebted borrowers have to sell their assets at the "Minsky moment." Liquidity dries up, asset prices collapse and the recession starts.

In his analysis Minsky distinguishes three types of borrowers (Shostak 2007). First, hedge borrowers pay interest and principal of their loans from their cash flows. Second, speculative borrowers pay interest but not principal from their cash flows, and as such, have to continuously roll over the principal of the loan. Third, Ponzi borrowers are not able to pay neither interest nor the original loan. These borrowers of the ultimate phase of the boom rely on the appreciation of the assets which they bought in order to use them as collateral to refinance themselves and/or lower interest rates.

An important similarity to the ABCT is that the cause of the business cycle is monetary: credit expansions (accompanied by financial innovations). Minsky´s theory is also an endogenous theory. Bubbles are seen endogenous to financial markets. ABCT acknowledges an increase in the fragility of the financial system as the credit expansion continues. However, here the similarities end. For Minsky the capitalist system itself is unstable. However, while ABCT is also an endogenous theory of the business cycle, the cause is not to be found in the free market. Rather, fractional reserve

---

5   For a recent Austrian assessment of Minsky´s financial instability hypothesis see Prychitko (2010).

banking and the production of fiduciary media cause the business cycle and as a side effect make the financial system ever more unstable. In other words, the financial instability is only the consequence of the underlying real causes such as the distortion of the structure of production. It is not credit or money per se that cause the crisis but the lack of real savings, when fiduciary media finance new investment projects. While Minsky recognizes a financial instability, he does not well explain why agents over-indebt themselves and why the crisis does not only affect the financial sector but also the real economy. He explains the bust—the financial break down—but not the boom of the real economy. He also fails to explain how the financial system ever re-stabilizes.

In contrast to Minsky's view, the problem is not credit (or its corollary debt) per se. Commodity credit—loans backed by real savings—is unproblematic. The problem is circulating credit—loans not backed by real savings. The main reason for Minsky's shortcomings is the lack of a developed capital theory that would allow him to analyze the effect of the manipulation of the interest rate on the real structure of production.

COMMON PROBLEMS IN MODERN BUSINESS CYCLE THEORY

Beside the already mentioned specific problems in the above modern cycle theories, they have in common some more fundamental problems.

First, their analysis is too aggregated. Modern business cycle theories try to find relations between macroeconomic aggregates. The focus on the aggregates hides the view on the real underlying microeconomic discoordination problems that ABCT does explain. One usually fails to notice the microeconomic adjustment problems trying to find relationships between aggregates such as aggregate demand, aggregate supply, the general price level and the money supply. In particular, the analysis of the effect of the rate of interest on the structure of production is prevented by the level of aggregation in modern business cycle theories.

Second, and related to the first point, in contrast to ABCT modern business cycle theories lack an elaborate intertemporal capital theory integrated with monetary theory. EBCT, for instance, follows Clark and Knight in the idea that capital is a homogenous and self-renewing fund.[6] The main

---

6   For the differences between Austrian capital theory and the capital theory of Clark and Knight see Huerta de Soto (2000, pp. 91–96), Machlup (1935), and Knight (1935).

shortcoming of modern cycle theories is that they neglect that production takes time. Not all investment projects are viable if people are not willing to wait for their completion but want to increase consumption earlier. The interest rate coordinates these saving and investment preferences. Due to the lack of a genuine capital theory, the discussed business cycle theories have a blind spot for intertemporal distortions in the structure of production caused by the production of fiduciary media.

Third, methodological differences set ABCT apart from modern business cycle theories. EBCT, or RBCT uses an representative maximizing agent, mathematical equilibrium models and homogenous capital. Minsky, Friedman and New Keynesians make very restrictive assumptions on human action. Minskian investors are prone to become over-indebted. Friedman´s workers adjust their expectations but do not anticipate policy changes. New Keynesians economic agents do not adopt or renegotiate prices in the wake of shocks.

In contrast, ABCT is based on individual human interaction. Individual entrepreneurs provided with fiduciary media at artificially low interest rates tend to engage in specific and rather long investment processes. These projects will turn out to be unsustainable as there is a lack of real resources. Individual consumption and saving behavior is not in line with entrepreneurial investment plans. The mathematical corset of EBCT, RBCT, NKBCT, monetarist business cycle theories make these theories both unrealistic and inflexible. The realism of the ABCT allows for a theoretical richness and makes is flexible for additions as the institutional environment changes.

Fourth, there is a lack of realism in modern business cycle theories.[7] These theories just explain changes in the general output due to (perceived) changes in general profitability. Moreover, these changes do not explain long enduring booms. Thus, EBCT diagnoses an overinvestment. NKBCT also points to a general increase or fall in business activity due to price stickiness. Modern theories can explain a general boom and a general bust of economic activity. But they cannot explain changes within the

---

7   As Roger Garrison (1989, 12) puts it: "Austrian theory has empirical content that is absent from rival theories." ABCT explains why more capital intensive industries suffer more in a recession. It takes into account that new money is introduced through credit markets, while in rival theories it just reaches individual cash balances. ABCT emphasize the different stages of production and the absence of complete vertical integration. With complete vertical integration it would be impossible for individual entrepreneurs to profit from different profit rates at the distinct stages.

structure of production. In the boom phase more capital intensive sectors have higher growth rates than consumer good related sectors, while in the recession the consumer sector fares relatively well in comparison to sectors far away from consumption. The change in relative profitability of different stages of the structure of production and the consequent adaption of the structure of production is only explained by ABCT. Only ABCT explains unemployment through the reallocation of resources that then may be prolonged by institutional rigidities. The level of aggregation prohibits modern business cycle theories to explain these phenomena we observe in reality. Changes in the general price level that many modern business cycle theories focus on, do not account for the severe restructuring occurring during the business cycle.

Is ABCT Still Up to Date?

As we have seen the similarities between ABCT and modern business cycle theories are only superficial while the differences abound and are profound. Modern business cycle theories have more in common with each other than with ABCT due to methodological differences.

Some ideas of ABCT reappear in modern business cycle theories but in a distorted way due to a too aggregate approach. EBCT, for instance, hinges on monetary illusion. Mises (1998, pp. 546–47) also mentions the possibility of a monetary illusion regarding entrepreneurs. Indeed, there may be an accounting illusion for entrepreneurs who think that their real profits have increased and do not realize that the increase in accounting profits is only due to price inflation. The inflationary generated "wealth effect" leads to capital consumption. For Mises this is only a possible but not necessary feature of the cycle. These accounting profits lead to an increase in consumption thereby increasing the discoordination of the structure of production.

The idea of price rigidities appearing in NKBCT has also been addressed by Austrian economists in context of the recovery in the form of institutional rigidities. Government interference with factor markets may prolong considerably the recession (Huerta de Soto 2009). After the boom factors of production are allocated at places where consumers do not want them to be. Consumers have more urgent desires. Consequently, factors of production must be re-shifted. Government regulations delay this adjustment process by causing institutional price rigidities.

Moreover, the idea that psychology may play a role in business cycles can also be easily fit in into ABCT. As mentioned, Mises himself uses the accounting profit illusion. Huerta de Soto speaks of an optimism with very harmful effects that develops during the boom due to wealth effects. Economic agents start to believe that they can get rich without saving through credit expansion. A phenomenon called herding behavior and asset price bubble may develop in turn (Bagus 2007, 2008b). Thus, some insights from behavioral finance are compatible with ABCT and may be enriching to a historical analysis of business cycles. In contrast to the traditional Keynesian approach (animal spirits), however, it is not exogenous changes in psychology that causes the business cycle. Euphoria and optimism are just possible ingredients that develop during a credit expansion. The cause of the boom is the credit expansion that feeds the euphoria which otherwise would most likely die out very quickly.

In short: In modern business cycle theories there are no new ideas that are good, and what is acceptable in modern business cycle theories has been better expressed and incorporated into ABCT.

Non-surprisingly, even though being the oldest of the mentioned cycle theories, the influence of ABCT has been rising recently as market commentators have used it to explain the crisis of 2008. Due to its realism and methodological approach ABCT is in one sense the youngest cycle theory as it is most flexible and can explain most recent events.

Its realism also allows ABCT to incorporate additions and updates to institutional changes. For instance, political business cycles are easy to incorporate. According to Nordhaus (1975, p. 185) politicians try to stimulate monetary growth in order to generate a boom that helps them to be reelected. When politicians can influence monetary institutions, such as the central bank, the possibility of an artificial boom increases before elections.

An update of ABCT is to incorporate the institution of investment banks that during the last decades increasingly engaged in excessive maturity mismatching (Bagus 2010; Bagus and Howden 2010). While U.S. investment banks cannot expand credit (they do not accept demand deposits), they borrowed short term on whole sale financial markets at low interest rates and invested long term at higher interest rates.

The risk of this behavior was already pointed out by Mises in 1912 (1953, p. 263, citing Knies [1876, p. 242]):

> For the activity of the banks as negotiators of credit the golden
> rule holds, that an organic connection must be created between

the credit transactions and the debit transactions. The credit
that the bank grants must correspond quantitatively and qualitatively to the credit that it takes up. More exactly expressed,
"The date on which the bank's obligations fall due must not pre-
cede the date on which its corresponding claims can be realized." Only thus can the danger of insolvency be avoided.

While Mises refers to the golden rule of matched maturities as a common sense rule to reduce risks, he does not apply this insight to his own
ABCT and intertemporally discoordination. However, this application is a
small step (Bagus 2010). When people save to increase their consumption
in six months, their savings can only be used sustainably in investment
projects that yield additional consumer goods in six month time. When
a bank lends the monetary savings for projects that yield additional consumer goods only in 10 years time, there is a distortion in the structure of
production. There is an artificial lengthening of the structure of production
that is not sustainable, because people do not save enough; or more precisely not long enough. The practice of maturity mismatching which has
been very pronounced during the last cycle and exacerbated the amount
of malinvestments would be reduced in a free market due to its entailing
risky nature pointed out by Mises. However, banks will excessively engage
in this behavior when there is a government to bail them out, or a central
bank that will rediscount their illiquid long term investments in times of
emergency. In a world of fractional reserves and continuous credit expansion, maturity mismatching also becomes less risky. As the money supply
is almost continuously increasing it is easier to find someone to roll-over
the short term debts invested long term. In recent times, maturity mismatching has amplified the traditional ABCT developed first by Ludwig
von Mises 100 years ago. Mises remarks almost hint at this extension.

It comes as no surprise that excessive maturity mismatching is easy to
add to the existing theory, because ABCT has always been based on realism. In this sense, it is the most modern of all business cycle theories.

REFERENCES

Alonso Neira, Miguel A., Philipp Bagus, and Juan Ramón Rallo Julián. 2011. "Teorías del ciclo economic: principales contribuciones y análisis a la luz de las aportaciones de la escuela austriaca de economía." In *Tendencia y nuevos desarrollos de la teoría económica, ICE,* January, February, No. 858.

Arena, Richard. 1994. "Hayek and modern business cycle theory." In *Economics of F.A. Hayek: Vol. 1 Money and Business Cycle.* Marina Colonna and Harold Hagemann, eds. Brookfield, Vt.: Edward Elgar. Pp. 203–17.

Bagus, Philipp. 2007. "Asset Prices—An Austrian Perspective." *Procesos de Mercado: Revista Europea de Economía Política* 4, no. 2: 57–93.

——. 2008a. *Österreichische Konjunkturtheorie aus heutiger Sicht.* Munich: Grin Verlag.

——. 2008b. "Monetary Policy as bad medicine: The volatile relationship between business cycles and asset prices." *Review of Austrian Economics* 21, no. 4: 283–300.

——. 2010. "Austrian Business Cycle Theory: Are 100 Percent Reserves Sufficient to Prevent a Business Cycle?" *Libertarian Papers* 2, no. 2.

Bagus, Philipp, and David Howden. 2010. "The Term Structure of Savings, The Yield Curve, and Maturity Mismatching." *Quarterly Journal of Austrian Economics* 13, no. 3: 64–85.

Becker, Gary. 2008. "Depressions Cause a Lot More Pain than Benefits." The Becker-Posner Blog. http://www.becker-posner-blog.com/archives/2008/11/depressions_cau.html#c097726

Bordo, Michael D. 1986. "Austrian Influence on Business Cycle Theory." *Cato Journal* 6, no. 2: 455–59.

Cagan, Phillip. 1956. "The Monetary Dynamics of Hyperinflation." In *Studies in the Quantity Theory of Money.* Milton Friedman, ed. Chicago: University of Chicago Press.

Clark, James, and James Keeler. 1990. "Misconceptions about Austrian Business Cycle Theory: A Comment." *The Review of Austrian Economics* 4: 208–11.

Friedman, Milton. 1968. "The Role of Monetary Policy: Presidential Address to AEA." *American Economic Review* 58: 4–17.

——. 1993. "The 'Plucking Model' of Business Fluctuations Revisited." *Economic Inquiry* 31, no. 2: 171–77.

Garrison, Roger W. 1989. "The Austrian Theory of the Business Cycle in the Light of Modern Macroeconomics." *The Review of Austrian Economics* 3: 3–30.

——. 1991. "New Classical and Old Austrian Economics: Equilibrium Business Cycle Theory in Perspective." *The Review of Austrian Economics* 5, no. 1: 91–103.

——. 2001. *Time and Money: The Macroeconomics of Capital Structure.* London: Routledge.

Hayek, F.A. von. 1929. *Geldtheorie und Konjunkturtheorie.* Vienna: Gustav Fischer.

——. 1931. *Prices and Production.* London: Routledge.

Huerta de Soto, Jesús. 2000. *La Escuela Austríaca, Mercado y Creatividad Empresarial.* Madrid: Editorial Síntesis.

——. 2009. *Money, Bank Credit, and Economic Cycles.* Auburn, Ala.: Ludwig von Mises Institute.

Hülsmann, Jörg Guido. 1998. "Toward a General Theory of Error Cycles." *Quarterly Journal of Austrian Economics* 1, no. 4: 1–23.

——. 2007. *Mises: The Last Knight of Liberalism.* Auburn, Ala.: Ludwig von Mises Institute.

Knies, Karl. 1876. *Geld und Kredit*, Vol. II. Berlin: Weidmann'sche Buchhandlung.

Knight, Frank H. 1935. "Comment." *The Journal of Political Economy* 43, no. 5 (October): 625–27.

Laidler, David. 1983. *Monetarist Perspective.* Linotron Times: The Camelot Press.

Lawson, Dominic. 2008. "It all went wrong when we left the gold standard." *The Independent.* 14th October. http://www.independent.co.uk

Lucas, Robert E., Jr. 1975. "An Equilibrium Model of the Business Cycle." *Journal of Political Economy* 83, no. 6: 1113–44.

——. 1977. "Understanding Business Cycles." In *Stabilization of the Domestic and International Economy.* Karl Brunner, Allan H. Meltzer, eds. Vol. 5. Amsterdam, New York, Oxford: North-Holland Publishing. Pp. 7–29.

Maanen, Peter van. 2004. "Monetarist Business Cycle Theories: A Critique." Working Paper. Auburn, Ala.: Ludwig von Mises Institute.

Machlup, Fritz. 1935. "Professor Knight and the 'Period of Production.'" *The Journal of Political Economy* 43, no. 5 (October): 577–624.

Masse, Martin. 2008. "Credit does not grow on trees." *Financial Post.* October 22nd.   http://network.nationalpost.com/np/blogs/fpcomment/archive/2008 /10/22/credit-does-not-grow-on-trees.aspx

Minsky, Hyman. 1974. "The Modelling of Financial Instability: An introduction." *Modelling and Simulation* 5, no. 1: 267–72.

——. 1992. "The Financial Instability Hypothesis." The Jerome Levy Economics Institute Working Paper No. 74.

Mises, Ludwig von. 1912. *Die Theorie des Geldes und der Umlaufsmittel.* Leipzig: Duncker und Humblodt.

——. 1928. *Geldwertstabilisierung und Konjunkturpolitik.* Vienna: Gustav Fischer.

——. 1953. *The Theory of Money and Credit.* New Haven, Conn.: Yale University Press.

——. 1998. *Human Action.* Scholar's Edition. Auburn, Ala.: Ludwig von Mises Institute.

Nordhaus, William D. 1975. "The Political Business Cycle." *Review of Economic Studies* 42, no. 130: 169–90.

Rothbard, Murray N. 2000. *America's Great Depression.* Auburn, Ala.: Ludwig von Mises Institute.

Prychitko, David L. 2010. "Competing explanations of the Minsky moment: The financial instability hypothesis in light of Austrian theory." *The Review of Austrian Economics* 23, no. 3: 199–221.

Shostak, Frank. 2007. "Does the Current Financial Crisis Vindicate the Economics of Hyman Minsky?" Ludwig von Mises Institute, http://mises.org/ story/2787

Snowdon, Brian, Vane, Howard, and Wynarczyk, Peter. 1994. *A Modern Guide to Macroeconomics: An Introduction to Competing Schools of Thought.* Brookfield, Vt.: Edward Elgar.

Warburton, Clark. 1966. "The Monetary Disequilibrium Hypothesis." In *Depression, Inflation, and Monetary Policies: Selected Papers: 1945–53.* John Hopkins University Press, Baltimore. Pp. 25–35.

Yeager, Leland. 1997. "The Significance of Monetary Disequilibrium." In *The Fluttering Veil*. Indianapolis: Liberty Fund. Pp. 217–51.

Zijp, Rudy van. 1993. *Austrian and New Classical Business Cycle Theories, A comparative study through the method of rational reconstruction*. Brookfield, Vt.: Edward Elgar.

12

The Monetary Theory in Current Textbooks in Light of *The Theory of Money and Credit*

THE THEORY OF MONEY AND CREDIT (thereafter: *TMC*) was published one century ago by a 31-year old Ludwig Mises, with a second edition in 1924. Today, this landmark treatise remains a must-read for anyone wishing to get acquainted with the Austrian monetary theory. Its contributions are deep and numerous[1] but only a few of them will be considered here, in relation to the most basic questions of monetary theory: (i) the definition of monetary theory, (ii) the functions of money, (iii) the typology of money, (iv) the determination of the purchasing power of money, (v) the demand for money, and (vi) the neutrality of money (on the other hand, the following topics go beyond the scope of the present paper and will not be addressed here: monetary and credit policy, the social consequences of inflation, and the theory of the business cycle). The present chapter will show that, in spite of the importance and continuing relevance of the approach and monetary theories of Mises, they are today almost completely unknown to standard neoclassical economists. The standard texts that are

RENAUD FILLIEULE is professor of sociology at the Université Lille Nord de France, and member of the CLERSE research unit.
1   See Hülsmann (2007, esp. chap. 6) and North (2012) for recent overviews of Mises's monetary theories.

247

going to be used in order to make this point are, first Mankiw's *Economic Principles* (2011), a well-known elementary textbook, second Romer's *Advanced Macroeconomics* (2006), and third Walsh's *Monetary Theory and Policy* (2010), an advanced textbook entirely devoted to monetary questions. Selected entries from the *New Palgrave Dictionary of Economics* will also be used, for instance on "Money" by Tobin, on "Inflation" by Parkin, on "Neutrality of Money" by Patinkin, etc. As we shall see, the comparison between the Misesian theories and those found in current textbooks does not turn to the advantage of the latter. Indeed, the limits and defects of monetary theory as it is taught today in the reference texts appear vividly in light of the great monetary treatise of Mises.

Monetary Theory

There is no sweeping difference between Mises and current authors as far as the conception of monetary theory is concerned. Mises clearly delineates monetary theory: it has a "chief problem" to solve, namely "that of explaining the exchange-ratios between money and other economic goods," or in other words that of explaining the purchasing power of money (*TMC*, pp. 63, 97). The main part of his treatise is, accordingly, devoted to the topic of the value of money. Mankiw (2011) and Romer (2006) do not define monetary theory as such (in fact, the expression "monetary theory" does not appear at all in Mankiw's textbook). The main focus of their monetary theory, however, is also quite clear. The very first question that they both try to answer is: Where does inflation (that they define as an increase in the price level) come from? This question is *narrower* than the one asked by Mises, but obviously belongs to the same framework, and it is furthermore quite understandable on account of the inflationist trend that has occurred since the beginning of the twentieth century. Walsh covers the same ground when he states that the "focus in monetary economics" emphasizes "price level determination, inflation, and the role of monetary policy" (2010, p. xvii).

The Functions of Money

Mises strongly emphasizes that money has *one* main or key function, which is to "facilitate the interchange of goods and services" (*TMC*, p. 34, and see Hülsmann 2007, p. 216). Other functions exist, of course, and he lists the facilitation of credit transactions and the transmission of value through time and space, but these functions are "secondary" in the sense that they can be deduced from the crucial one of serving as a "common medium of exchange." Current standard authors do not endorse this idea of a hierarchy between a primary function and subsidiary or derivative functions. Mankiw (2011, p. 621) lists the three usual standard functions—medium of exchange, unit of account, and store of value—without saying if one is more important than the others. And indeed, in his intermediate-level textbook (Mankiw 2002, pp. 76–77), he lists these three functions in a different order. The more advanced textbook by Romer (2006) does not even mention the functions of money. Walsh only briefly evokes the distinction between money as a medium of exchange and money as a store of value (2010, p. xviii).

Neil Wallace, one of the prominent standard monetary theorists, begins his *New Palgrave* entry on "Fiat Money" with the following sentence: "An object is often said to qualify as *money* if it plays one or more of the following roles: a unit of account, a medium of exchange, a store of value." And he adds: "The first and third seem insufficient." By using the verb "seem," Wallace indicates that he tends to think that they are insufficient—but is not absolutely sure or does not want to give the impression that he is absolutely sure. Mises would undoubtedly have stated that they are, not only insufficient, but in fact derivative: a medium of exchange, because it is a medium of exchange, will tend to be used as a unit of account; furthermore, a medium of exchange is chosen among durable goods of stable value and is therefore also suitable as a store of value. In his *New Palgrave* entry on "Money," Tobin characteristically lists the triad of functions as "(1) unit of account, or *numéraire*, (2) means of payment, or medium of exchange, and (3) store of value," and just like Wallace he begins his enumeration with a subordinate function.[2] The convincing Misesian idea of one main and other subordinate functions of money has not made it through the current mainstream.

THE TYPOLOGY OF MONEY

Mises crafts in *TMC* a *systematic* and very useful typology of money (*TMC*, p. 483). He distinguishes between three kinds of moneys in the

---

2   The advent of the euro clearly showed the difference between money and a unit of account. Many people were accustomed to counting in French francs (for instance) and just kept doing so in spite of the fact that they were using the euro as a medium of exchange. A multiplication by 6.55 was required to calculate prices in francs, but their unit of account was indeed the franc and not the euro.

narrower sense (commodity money, credit money, and fiat money), two kinds of money substitutes (money certificates and fiduciary media), and two kinds of fiduciary media (token money and uncovered bank deposits and notes). In distinct contrast with Mises's carefully elaborated classification, the current textbooks only offer very rudimentary typologies. Mankiw (2011, pp. 621–622) devotes a few paragraphs to the distinction between commodity money and fiat money, and defines the latter as a money without any "intrinsic value" and "established as money by government decree." He notes, however, that a government decree is insufficient to induce people to use a fiat money: "expectations and social convention" are according to him as important a factor in the acceptance of a fiat money. Mises went one step further and asserted that even in the case of commodity money it is the "common practice," not the state, that is the essential element in the adoption of a money.[3]

Romer (2006) and Walsh (2010) never evoke commodity moneys. They probably both believe that there is no need to talk about a kind of money that is not used anymore. And indeed, we read in the entry on "Commodity Money" in the *New Palgrave* that "Commodity money is a thing of the past; countries worldwide now use fiat money standards." It is odd but significant that this exact same sentence is repeated twice in the article, once in the introduction and once in the conclusion, as if the key message to be conveyed was that "Commodity money is a thing of the past"—a message that most Austrian economists today try to invalidate by arguing and fighting for the return to commodity (i.e., sound) moneys![4]

The main distinction developed by Mises is between money (or money "in the narrower sense") and money substitutes. This distinction is indeed crucial in the case of a commodity money, for instance between gold coins (money in the narrower sense) and gold certificates ("perfectly secure claims" to gold coins, 100 percent covered by the coins deposited in the banks' vaults). The third part of Mises's treatise is devoted to the analysis of the consequences of the use of a special kind of money substitute that he calls "fiduciary money" and that is a legal claim on money in the narrower sense, but not fully covered by money in the narrower sense due to fractional reserve banking. Under

---

3   "Business usage alone can transform a commodity into a common medium of exchange. It is not the State, but the common practice of all those who have dealings in the market, that creates money" (*TMC*, pp. 77–78).

4   See for instance the critiques against fiat money by Hülsmann (2008), Salerno (2010, Introduction), and Polleit (2011).

current monetary systems based upon fiat money and central banking, this distinction between money and money substitutes is still relevant. The so-called "monetary base" or *high-powered-money* is money in the narrower sense, comprised of currency held by the nonbank public plus banks' reserves held on deposit with the central bank. Walsh (2010, p. 137) briefly defines high-powered money, but never contrasts it with low-powered money (this expression does not appear in his text), and thus does not offer any explicit typology of money in his 613-pages long monetary textbook.

THE PURCHASING POWER OF MONEY (PPM)

The Subjectivist Explanation

The core of monetary theory is the study of the determination of the purchasing power of money (PPM). Even though it may come as a surprise, *Mankiw expounds a subjectivist theory of the PPM that is quite similar to the theory developed by Mises in TMC.*[5] There are however important differences that will be underlined below between their respective theories.

Mankiw (2011, pp. 645–49) explains that the purchasing power of money is determined by the interplay between the demand for and the supply of money. The demand for money is a demand for cash balances ("Most fundamentally, the demand for money reflects how much wealth people want to hold in liquid form"), and even though this demand depends on a number of different elements, the PPM is an especially important factor ("one variable stands out in importance: the average level of prices in the economy"). If the PPM is lower, i.e., if the level of prices is higher, then people will tend to need a greater quantity of money ("The higher prices are, the more money the typical transaction requires, and the more money people will choose to hold in their wallets and checking accounts"). The demand for money is thus decreasing with the PPM, everything else equal. The supply of money is the quantity M1 (currency + deposits), by hypothesis here determined and controlled by the central bank.

Mankiw then shows that there is a tendency for the PPM to converge toward the equilibrium level that equalizes the demand for and the supply of money (see Figure 1a): if the PPM is above its equilibrium level, it means that the stocks of money of the individuals exceed their demand

---

5   Strictly speaking, Mankiw seeks to explain the price level, not the PPM in the Misesian sense: see the remark (1) below.

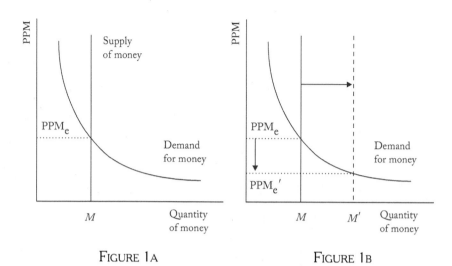

FIGURE 1A

The Equilibrium Price Level
(adapted from Mankiw, 2011, p. 647)

FIGURE 1B

An Increase in the Money Stock
(adapted from Mankiw, 2011, p. 648)

and they begin to spend more, thus raising the prices and reducing the PPM; if the PPM is below its equilibrium level, then for symmetrical reasons people tend to reduce their monetary spending, prices diminish and the PPM increases. The consequences of an increase in the quantity of money are then easily explained and depicted (see Figure 1b): when the quantity of money increases, the individual stocks of money come to exceed the individual demands for money; consequently, people spend greater quantities of money and prices rise—the PPM falls until it reaches its new and lower equilibrium value at the intersection of the aggregate demand for and supply of money.

This presentation by Mankiw is, in fact, *identical* to the one offered by Rothbard in *Man, Economy, and State* (2009 [1962], pp. 756–64).[6] Both authors draw the very same Figures 1a and 1b in order to show the equilibrium point and the effect of an increase in the quantity of money. Furthermore, their explanation of the adjustment process is exactly the same— and also the same as the explanation provided by Mises in *TMC*. It is very unlikely that Mankiw ever read Rothbard's treatise. And yet the striking

---

6   The only notable difference is that Rothbard analyzes the total demand for money D_t as the sum of two components, the exchange-demand D_e and the reservation or cash-balance demand D_r.

similarity between their respective theories seems to indicate that Rothbard (and thus ultimately Mises) may have had an *indirect* influence upon Mankiw. Since the latter does not cite any author, the channels of this possible influence are unknown to us.

Let us now turn to Mises. His concept of the demand for money as a demand for cash balances[7] and his theory of the adjustment process following an increase in the quantity of money (*TMC*, p. 139) are similar to those used by Mankiw. Nonetheless, significant differences exist between the two presentations.

(1) Mises offers a *purely subjectivist account* of the determination of the purchasing power of money. There is no "price level" in his presentation and the PPM cannot be calculated as a single number (the PPM is the array of the quantities of goods that a given sum of money can buy; even though Mises does not develop this point, each individual can have his own evaluation of the PPM based on a personal knowledge of relevant past prices). The aggregate demand for and supply of money exist at every moment, as they are the sums respectively of the individual demands and of the individual stocks. But Mises never makes any reasoning based on these aggregate functions. He always starts with the individual subjective scales of preferences and the decisions by each individual to change or to preserve his own monetary relation (*TMC*, pp. 134–35). Either the demand for money of an individual "exceeds his stock of it" and he will buy less goods in order to replenish his cash reserves (hence a tendency for the monetary prices to fall and the PPM to rise), or the stock exceeds the demand and he will spend more money (hence a tendency for the prices to rise and the PPM to fall), or, finally, the demand and the stock are equal. In normal times, the individual changes offset one another and have no overall impact the purchasing power of money. But when the demands or the supplies of many people are affected in the same direction, their cumulative actions based on their subjective evaluations will lead to a change in the PPM.

(2) Since the theory developed by Mises is based upon individual decisions and actions, it cannot be separated from the *diffusion process of the new money* through the economic system. And indeed, when he analyzes the effects of an increase in the quantity of money, Mises immediately takes into account the fact that the new monetary units enter into the economic

---

7   Mises's conception of the demand for money is explored in greater detail in the next section.

system through the cash balances of specific individuals.[8] The first persons who receive the new monetary units "have a relative superfluity of money and a relative shortage of other economic goods," they increase their monetary spending, the prices of the goods they buy tend to rise, the sellers of these goods get the new money and then in turn spend it, and so on and so forth. Mankiw, on the other hand, totally neglects the question of who gets the new money first and how these additional monetary units propagate through the economic system. He just moves the aggregate supply curve to the right and explains the lowering in "the" PPM as shown in Figure 1b. The main problem with this kind of aggregate reasoning is that it conceals the *redistribution effect* that occurs during the diffusion process of the new money: the first actors who get the new money benefit from an increase in real income, compensated by the diminished real income of the last actors who get the new money; the economic disadvantage of the latter results from the fact that they must temporarily pay higher prices (due to the diffusion of the new money through the economic system) while their incomes have not yet increased (*TMC*, pp. 208–09). Mankiw never evokes this redistribution effect in his textbook.

(3) According to Mankiw, it is only *in the long run* that the PPM adjusts to balance the money demand and supply. In the short run, the PPM cannot play any equilibrating role because "many prices are slow to adjust to changes in the money supply" and therefore the price level "is stuck at some level" (2011, p. 762). The money demand and supply, then, are balanced in the short run by changes in the interest rate, as explained by the Keynesian theory of liquidity preference ("An increase in the interest rate raises the cost of holding money and, as a result, reduces the quantity of money demanded"). *So Mankiw puts forward two entirely different adjustment processes of the money demand and supply, through the interest rate in the short run and through the PPM in the long run.* From a Misesian perspective, this standard framework is highly questionable. The chief aim of monetary theory is to explain the PPM. Obviously, the Keynesian theory of liquidity preference does not contribute at all to this aim since it explains the interest rate and presupposes that (in the short run) the PPM is an exogenous and given data. Is it true, as Mankiw claims, that the PPM

---

8   "An increase in a community's stock of money always means an increase in the amount of money held by a number of economic agents, whether these are the issuers of fiat or credit money or the producers of the substance of which commodity money is made" (*TMC*, p. 139).

is "stuck at some level" in the short run? No, it is not. Many prices are free to move and will move in the short run if the quantity of money increases. Admittedly, quite a lot of prices are contractually fixed in the short run. So if an unanticipated increase in the quantity of money occurs, the PPM will not change at first as quickly as it would if all prices were flexible (or if the change had been anticipated). In this sense, it can indeed be said that the initial movement of the PPM is "slow." But the PPM will nevertheless *immediately* begin to fall; it is not fixed and exogenous in the short run. In *TMC*, the decrease in the value of money that follows a growth of the money supply is both a short run *and* a long run phenomenon. It is a process that begins as soon as the first people who receive the new money spend it on markets where prices are flexible,[9] a process that goes on while these additional money units are received and spent, affecting more and more prices through the economic system, until a stable whole new spending pattern finally emerges in the long run.

(4) Last but not least, Mises clearly explains in *TMC* that money prices have a *historical component* (he credits Wieser with this discovery). When people spend their money to buy goods, they compare the marginal utility of the goods they demand with the marginal utility of the money that they offer in exchange. In order to evaluate the marginal utility of money, they need to assess its purchasing power. Since they only know past prices, their evaluation is based on the PPM of the immediately preceding "period" ("The valuation of money by the market can only start from a value possessed by the money in the past," *TMC*, p. 114). Consequently, the PPM of the current period depends on the PPM of the previous period, which depends in turn on the PPM of the still earlier period, and so on and so forth.[10] Now, *the historical component of the PPM is not taken into account in Figures 1a and 1b*, where the PPM is implicitly the current one. The demand for money, however, cannot depend on the current PPM since it is still unknown to the economic agents. It depends on the PPM of the previous period, and this time lag needs to be explicitly acknowledged in the theory and the graphical representations.

---

9   If the new influx of money has been correctly anticipated by the first sellers who will get the additional money units spent by the first recipients, then prices might even begin to move up shortly *before* any additional spending has taken place.

10   The historical component of money prices ultimately goes back to the period when the good used as money had not yet begun to be used as a medium of exchange—this is the important *regression theorem* discovered by Mises and expounded in *TMC*.

For all the reasons given above, Mises would probably have considered that the Figures 1a and 1b are very poor representations of the theory of the purchasing power of money, and that they elude some of the most important questions raised by monetary theory. There is no doubt that Mises's subjectivist theory of the PPM is vastly superior to the textbook version offered by Mankiw a century later.

The Holistic Explanation: The Equation of Exchange

One of the main contributions of Mises's *TMC* is his trenchant criticism of the classical equation of exchange $MV = PT$. This equation, however, is still used today in every standard textbook—what is more, it is often the *only* formulation of the quantitative theory of money that is offered to students. The criticism by Mises is clearly unknown to the current writers belonging to the "orthodox" paradigm. This is unfortunate because Mises has convincingly shown that the equation of exchange is a superficial and ultimately unsatisfactory theory of the purchasing power of money. His main criticism is aimed at the concept of velocity of money: counting how many times a unit of money changes hands on average in a year cannot replace the concept of the subjective demand for money. The velocity of money is only a manifestation of the *effects* of the demand for money, and it obfuscates the causal processes through which the value of money is determined. The concept of the subjective demand for money is, as we have seen in the previous section, the necessary foundation for an explanation of the PPM. Mankiw (2011) and Milton Friedman (in his entry "Quantity Theory of Money" in the *New Palgrave*) both recognize this fact. They begin their respective presentations of the quantity theory with the subjectivist theory expounded above, but then they fall back and focus on the holistic and mathematical equation only.

The way Mankiw addresses this issue is telling. There are two versions of his textbook, an elementary introductory-level version (Mankiw 2011) and a more advanced intermediate-level version (Mankiw 2002). The subjectivist account of the determination of the value of money is presented in his elementary-level textbook (see Figures 1a and 1b above). But this quasi-Misesian account *completely disappears* in the intermediate-level textbook, in which only the equation of exchange is explained and the demand for money is defined as the ratio of the quantity of money M to the level of prices P: all the subjectivist elements are removed (Mankiw 2002, pp. 81–85). So if we follow Mankiw's presentation, the subjectivist or Misesian explanation of the determination of the PPM is intended for beginners, but it is not required—is it too simplistic?—for more advanced students. In this presentation, a holistic equation is somehow considered as more elaborated than a subjectivist theory. But the opposite is true, of course. The Misesian theory is much more sophisticated than the equation of exchange. Mises develops a general theoretical framework in which the deductions from the equation of exchange appear as simplistic at best. It is true that a doubling (for instance) of the quantity of money will roughly lead to a doubling of the price level—a halving of the PPM—everything else being equal. But first, this is only an approximate result. And second, some essential theoretical elements are impossible to express with the equation, such as the subjectivist foundation of the PPM, the historical component in the determination of the PPM, and the diffusion process of the money through the economic system.

To sum up, Mises offers in *TMC* a much more general, improved, and theoretically sound version of the quantity theory of money than the equation of exchange. To this extent, it is all the more unjustifiable that Milton Friedman (2008) acknowledges Keynes as "a major contributor to the quantity theory" (for his book *A Tract on Monetary Reform*, 1971 [1923]) but totally neglects Mises's contribution and does not cite him even once.[11]

THE INDIVIDUAL DEMAND FOR MONEY

Why do people demand money? More precisely, why do they choose to hold a stock of money? The answer given by Mises in *TMC* is not entirely satisfactory in that it lacks consistency (see Hülsmann 2007, pp. 785–86). In one place, he states that the subjective use-value of money "is nothing but the anticipated use-value of the things that are to be bought with it" (*TMC*, p. 108). But this account is too narrow. Money is intended to be exchanged against goods, of course, but people do not strive to spend all of their money as soon as possible. They hold a part of their wealth as a stock

---

11   The *Tract* by Keynes is a clear and interesting text (it contains the infamous quote "*In the long run* we are all dead," p. 65). But the presentation that it offers of the quantity theory is much shorter and much less thorough than the one provided by Mises. Furthermore, Keynes expounds a quite standard version of the quantity theory and it is a bit difficult to see how this qualifies him as a "major contributor" to this theory. Mises, on the other hand, develops a new and more encompassing monetary paradigm in which the qualities and especially the defects of the standard (i.e., Fisherian) version of the theory are illuminated. Keynes does nothing of the kind in his *Tract on Monetary Reform*.

of money of a chosen size. These stocks as such, therefore, have a subjective value for their owners. Mises perfectly recognizes this fact in other parts of his monetary treatise, for instance when he writes that "What is called storing money is a way of using wealth" (*TMC*, p. 147). He also clearly explains the usefulness of holding a stock of money in order to deal with the *uncertainty of the future*: keeping a stock of money is a suitable way to fulfill urgent but yet unanticipated needs that may arise out of future and still unknown circumstances.[12] Even though the demand for money originates in the subjective preferences, a number of external factors can contribute to increase or to decrease it. Among the factors that tend to enlarge the demand for money, Mises lists the multiplication of monetary transactions that goes with the intensification of the division of labor and population growth. Among the factors that tend to diminish it, he lists the reliability of markets (especially of securities markets) and the system of clearinghouses (*TMC*, pp. 300–03). In *Human Action*, Mises resolves the contradiction that affects *TMC* and conclusively adopts the idea that the demand for money is a demand for cash balances that is fundamentally explained by the radical uncertainty of the future.

How is the individual demand for money understood in current text-books? Mankiw offers a correct but very brief statement—just one sen-tence!—that has already been quoted ("Most fundamentally, the demand for money reflects how much wealth people want to hold in liquid form," 2011, p. 646). Romer (2006, p. 226) only studies the aggregate demand for money in the framework of the equation of exchange. The advanced monetary textbook by Walsh, on the other hand, offers long developments about the individual demand for money. Two main models have been elaborated in the standard framework in order to integrate the individual demand for money into the general equilibrium paradigm: the money-in-the-utility-function or *MIU model* and the cash-in-advance or *CIA model*. Walsh writes—and this starting point of his presentation is fine from a Misesian perspective—that "a role for money must be specified so that the agents will wish to hold positive quantities of money" (2010, p. 33). The

---

12   "The uncertainty of the future makes it seem advisable to hold a larger or smaller part of one's possessions in a form that will facilitate a change from one way of using wealth to another, or transition from the ownership of one good to that of another, in order to preserve the opportunity of being able without difficulty to satisfy urgent demands that may possibly arise in the future for goods that will have to be obtained by way of ex-change" (*TMC*, p. 147).

problem, as we shall see, is that none of the two main standard models gives a satisfactory explanation of the subjective value of cash balances; none of them convincingly explains why people "will wish to hold positive quantities of money."

The Money-in-the-Utility-Function Model (MIU)

In the MIU model, the demand for money is directly integrated into the utility function u_t of the representative household: instead of a utility function $u_t = u(c_t)$, where c_t is consumption at time t, the function becomes $u_t = u(c_t, m_t)$, where m_t is the stock of money (in real terms) held by the household at time t.[13] So here, by hypothesis, a stock of money (in real terms) m_t brings in utility. But why does it bring utility? As Walsh openly and repeatedly concedes, the model does not answer this question:

> In the MIU model, there is a clearly defined reason for individuals to hold money—it provides utility. However, this essentially solves the problem of generating a positive demand for money by assumption; *it doesn't address the reasons that money*, particularly money in the form of unbacked pieces of paper, *might yield utility.* (Walsh, 2010, p. 52, emphases added; see also p. 75)

So the utility of money here is *postulated* but in no way explained. This model is in this regard highly artificial and does not even try to deal with the initial question of why the agents choose to "hold positive quantities of money." There is money in the economic system—but we do not know why. And it brings utility—but we do not know why either. The problem, however, is even more serious because in this model the uncertainty of the future has been ruled out by hypothesis. Consequently, holding money is in fact totally *useless.*[14] The conceptual foundations of the MIU model suffer

---

13   The household real money stock m_t is defined as the ratio of the total quantity of money M_t to the number of households N and to the price level P_t: $m_t = (M_t/N_t P_t)$. From a Misesian perspective, this definition of the real money balance is problematical because the nominal quantity of money M/N is associated to a *simultaneous* purchasing power $(1/P_t)$ (P_t units of money buy one unit of good, one unit of money buys $1/P_t$ unit of good). But when an individual holds money, he does not yet know with certainty what the prices will be for the goods that he will purchase *in the future* with this money. Standard economists completely neglect this time lag. In other words, they are not aware of the problem of the historical component of money prices.

14   Mises trenchantly makes this point when he writes that "Where there is no uncertainty concerning the future, there is no need for any cash holding. As money must

from insuperable difficulties that can be summed up by saying that, in this model, holding a stock of money is arbitrarily supposed to bring utility in a universe of certainty where money as such is useless.

In spite of these deep conceptual problems, and because it fits nicely within the standard framework of general equilibrium and of Solow's growth theory, the MIU model has been elaborated for more than three decades now by mainstream economists. Other comments pertaining to its content and results will be made below.

The Cash-in-Advance Model (CIA)

The CIA model addresses the main conceptual problem affecting the MIU model, namely the lack of any explanation of the subjective value of money. In the CIA model:

> [Money] is valued because it is useful in facilitating transactions to obtain the consumption goods that do directly provide utility. . . . A medium of exchange that facilitates transactions yields utility indirectly by allowing certain transactions to be made that would not otherwise occur or by reducing the costs associated with transactions . . . the demand for money arises from its use in carrying out transactions. (Walsh 2010, p. 91)

In other words, money is useful because it lowers the transaction costs or allows some transactions to be made that could not take place without it. Here, people supposedly need a sum of money at the beginning of each period—hence the name "cash-in-advance"—in order to proceed to the monetary transactions that they have planned for this period. As far as the conceptual foundations are concerned, this model is an improvement over the MIU model, because an explanation is now offered for the existence of money in the economic system. This explanation is inspired by the theory of the origin of money developed by Menger (2007 [1871]), and to this extent it is satisfactory from an Austrian point of view. Nevertheless, the CIA model shares with the MIU model a very problematic characteristic, namely that there is *no uncertainty* of the future. As Mises asserted in *TMC* and convincingly argued in *Human Action*, in a context where there is no uncertainty of the future, the demand for money is zero (see note 14). Even if we suppose that people need money for their transactions,

---

necessarily be kept by people in their cash holdings, there cannot be any money. The use of media of exchange and the keeping of cash holdings are conditioned by the changeability of economic data" (1998 [1949], p. 414).

they will try to maximize their interest returns by withdrawing at the last moment from their savings accounts the exact sum of money that they need in order to spend it immediately as planned. And this means that in between payments they need no money at all: they do not hold any cash balance because they prefer to invest all of their money. In other words, without uncertainty, people do not use any cash-in-advance: outside of the moments when exchanges are made *no one* wants to hold money, so ultimately there is just no demand for money and thus no money in the economic system. *The fact that money is useful in facilitating transactions cannot by itself explain the positive individual demand for money*, and the CIA model is thus unsatisfactory.

Finally, the question "Why do people hold cash balances?" does not receive any suitable answer either from the MIU or the CIA model, a problem acknowledged by Walsh when he writes that "neither approach is very specific about the exact role played by money" (2010, p. 115). It is amazing to observe that the two main standard neoclassical models in the theory of money are unable to explain why there is a demand for money in the economic system. From a Misesian perspective, however, this is not at all surprising since these models are not conceived to take the radical uncertainty of the future into account.

The Neutrality of Money

The term "neutrality" of money does not appear in *TMC* and this is understandable since (according to Patinkin 2008) it was first used at the end of the 1920s—a few years after the publication of the last edition of Mises's treatise in 1924. But even if the term is missing, the issue is addressed in depth by Mises. He begins by criticizing the classical arguments made by Hume and Stuart Mill. The latter tried to show that money could in some circumstances be neutral in the sense that an increase in the quantity of money would have a proportionate effect on all prices while the quantities produced and sold would not change at all. Mises demonstrates that their arguments are mistaken. However the increase is effected—whether through giving the same sum to everyone, giving a sum proportional to the income or to the wealth or to the cash balance, or in any other way—it will always alter the relations between the prices and affect the quantities produced.

The essential reason for the non-neutrality of money is that the valuation of the money units is subjective and "will depend upon a whole series of individual circumstances" (*TMC*, p. 141). In the real world, it can simply not happen that the spending patterns all change simultaneously and in the same proportion, because spending decisions are based upon subjective preferences between units of money and units of goods. When a quantity of money is added to the cash balance of one individual, his evaluation of a unit of money decreases and he will spend more, but it is impossible to predict how much more and on which goods. Another individual endowed with the same additional quantity of money, even if placed in similar circumstances, will spend different sums on different goods. Consequently, the initial equilibrium will necessarily be disturbed as different quantities of goods will be demanded and produced. Another (secondary) argument reinforces this conclusion, namely that the additional money enters into the economic system at specific points: the diffusion process that follows necessarily also alters the relative prices since the demands for specific goods are affected first. The conclusion is unmistakable. An increase in the quantity of money will never lead to a proportionate increase in all prices or to a proportionate decrease in the purchasing power of money. Briefly, *money can never be neutral.* Some decades later, in *Human Action*, Mises scoffs at "the fable of money neutrality" (1998 [1949], p. 203) and at "the spurious idea of the supposed neutrality of money" (p. 395), and holds that "the notion of a neutral money is unrealizable and inconceivable in itself" (p. 250).

Let us now turn to standard textbooks. Mankiw briefly defines monetary neutrality as "the proposition that changes in the money supply do not affect real variables" (2011, p. 650). Romer adopts a similar definition: "an increase in m leads to an increase in all p_i's, and hence in the overall price index, p. No real variables are affected" (2006, p. 276). Walsh (2010) does not offer a formal definition, but writes that when money is neutral "proportional changes in the *level* of nominal money balances and prices have no real effects" (2010, p. 43).

In this section, we will first analyze a core idea found across the standard texts, according to which money is not neutral in the short run but nevertheless neutral in the long run.[15] We then address two more technical points: the conception of neutrality in the standard MIU model, and Patinkin's argument purporting to demonstrate that money can be neutral in certain definite circumstances.

---

15   On this point, see Salerno (2010, chap. 8).

A standard principle: money is non-neutral in the short run, but neutral in the long run

Standard economists perfectly agree that money is not neutral in the short run. Their arguments, however, are not at all the same as those put forward by Mises.

(1) Their first argument is that people can be *confused* by a change in prices: consumers fall prey to the "money illusion" and confuse a simple increase in prices with a greater scarcity of goods; producers observe a rise in the money demand for their product and mistakenly believe that this rise is limited to their branch, when it is in fact a general phenomenon, so that they will erroneously think that their real profit has risen and act accordingly (Mankiw 2011, pp. 650, 737, and see the next subsection).

(2) The second main standard argument is that some prices are *sticky*: wages, for instance, adjust slowly because of the labor contracts; some other selling prices are sticky because it is costly to change them (due to so-called "menu costs"); in both cases, stickiness prevents a quick and proportionate adjustment of all prices to the increased quantity of money.

So the non-neutrality of money in the short run is explained either by mistakes and misperceptions (errors of expectations) or by sticky prices. All these arguments are correct and relevant, but *the demonstration by Mises is much more general.* He shows that, on account of the subjectivity of the individual demands for money and of the fact that money enters in the economic system at specific points, even if people do not commit any mistake and if prices are flexible, money will not be neutral. So the standard arguments are interesting and deserve consideration, but they are subordinate in that they miss the essential reasons why money can never be neutral.

So far, and in spite of dissimilar arguments, there is a kind of agreement between Mises and current standard authors. But then a big problem arises. Standard economists argue that, while money is not neutral in the short run, somehow it can still be *neutral in the long run.* Writes Walsh:

> If prices do not adjust immediately in response to a change in M, then a model might display non-neutrality with respect to changes in M in the short run but still exhibit monetary neutrality in the long run, once all prices have adjusted. (2010, p. 42)

Now, strictly speaking this result is highly questionable if not outright *impossible.* If the productive relations have been altered in the short run by an increase in the quantity of money, with non-proportionate changes in prices, then these changes *cannot* magically all become proportionate again in the long run. The limits of the standard approach clearly appear in the following quote by Parkin in his entry on "Inflation" in the *New Palgrave*.

> [In] the case of anticipated inflation and] abstracting from transitory adjustment paths, all economic theories predict monetary neutrality: a one-shot change in the quantity of money leads to a proportionate change in the levels of all prices (and wages) and has no real effects. (Parkin 2008)

First of all, *not* "all" theories predict monetary neutrality, even in the case when anticipations are correct. And second, "abstracting from transitory adjustment paths" amounts to neglecting the real economic processes that follow a change in the quantity of money. Of course, if the fact that money is not neutral in the short run is neglected, then it can logically be concluded that money is neutral in the long run! But such reasoning ignores the economic reality that it is supposed to analyze. Saying that money is neutral if and only if expectations are correct and all adjustments take place instantly is another way of saying that, indeed, money cannot be neutral *in the real world*. Mises's criticism against the neutrality of money was always grounded in a realistic framework and never pertained to a purely imaginary or theoretical world where instantaneous and perfect adjustments can take place.

To be fair, when standard economists speak of long-run neutrality, they sometimes use a *weak definition of neutrality*. They mean in fact that changes in the quantity of money will not affect the long-run evolution of the real GDP (rate of real growth), nor the natural unemployment rate (vertical long-run Phillips curve). In this sense, long-run neutrality does not imply a proportionate change in all prices, since it rests upon a very simplified macroeconomic reasoning in which there is just one kind of consumer good. This difference in perspective explains the different conclusions reached, by Mises that money is never neutral and by standard macroeconomists that it is neutral in the long run. This point is elaborated in the following subsection.

Neutrality in the MIU Model

In order to properly understand the way standard economists approach the topic of the neutrality of money, it is necessary to come back to the MIU model and to offer a brief overview of the highly technical chapters that Walsh devotes to this subject matter (2010, chap. 2, chap. 5–6). We

have already seen that the MIU model is unable to explain the very existence of money. It is just as ill-suited to the study of the neutrality of money,
for three simple reasons. First, in this model there is just *one consumer
good* (or one fixed basket of consumer goods) and it is thus impossible to
analyze the effects of a change in the quantity of money on the prices of
different commodities. Second, the capital goods are represented by their
aggregate value K, so that again there is no distinction between the prices
of the different factors of production. And third, the differences between
individuals are completely removed: the optimizing consumption decision is made by a *representative household* that maximizes an intertemporal utility function on an infinite time horizon and under a budget constraint (a constraint that takes money balances and return from investment
into account). More specifically (Walsh 2010, p. 35), the utility function is
$\Sigma \beta^t u(c_t, m_t)$, with $0 < \beta < 1$, c_t the quantity consumed at time t, and $m_t =$
$(M_t/N_t P_t)$ the money balance in real terms at time t (M_t is the total quantity
of money, N_t the number of households, and P_t the price level). When the
supply of money is increased by the State (ΔM), a lump sum is directly
received by the representative household ($\Delta M/N_t$). If the real money stock
demanded does not change (and neither does the number of households
N_t), then a change in the quantity of money M_t is instantaneously matched
by a proportional change in the price level P_t (i.e., in the price of the consumer good). Likewise, any change in the real stock of money demanded
m_t (M_t and N_t remaining constant) is instantly translated in an inversely
proportional change in the price level P_t.

    As this presentation makes clear, the basic MIU model is not at all con-
ceived to analyze the non-neutrality of money. The non-neutrality comes
from the existence of different prices for the different consumer and capital
goods, from the specific situation and subjective preferences of each individual, and from the diffusion process of the additional units of money
through the economic system. All these characteristics that make money
non-neutral in the Misesian theory (and in the real world!) are excluded
from this model.

    Walsh raises the issue of money neutrality nonetheless. He shows that,
in the MIU model, money is neutral (2010, pp. 41–43). But money neutrality here has a very specific meaning: it means that the real equilibrium values of consumption, output and capital *in the steady state* are not affected
by a change in the quantity of money M. In the steady state: consumption,
output, capital stock, and money balances are constant. Walsh writes down
the equations defining the steady state equilibrium and observes that their

real solutions do not depend on M. He concludes that money is neutral.[16] Furthermore, in the steady state the real money balance $m_t = (M_t/N_tP_t)$ of the representative household is constant through time; if population does not change ($N_t = N$), the logical implication is that the price level P_t grows at exactly the same rate and at exactly the same moment as the quantity of money M_t. From a Misesian perspective, the question is: what about disequilibrium or the path toward equilibrium? But Walsh never evokes the disequilibrium case and sticks to the framework of a "static" conception of money neutrality (the following subsection will show that Patinkin does exactly the same). It was explained above that money is useless when there is no uncertainty. It is even more useless—so to speak—in a steady equilibrium in which all the real variables are constant and only nominal prices change.

Now standard economists are perfectly aware that changes in the quantity of money can and do affect the functioning of the economic system. More specifically, an increase in the quantity of money can temporarily boost employment and output. Writes Walsh:

> The empirical evidence from the United States is consistent with the notion that positive monetary shocks lead to a hump-shaped positive response of output that persists for appreciable periods of time. (2010, p. 195)

So in the short run at least, money is definitely not neutral and the MIU model needs to be amended in order to account for this well-known phenomenon. It has been enriched indeed, from the early 1970s on, in a series of technical contributions by Lucas, Sargent, Barro, and other New Classical, and (later) New Keynesian economists. Their models provide the foundations for the reasoning of the previous subsection, namely that if prices are flexible then the output disturbances caused by monetary changes are the consequences of "informational rigidities" (i.e., of *mistakes* committed by the economic actors), and if prices and wages are sticky then the effect on output is the result of the delayed adjustments in prices. In the model by Lucas, for instance, a general rise in price is mistakenly analyzed by some firms as a rise in the relative price of their own products; these firms falsely believe that they are making a profit, they rise wages in

---

16   In some cases, money is even *superneutral*, in the sense that the real variables are not affected by a change in the rate of growth of the quantity of money (the term "superneutrality" appears 28 times in Walsh's textbook!).

order to increase production and thus attract more labor in the economic system, hence the rise in total output. This effect is only temporary, since these firms eventually realize that they have confused a monetary with a real effect. When, on the other hand, the changes in the quantity of money are correctly anticipated, then no such real effect occurs and variations in the quantity of money have no consequences on the real variables of the economic system. In his theory of the business cycle, Mises also explains how monetary creation (credit expansion) can lead at first to an increase in real wage (see Salerno 2010, p. 208).

Here are a few concluding remarks on the very influential MIU model and its weird—weird, that is, from a Misesian perspective—approach to the neutrality of money.

(1) In the basic version of the MIU model, money is neutral (as long as there is no uncertainty and the economic system remains in a steady state). Neutrality is thus the starting point of the model, and non-neutrality can only be obtained through an elaboration and complexification of the basic model. In Mises's theory, by contrast, the starting point is non-neutrality and the concept of neutrality is evoked only so that it can be immediately rejected: seeking for the conditions in which money can be neutral (or superneutral!) is a futile endeavor.

(2) Traditionally (with Hume, Stuart Mill, Mises) the question of the neutrality of money is analyzed in terms of *relative prices*. Now in the MIU model there are no relative prices (since there is just one consumer good or basket) and money non-neutrality is understood in a very limited and exclusively *macroeconomic* sense, through the impact of monetary changes upon the total output (not upon the composition of the output). So in the short run an increase in the quantity of money can in some cases (unanticipated inflation) boost the economic growth rate above its average level, but in the long run (anticipated inflation) the increases in the quantity of money will not affect the growth rate anymore. This is the meaning of the standard idea that money can be non-neutral in the short run and still be neutral in the long run—an idea that appears nonsensical in the Misesian framework of relative prices.

(3) The mathematical formalization and rigor characterizing the MIU model are impressive (with the demonstration of the existence of a steady state equilibrium), but they rest upon the highly questionable hypotheses of a representative household and of an instantaneous adjustment of the price level to the changes in the quantity of or demand for money. Mises would certainly have considered that, with such simplifying assumptions,

the MIU model bypasses some of the deepest and most important problems of monetary theory (for instance the historical component in money prices).

Patinkin's Conception of the Neutrality of Money

Let us now turn to the entry "Neutrality of Money" by Patinkin in the *New Palgrave*. There, he explains that people will not suffer from the "money illusion" if and only if they make their choices, not according to the nominal prices p_1, p_2, p_3, etc., p_n, of the n goods, but rather according to the relative prices p_1/p, p_2/p, p_3/p, etc., p_n/p (p being an average index of prices: $p = \Sigma w_i p_i$), the interest rate r, and their real wealth ($K + B/p + M/p$). In this case, the demand and supply functions depend entirely on relative (and not on nominal) prices. A change in the unit of money, such as the introduction of the "new franc" in France in 1960 (one new franc represented 100 "old" francs), would then have no effect at all on real variables. There would be no money illusion whatsoever.

Patinkin then combines this hypothesis (the choices are entirely determined by relative prices, the interest rate, and the real wealth of each individual) with the general equilibrium equations. The initial economic system is in a general equilibrium, with prices p_1, p_2, p_3, . . . , p_n, p, and an interest rate r. The quantity of money M is changed to kM, and here is what would happen according to Patinkin (this quote is slightly edited as far as the mathematical notations are concerned):

> From the preceding system of equations we can immediately see that (on the further assumption that the system is stable) the economy will reach a new equilibrium position with money prices kp_1, . . . , kp_n, kp and an unchanged rate of interest r. . . . Thus the increased quantity of money does not affect any of the real variables of the system, namely, relative prices, the rate of interest, the real value of money balances, and hence the respective outputs of the n goods. In brief, *money is neutral.* (Patinkin 2008, emphases added)

Now there are a few problems with this demonstration of the neutrality of money. It must first be realized that it rests upon a highly unrealistic assumption, namely that people only take relative prices and real wealth into account. It is obvious that this hypothesis will never hold in the real world, and this fact alone proves the impossibility for money to be neutral in an actual economic system.

But there is another—and a greater—difficulty. Patinkin does not take the *adjustment process* from the first general equilibrium to the second one into account. It is true that if the prices $p_1, p_2, p_3, \ldots, p_n$, are the solutions of the general equilibrium system of equations, then under the hypotheses postulated the prices $kp_1, kp_2, kp_3, \ldots, kp_n$, will also solve this very same system of equations. But in the dynamic process that leads from one equilibrium to another, the initial relations between prices will be altered and the proportionality will not be maintained—even if people are not fooled by any money illusion. Patinkin falls here in the trap that Mises had warned against in *TMC*, namely the *confusion between a dynamic and a static problem*. Patinkin compares two static systems, one with prices p_i and a quantity of money M, the other with prices kp_i and a quantity of money kM, and concludes that since people are free from any money illusion the change in the quantity of money from M to kM leads from the first one to the second one. But as Mises writes, "every variation of the quantity of money introduces a dynamic factor into the static economic system" (*TMC*, p. 145). In other words, the change in the quantity of money disturbs the initial equilibrium, so that the new equilibrium will not be characterized by prices that are proportionate to the old ones. Money is *not* neutral and Patinkin's demonstration fails to take the dynamic nature of money into account.[17] Patinkin, however, seems to acknowledge this problem when he writes that "The conclusions of the foregoing analysis are clearly those of long-run comparative-statics analysis." So he falls back on the standard but questionable idea that money can be neutral in the long run even though it is not neutral in the short run.

CONCLUSION

It is a striking and unfortunate result of this inquiry that *none of the most important insights originating in Mises's* The Theory of Money and Credit *is to be found in contemporary textbooks or reference texts*. It can even be observed that the more advanced the standard textbook, the more unsatisfying the presentation of monetary theory from an Austrian perspective. There is more Mises, so to speak, in the elementary textbook by Mankiw than in the very advanced one by Walsh. This is unfortunate

---

17   Mises (*TMC*, p. 144) had also very clearly explained that the problem of the effects of a change in the quantity of money must not be confused with the problem of the effects of a simple change in the denomination of money (money illusion).

because the Misesian theories of the determination of the purchasing power of money and of the neutrality of money are much sounder than their standard neoclassical counterparts. Of course, from a mathematical point of view Mises's theories are not as impressive as standard models (such as the MIU model). But mathematics is only a tool. It should never be given precedence over theoretical relevance. And as far as theoretical relevance is concerned, one century after its publication the monetary treatise of Mises is as significant as ever—perhaps more significant than ever.

REFERENCES

Friedman, Milton. 2008. "Quantity Theory of Money." In *The New Palgrave Dictionary of Economics*. 2nd ed. New York: Macmillan.

Hülsmann, Jörg G. 2007. *Mises: The Last Knight of Liberalism*. Auburn, Ala.: Ludwig von Mises Institute.

——. 2008. *The Ethics of Money Production*. Auburn, Ala.: Ludwig von Mises Institute.

Keynes, John M. [1923] 1971. *A Tract on Monetary Reform*. *The Collected Writings of John Maynard Keynes*. Vol. 4. London: Macmillan.

Mankiw, Gregory N. 2002. *Macroeconomics*. 5th ed. New York: Worth Publishers.

——. 2011. *Principles of Economics*. 6th ed. South-Western Cengage Learning.

Menger, Carl. [1871] 2007. *Principles of Economics*. Auburn Ala.: Ludwig von Mises Institute.

Mises, Ludwig von. [1924] 1953. *The Theory of Money and Credit*. 2nd ed. New Haven, Conn.: Yale University Press. http://mises.org/books/tmc.pdf

——. [1949] 1998. *Human Action: A Treatise on Economics*. Auburn, Ala.: Ludwig Mises von Institute. http://mises.org/books/humanactionscholars.pdf

North, Gary. 2012. *Mises on Money*. Auburn, Ala.: Ludwig von Mises Institute.

Parkin, Michael. 2008. "Inflation." In *The New Palgrave Dictionary of Economics*. 2nd ed. New York: Macmillan.

Patinkin, Don. 2008. "Neutrality of Money." In *The New Palgrave Dictionary of Economics*. 2nd ed. New York: Macmillan.

Polleit, Thorsten. 2011. "Fiat Money and Collective Corruption." *Quarterly Journal of Austrian Economics* 14, no. 4: 397–415.

Romer, David. 2006. *Advanced Macroeconomics*. 3rd ed. New York: McGaw-Hill.

Rothbard, Murray N. [1962] 2009. *Man, Economy, and State with Power and Market.* 2nd ed. Auburn, Ala.: Ludwig von Mises Institute. http://mises.org/books/mespm.pdf

Salerno, Joseph T. 2010. *Money: Sound and Unsound.* Auburn, Ala.: Ludwig von Mises Institute.

Tobin, James. 2008. Money. In *The New Palgrave Dictionary of Economics.* 2nd ed. New York: Macmillan.

Velde, François R., and Warren Weber. 2008. Commodity Money. In *The New Palgrave Dictionary of Economics.* 2nd ed. New York: Macmillan.

Wallace, Neil. 2008. "Fiat Money." In *The New Palgrave Dictionary of Economics.* 2nd ed. New York: Macmillan.

Walsh, Carl E. 2010. *Monetary Theory and Policy.* 3rd ed. Cambridge, Mass.: MIT Press.

13

THORSTEN POLLEIT

Mises's *Theory of Money and Credit*: Arguments Against Central Banking

I. INTRODUCTION

"THE AUSTRIAN THEORY OF MONEY virtually begins and ends with Ludwig von Mises's monumental *Theory of Money and Credit*, published in 1912."[1] Mises's *Theory of Money and Credit* (*TM&C*) is indeed a most remarkable contribution to monetary theory. In the book Mises extended the marginal utility theory to the value of money; showed that money cannot, be "neutral"; corrected the commonly used interpretation of the quantity theory of money and exploded the "price index regime" developed by Irving Fisher (1867–1947) as unscientific; provided an economically sound explanation of inflation and deflation; and developed, in particular in the second edition of *TM&C* published in 1924, the foundations of the Austrian trade cycle theory. On the basis of his monetary theory insights Mises called for free banking with a 100-percent gold backed currency, which effectively amounts to ending central banking—which is what Mises did in his 1952

THORSTEN POLLEIT is Honorary Professor at the Frankfurt School of Finance & Management, Frankfurt, Germany.

1   Rothbard (2011), "The Austrian Theory of Money," p. 685; see also Salerno (2010), "Ludwig von Mises's Monetary Theory in Light of Modern Monetary Thought"; also Rothbard (1999), "Ludwig von Mises: The Dean of the Austrian School," esp. pp. 146–55; Hülsmann (2007), *The Last Knight of Liberalism*, pp. 211–54.

essay *Monetary Reconstruction*, which was added as part four in the second English edition of *TM&C*.

Mises's theoretical findings and conclusions stand in sharp contrast to today's mainstream economics point of view, which considers central banking as the *state-of-the-art concept* for organizing monetary affairs. In short, central banking rests on four main characteristics: (1) a state sponsored central bank holds the money production monopoly, (2) the commercial banking sector operates on fractional reserves, (3) money is produced through bank lending, and (4) money is irredeemable into anything, that is it is unbacked paper, or *fiat*, money. Central banking is typically perceived as securing the purchasing power of money, thereby contributing to output and employment gains, helping to smooth business cycles and serving as a "policy instrument" for "fighting" financial and economic crises (with the central bank acting as a "lender of last resort").[2]

Firmly rooted in the monetary theory as laid out in *TM&C* and fully integrated in the libertarian philosophy based on Mises's *praxeology*, Murray N. Rothbard (1926–1995) demystified central banking, laying bare its economic and ethical deficiencies:

> The Central Bank eliminates hard and noninflated money, and substitutes a coordinated bank credit inflation throughout the nation. That is precisely its purpose. In short, the Central Bank functions as a government cartelizing device to coordinate the banks so that they can evade the restrictions of free markets and free banking and inflate uniformly together. The banks do not chafe under central banking control; instead, they lobby for and welcome it. It is their passport to inflation and easy money.[3]

The objective of this article is to review the major monetary theory insights developed in *TM&C* and contrast them with today's mainstream-economic point of view. It will be shown that *TM&C* actually contains all the (logical-) theoretical arguments for making a convincing economic and ethical case against central banking. The rest of this article has been structured as follows. The major characteristics of today's central banking regime will be outlined in section II. Then in section III money will be defined, and it will be explained why any quantity of money is "sufficient." Mises's view

---

2   For an overview see, for instance, Bank for International Settlement (2009), pp. 17–55.

3   Rothbard (2008), *The Mystery of Banking*, pp. 133–34. See in this context also the important work of Hoppe (1995), *Economic Science and the Austrian Method*.

regarding inflation and deflation is explained in section IV. What then follows is a critique of the theory underlying price-level stabilization policies in section V, and a brief explanation of the Austrian trade cycle theory in section VI. Mises's regression theorem will briefly be reconsidered in section VII, revealing the unethical nature of central banking. Section VIII concludes with taking a look ahead.

II. THE CENTRAL BANKING REGIME

In today's *mainstream economics*, central banking is considered the *state-of-the-art* organization of monetary affairs. Central banking is widely seen as an indispensable institution for safeguarding "stable money" and "financial market stability" and "fighting" financial and economic crises.[4] Over the last decades, central banking has become increasingly uniform across most currency areas in terms of policy goals, policy instruments, and actual policy making. In fact, one can identify at least seven elements that form the core of today's central banking regimes.

1. Central banks are government owned agencies that hold the *money production monopoly*. They determine the quantity of base money, and they also determine part of the demand for base money through setting minimum reserve requirements.

2. In a central banking regime, commercial banks are allowed to create additional money (commercial bank money), heaped on top of the quantity of base money.

3. Under central banking, money is typically produced through the expansion of bank credit, or in Mises's terminology, *bank circulation credit*, meaning that the quantity of money is increased if and when banks extend loans.

4. Commercial banks operate on the basis of *fractional reserves*, thereby creating additional commercial bank money through lending which is not backed by real savings.

---

4   Contributions like, for instance, made by Vera C. Smith *The Rationale of Central Banking and the Free Banking Alternative* (1936), which point out the severely adverse economic and political effects of central banking, have not made much of an impact; nor did Rothbard's *The Mystery of Banking* (2008), which also lays bare the ethical deficiencies of central banking and paper, or fiat, money.

5.   The primary objective of central banking has become to maintain price *level* stability, which typically means that the annual increase in the consumer price index shall remain within the range of, say, zero to 3 percent.

6.   To achieve their policy goals, central banks have a number of *instruments*. For instance, they set short- and long-term interest rates for loans granted to commercial banks, thereby exerting a major influence on other market interest rates. By setting minimum reserve requirements, central banks influence the scope of commercial banks' credit expansion and their credit funding costs and thus the funding costs in credit markets in general.

7.   Central banks have been made *politically independent*, for this is said to ensure lower inflation and thus a more stable economic and financial environment:[5] Monetary policy decision makers are not allowed to take instructions from government representatives or special interest groups.

Central banking has not developed in an ideological-political and theoretical vacuum. In particular mainstream economic theory has been instrumental in legitimizing central banking and shaping its objectives, instruments, and policy responses to economic and financial developments. However, the theoretical insights Mises developed in his groundbreaking *TM&C* amount to a refutation of basically all mainstream political-economic arguments in favor of central banking—and Mises published his work at a time when monetary affairs had only a faint resemblance with today's central banking regime. To set the ball rolling, one should start with addressing a very fundamental question: *What is money?*

---

5   Typically, three lines of arguments are put forward that political independence of the central bank brings lower inflation: (1) public choice arguments, (2) the theory of Sargent and Wallace (1981), according to which a politically dependent central bank will be forced by government to monetize its debt, and (3) the time-inconsistency issue popularized by Kydland and Prescott (1977), Calvo (1978), and Barro and Gordon (1983). For an overview of the issue of central bank independence see, for instance, Eijffinger and De Han (1996), "The Political Economy of Central-Bank Independence."

III. What Money Is, and Why any Existing Quantity of Money is "Sufficient"

It is a widely held view that money has four functions in the economy: exchange function, unit of account function, store of value function, and means of deferred payment function. In *TM&C* Mises disagreed. He pointed out that money, the universally accepted means of exchange, has only *one* function: the means of exchange function. The unit of account function, the store of value function, and the function as a means of deferred payment are simply sub-functions (or: *secondary* functions) of money's means of payment function.[6]

Mises argued that money is neither a production nor a consumption good, but that it represents a third category: a medium of exchange—thereby siding with the position expressed by Karl G. A. Knies (1821–1898) in his *Geld und Credit* (1885).[7]

To Mises, money is an economic good. As such, it is subject to the irrefutably true *law of diminishing marginal utility*.[8] Because of the importance of this insight it seems worthwhile to briefly review Mises's line of argumentation for integrating the value of money into the marginal utility theory.

To start with, Mises distinguishes between an objective use-value, a subjective use-value, and an objective exchange-value of money. The effectively technologically-determined *objective use-value* denotes whether a good is a means for attaining a definitive end.

The *subjective use-value* denotes a good's position on an individual's value scale (and is not always based on the good's true objective use-value); and the *objective exchange-value,* which is a good's purchasing power—its command over other goods—as established in the market place.

---

6   See Mises (1953), *TM&C*, pp. 34–37.

7   See the comprehensive discussion in Mises (1953), *TM&C*, pp. 79–90. In his *Geld und Credit* (1885), Knies noted (in German, p. 21). "Um so mehr kann es zunächst als empfohlen erscheinen, an die Stelle jener Zweiteilung—Produktionsmittel und Genussmittel—zur Eingliederung auch des Geldes die Dreiteilung treten zu lassen in Produktions-, Genuss- und Tausch-Mittel."

8   There are actually two insights that come with the law of diminishing marginal utility as derived from the axiom of human action: (1) the marginal utility of each unit decreases as the supply of its units increase (given the size of a unit of a good), and (2) the marginal utility of a larger-sized unit is greater than the marginal utility of a smaller-sized unit. See Rothbard (2001), *Man, Economy and State*, pp. 268–71; Mises (1996), *Human Action*, pp. 119–27.

As money's sole function is the means of exchange function, Mises concludes: "In the case of money, subjective use-value and subjective exchange value coincide."[9]

And further: "[T]he subjective estimates of individuals are the basis of the economic valuation of money just as of that of other goods."[10] From the law of diminishing marginal utility it follows that any rise in the quantity of money in someone's portfolio must necessarily lead to a decline in the marginal utility of the money unit.

As money will then be increasingly exchanged for goods and services, the money prices of these vendible items will rise (above the level that would prevail had the quantity of money remained unchanged); likewise, any decline in the quantity of money must be accompanied by a rise in the marginal utility of the money unit, leading to a decline in the money prices of goods.[11]

---

9   Mises (1953), *TM&C*, p. 97.

10   Ibid., p. 97; see also pp. 97–107.

11   Given the importance of this insight, a somewhat extensive citation of Mises's words seems to be required here (*TM&C*, p. 139):

> An increase in a community's stock of money always means an increase in the amount of money held by a number of economic agents, whether these are the issuers of fiat or credit money or the producers of the substance of which commodity money is made. For these persons, the ratio between the demand for money and the stock of it is altered; they have a relative superfluity of money and a relative shortage of other economic goods. The immediate consequence of both circumstances is that the marginal utility to them of the monetary unit diminishes. This necessarily influences their behavior in the market. They are in a stronger position as buyers. They will now express in the market their demand for the objects they desire more intensively than before; they are able to offer more money for the commodities that they wish to acquire. It will be the obvious result of this that the prices of the goods concerned will rise, and that the objective exchange value of money will fall in comparison. But this rise of prices will by no means be restricted to the market for those goods that are desired by those who originally have the new money at their disposal. In addition, those who have brought these goods to market will have their incomes and their proportionate stocks of money increased and, in their turn, will be in a position to demand more intensively the goods they want, so that these goods will also rise in price. Thus the increase of prices continues, having a diminishing effect, until all commodities, some to a greater and some to a lesser extent, are reached by it.

This, in turn, yields a highly important (and actually praxeological) insight, namely that any prevailing quantity of money in the economy is "sufficient," meaning that any change in the economy's money stock doesn't confer any social benefit.[12]

Such a conclusion stands in sharp contrast to today's monetary policy doctrine, which deliberately seeks to expand the quantity of money over time. The explanation is that money's sole function is the means of exchange function. An increase in the quantity of money dilutes the exchange value of money—which follows from the law of diminishing marginal utility—, thereby reducing money's effectiveness for exchange purposes.

What an increase in the quantity of money does is to benefit some at the expense of others—an insight often referred to as "Cantillon Effect." Writes Mises in *TM&C*:

> The increase in the quantity of money does not mean an increase of income for all individuals. On the contrary, those sections of the community that are the last to be reached by the additional quantity of money have their incomes reduced, as a consequence of the decrease in the value of money called forth by the increase in its quantity ...[13]

From this it follows that an expansion of the quantity of money through central bank action is, and necessarily so, a form of (as will be pointed out later: coercive) redistribution of income and wealth among market participants—where the early receivers benefit at the expense of those who receive the new money at a later point or do not receive anything from the new money at all:

> As money can never be neutral and stable in purchasing power, a government's plans concerning the determination of the quantity of money can never be impartial and fair to all members of society. Whatever a government does in the pursuit of aims to influence the height of purchasing power depends necessarily upon the rulers' personal value judgments. It always furthers the interests of some groups of people at the expense of other

---

12   It should be noted that this conclusion holds in a commodity as well as in a paper money regime. In a commodity money regime, where the commodity can be shifted from the sphere of non-monetary use to the sphere of monetary use and vice versa, a rise in the commodity serving as money can be socially beneficial. This is not the case in a pure paper, or fiat, money regime.

13   Mises (1953), *TM&C*, p. 139.

groups. It never serves what is called the commonweal or the public welfare.[14]

That said, central banking is never "neutral," it creates winners and losers, and necessarily so.

IV. ON INFLATION AND DEFLATION

Central banks' monetary policies by and large aim at achieving *price (level) stability*, with the latter typically denoting the absence of inflation and deflation. In *mainstream economics*, inflation and deflation are defined in terms of changes in the economy's consumer price level: Inflation denotes an ongoing rise in the price index (of no more than, say, 2 or 3 percent per annum), deflation refers to an ongoing decline in the price index over time. In *TM&C* Mises took the side of defining inflation and deflation in terms of changes in the purchasing power of money.[15] He noted:

> In theoretical investigation there is only one meaning that can rationally be attached to the expression Inflation: an increase in the quantity of money (in the broader sense of the term, so as to include fiduciary media as well), that is not offset by a corresponding increase in the need for money (again in the broader sense of the term), so that a fall in the objective exchange-value of money must occur. Again, Deflation (or Restriction, or Contraction) signifies: a diminution of the quantity of money (in the broader sense) which is not offset by a corresponding diminution of the demand for money (in the broader sense), so that an increase in the objective exchange-value of money must occur.[16]

At the same time, however, Mises saw that the terms inflation and deflation were actually contradictory, as there could be no thing as stable money: "If we so define these concepts, it follows that either inflation or deflation is constantly going on, for a situation in which the objective exchange value of money did not alter could hardly ever exist for very long."[17] Mises was already relatively close to the viewpoint he would develop later on when

---

14   Mises (1996), *Human Action*, p. 422.

15   In this context see, for instance, Cachanosky (2009), "The Definition of Inflation According to Mises: Implication for the Debate on Free Banking."

16   Mises (1953), *TM&C*, p. 240.

17   Ibid.

his praxeological approach to the science of human action had been fully developed.[18]

In *Human Action*, published in 1949 as the rewritten English version of *Nationalökonomie* (1940), Mises identified inflation and deflation with changes in the quantity of money (which he termed "cash-induced changes"): "[I]nflation was applied to signify cash-induced changes resulting in a drop in purchasing power, and the term deflation to signify cash-induced changes resulting in a rise in purchasing power."[19] Such a definition of inflation and deflation is not only broader than the one put forward in *TM&C*. It also captures the effect a change of the quantity of money has on money's exchange value, including the *counterfactuals* from a change in the quantity of money: namely the forgone effects on the exchange value of money had there been no change in the quantity of money.

Perhaps the most important point Mises made in the debate about inflation and deflation is that the subjective exchange value of money is not, and cannot be constant, or stable over time: "[T]he increase in individuals' stocks of money which results from the inflow of the additional quantity of money must bring about a change in the subjective valuations of the individuals, and that this occurs immediately and begins immediately to have an effect in the market, can hardly be denied."[20] The latter is expressive of Mises's insight that, from the individual viewpoint, the value of money is subjective and determined by the law of diminishing marginal utility.

In *Human Action*, with his praxeology fully developed, Mises emphasized that changes in the (objective) exchange value of money are the logical consequence of human action. In fact, changes in the exchange value of money, which are termed inflation or deflation in today's terminology, are inevitable:

> The notions of inflation and deflation are not praxeological concepts. They were not created by economists, but by the mundane speech of the public and of politicians. They implied the popular

---

18   Mises published his views on the logical and epistemological status of the social science in journal articles between 1928 and 1931, and published them, after having added two more chapters, as a book in 1933 (German title: *Grundprobleme der Nationalökonomie*). It was only in 1960 that an English translation was published as *Epistemological Problems of Economics*. See Hülsmann's Introduction to Mises's *Epistemological Problems of Economics* (2003), pp. ix–lv.

19   Mises (1996), *Human Action*, p. 422.

20   Mises (1953), *TM&C*, p. 149.

fallacy that there is such a thing as neutral money or money of stable purchasing power and that sound money should be neutral and stable in purchasing power.[21]

Finally it should be noted here that in *Human Action* Mises emphasized the (political-economic) problems that result if and when people do not have a sound understanding of the causes and the symptoms of inflation or deflation, that is if people identify inflation and deflation with changes in prices rather than changes in the quantity of money:

> What many people today call inflation or deflation is no longer the great increase or decrease in the supply of money, but its inexorable consequences, the general tendency toward a rise or a fall in commodity prices and wage rates. This innovation is by no means harmless. It plays an important role in fomenting the popular tendencies toward inflationism.[22]

In other words: The lack of a clear-cut understanding of the true cause of inflation and deflation, said Mises, can be politically instrumentalized: Inflation will be blamed, for instance, on greedy businessmen, unyielding trade unions, excess demand, capitalism, or even bad weather; deflation will be blamed on a lack of aggregate demand, excess supply or a lack of government spending. All these explanations effectively work in favor of more government interventionism for "fighting" the politically undesirable effects ascribed to inflation and deflation. However, it is impossible for the quantity of money to increase or decrease according to any of these politically instrumentalized explanations.

V. CRITIQUE OF PRICE LEVEL STABILIZATION

In mainstream economics a stable *price level* is seen as contributing positively to economic growth and employment gains. As a result, virtually all central banks have nowadays adopted the monetary policy of "inflation targeting."[23] At the heart of inflation targeting is keeping a price index,

---

21   Mises (1996), *Human Action*, p. 422.

22   Ibid., p. 423.

23   Inflation targeting basically means that central banks change their policy instruments (1) in response to actual inflation deviating from envisaged (or: targeted) inflation or (2) change their policy in response to "intermediate variables" (such as, for instance, the quantity of money) which have a reliable relation to future changes in envisaged inflation. In the first case, inflation targeting denotes a policy concept that considers actual inflation

typically a consumer price index, stable over time. The idea is to prevent the price index from rising (persistently) by more than, say, 2 percent on an annual basis, and preventing it from (persistently) declining over time.

The idea of "stabilizing" the economy's price level goes back to the American economist Irving Fisher (1867–1947).[24] In *The Purchasing Power of Money* (1911) Fisher put forward his concept of a "compensated dollar"—meant to give the U.S. dollar a constant purchasing power and ending its definition in terms of the weight of gold. Fisher saw a *price level stabilization policy* as a way to eliminate, or at least mitigate, economic crises. By arguing that a rise or fall in the economy's price level is harmful, he called for monetary interventionism: that is increasing the quantity of money whenever prices fall (and thus money's purchasing power rises), and decreasing it whenever prices rise (and thus money's purchasing power drops).

In *TM&C* Mises had, in an impressively foresighted manner, already seen the severe economic problems that would come if and when Fisher's price index concept would become a generally accepted doctrine. Mises pointed out that Fisher's whole idea rested on an erroneous and contradictory notion, namely that there could be a good—in this case money—of unchanging (objective) exchange value:

> The fact that such goods are inconceivable needs no further elucidation. For a good of this sort could exist only if all the exchange-ratios between all goods were entirely free from variations. With the continually varying foundations on which the exchange-ratios of the market ultimately rest, this presumption can never be true of a social order based upon the free exchange of goods.[25]

From the false notion of money having an unchanged exchange value springs the equally false idea of money being a *measure of value*: "So long as the subjective theory of value is accepted, this question of measurement cannot arise."[26] The explanation is that when it comes to subjective value,

---

as being the "policy variable" to act on, whereas in the second case inflation is seen as the final objective of policy making.

24   For further explanation see Patinkin (1993), "Irving Fisher and His Compensated Dollar Plan"; also Humphrey (1997), "Fisher and Wicksell on the Quantity of Theory."

25   Mises (1953), *TM&C*, p. 189.

26   Ibid., p. 38.

there is only grading on an individual's value scale, but no measuring. Nor is money a measure of price, as Fisher maintains[27]: "Neither is objective exchange-value measurable, for it too is the result of the comparisons derived from the valuations of individuals."[28] That said, Mises exploded Fisher's idea of measuring the subjective use-value of money by the mathematical method as scientifically untenable: "All index-number systems . . . are based upon the idea of measuring the utility of a certain quantity of money."[29] "For this, recourse must be had to the quite nebulous and illegitimate fiction of an eternal human with invariable valuations."[30]

Mises also pointed out that the exchange ratio between the money unit and vendible items originates from the money side and/or commodity side. This is an important analytical insight, as the idea of keeping a price index unchanged over time is based on the notion that changes stemming from the commodity side, and which affect money prices, cancel each other out—if and when the quantity of money and the income velocity of money remain constant as the quantity theory assumes.[31] For keeping the purchasing power of a money unit stable, Fisher recommended to increase (decrease) the quantity of money whenever the purchasing power of a money unit rises (falls).[32]

---

27   In sharp contrast to Mises, Fisher (1911, p. 220) argued: "A price is an objective datum, susceptible of measurement, and the same for all men." And further: "The purchasing power of money in the objective sense is, therefore, an ascertainable magnitude with a meaning common to all men."

28   Mises (1953), *TM&C*, p. 48.

29   Ibid., p. 193.

30   Ibid.

31   In the foreword of this book, Fisher (1911, p. vii) noted: "The main contentions of this book are at bottom simply a restatement and amplification of the old 'quantity theory' of money. With certain corrections in the usual statements of that theory, it may still be called fundamentally sound. What has long been needed is a candid reexamination and revision of that venerable theory rather than its repudiation."

32   The transaction equation has the following form: $M \cdot V = Y \cdot P$, where M = quantity of money, V = income velocity of money, Y = output (or transaction volume), and P = price level. By assuming that (1) the economy runs at full capacity (with $Y = Y^*$, where the asterisk denotes the long-run, or equilibrium, level) and (2) the income velocity of money is stable ($V = V^*$), one arrives at the quantity theory: namely that a rise in M will show up in higher P. Taking logarithms and calculating first differences (denoted by Δ), one yields: $\Delta m + \Delta v^* = \Delta y^* + \Delta p$, or: $\Delta p = \Delta m + \Delta v^* - \Delta y^*$. It says that if the increase in the quantity of money exceeds the growth in (potential) output adjusted for the (trend) change in the income velocity of money, prices increase. For further explanation see Polleit and Gerdesmeier

However, Mises rejected the "mechanistic" interpretation of the quantity theory, which assumes that a constant relation exists between changes in the quantity of money and changes in the money unit's purchasing power: "Thorough comprehension of the mechanism by means of which the quantity of money affects the prices of commodities makes their point of view altogether untenable."[33] Mises argued that a rise in the quantity of money will, and necessarily so, affect different prices at different times and to a different degree. A rise in the quantity of money does therefore not have a proportional effect on prices (and thus the purchasing power of the money unit). Mises thereby actually refuted the notion of the *neutrality of money*, which holds that an increase in the quantity of money (above the increase in output, adjusted for the change in the income velocity of money) will only affect prices but leave output unchanged.

Mises explains:

> Since the increased quantity of money is received in the first place by a limited number of economic agents only and not by all, the increase of prices at first embraces only those goods that are demanded by these persons; further, it affects these goods more than it afterwards affects any others. When the increase of prices spreads farther, if the increase in the quantity of money is only a single transient phenomenon, it will not be possible for the differential increase of prices of these goods to be completely maintained; a certain degree of adjustment will take place. But there will not be such a complete adjustment of the increases that all prices increase in the same proportion. The prices of commodities after the rise of prices will not bear the same relation to each other as before its commencement; the decrease in the purchasing power of money will not be uniform with regard to different economic goods.[34]

Mises's rejection of the notion of a constant relation between changes in the quantity of money and changes in prices (and thus the purchasing power of money) makes central banking pursuing "inflation targeting" a source of economic destabilization.[35] Finally, at a more statistical-technical

---

(2005); also Belke and Polleit (2009), *Monetary Economics in Globalised Financial Markets*, pp. 675–92.

33   Mises (1953), *TM&C*, p. 140.

34   Ibid.

35   It should be mentioned that even a stable price level would by no means be an

level, Mises saw insurmountable problems of identifying and calculating an appropriate price index. First, including prices of vendible items paid at different places and different times would be appropriate only if and when these goods would have the same quality from the viewpoint of the individuals; lumping together those goods which are said to be of equal quality due to statistical-technological concepts wouldn't be a scientifically satisfying procedure. Second, deciding about the coefficients of importance (weightings) of the goods included in the index is, and necessarily so, arbitrary. A statistical price index, by whatever "ideal formula" it is calculated, would therefore be devoid of any scientific meaning.[36] Of course, the unscientific nature of the price index concept makes it particularly susceptible to political manipulation.[37]

On the Role of Asset Prices in Today's Monetary Policy

The majority of the supporters of the price index regime argues for using consumer price indices as central banks' "target variable." It is a widely held view that asset prices (that are the prices for stocks, bonds, real estate, etc.) should not be included in such a price index—in contrast to, for instance, the seminal work of Alchian and Klein (1973), who wrote: "The analysis in this paper bases a price index on the Fisherian tradition of a proper definition of intertemporal consumption and leads to the conclusion that a price index used to measure inflation must include asset prices."[38]

---

adequate protection against macroeconomic crises. See in this context, for instance, White (2006), *Is Price Stability Enough?*

36   For a critical assessment see Rothbard (2001), *Man, Economy, and State*, pp. 844–47.

37   For instance, the debate about "headline inflation" and "core inflation" measures is a case in point; likewise is the debate about whether or not including asset prices in price indices that serve as "target variables" of central banking.

38   Alchien and Klein (1973), p. 173. Goodhart argued that the theoretical argument put forward by Alchian and Klein in favor of including asset prices in the price index hasn't been refuted. For an overview of the mainstream economic view see Cecchetti, Genberg, Lipsky, and Wadhwani (2000), "Asset Prices and Central Bank Policy"; also European Central Bank (2005), *Asset Price Bubbles and Monetary Policy*. See also Kohn (2009), *Monetary Policy and Asset Prices Revisited*; for a somewhat more critical perspective see Issing (2009), "Asset Prices and Monetary Policy."

U.S. Profits: Financial Sector and Total Corporate Sector:
Q1 1950 to Q2 2012*

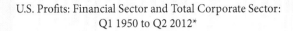

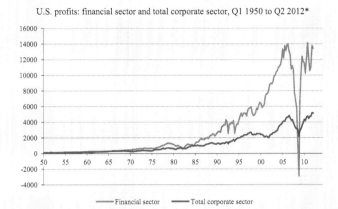

Source: Bloomberg, own calculations. Profits with inventory valuation and capital consumption adjustment. All indices are seasonally adjusted at annual rates. *Series are indexed (Q1 1950 = 100).

While it is beyond the scope of this article to provide a detailed overview about the arguments in the debate about how monetary policy should deal with changes in asset prices, it should be noted here that confining "inflation targeting" to keeping a consumer price index stable over time has a great attraction for those benefitting from "asset price inflation." This is because excluding asset prices from the price index targeted by the central bank actually allows for a fairly inflationary policy.

Consider the case in which the central bank expands, via an increase in bank circulation credit, the quantity of money (fiduciary media). Assume further that the rising quantity of money does not show up in higher consumer prices but leads to rising prices for, say, stocks and housing. In such a situation the central bank, if and when its policy is determined by changes in consumer prices, will continue to allow banks to churn out ever more money—which, in turn, keeps inflating asset prices.

Such an inflationary monetary policy is of course beneficial to the financial industry and the banking industry in particular. An increase in bank circulation credit is, first and foremost, a profitable business for banks. In addition, a growing quantity of credit and money results in a growing financial market. It brings additional profitable business opportunities such as, for instance, trading, hedging, settlement, and custodian services.

The finding that central banking and money creation through bank circulation credit expansion benefits, in particular, the financial industry, especially when asset price inflation is basically ignored by central banks, can be illustrated quite nicely by, for instance, U.S. data. After the end of (what little was left of) the (pseudo-) gold standard in August 1971, which resulted in a world-wide unfettered paper money regime, profit growth in the financial industry as a whole started outpacing profit growth of the total economy, especially from the middle of the 1980s.

VI. THE DESTABILIZING EFFECTS OF CENTRAL BANKING —THE "BOOM-AND-BUST CYCLE"

In *TM&C* Mises had already refuted the notion that money can have "stable value": By having succeeded in extending marginal utility theory to the value of money, Mises showed that any notion of "stable money" would be an "empty and contradictory notion,"[39] as he put it later. This insight is actually derived from praxeology, as the very notion of stability in human affairs is:

> founded on the illusory image of an eternal and immutable being who determines by the application of an immutable standard the quantity of satisfaction which a unit of money conveys to him. It is a poor justification of this ill-thought idea that what is wanted is merely to measure changes in the purchasing power of money. The crux of the stability notion lies precisely in *this* concept of purchasing power.[40]

In *Human Action*, Mises put forward an explanation of the popularity of the notion of stable money, namely that people are in favor of stabilization policies because they would not understand that it is government, not the free market, that is held to be responsible for causing financial and economic crises: "Shortcomings in the governments' handling of

---

39   Mises (1996), *Human Action*, p. 219.
40   Ibid., p. 220.

monetary matters and the disastrous consequences of policies aimed at lowering the rate of interest and at encouraging business activities through credit expansion gave birth to the ideas which finally generated the slogan "stabilization."[41] Mises saw that the erroneous notion of stable money would not only pave the way towards even more interventionism in monetary affairs, it would also provide government with a legitimization to monopolize money production and replace commodity money with unbacked paper, or: *fiat*, money.[42] Money will then be produced through *bank credit expansion*, thereby creating *fiduciary media*: money not backed by *real savings*. The issuance of fiduciary media through bank credit is at the heart of the Austrian monetary trade cycle theory, which was developed in the *TM&C* by integrating three hitherto separated theories: (1) the *Currency School*, (2) the capital and interest rate theory of Eugen von Böhm-Bawerk (1851–1914), and (3) the theory of the divergence of the market interest rate from the "natural interest rate" as developed by Knut Wicksell (1851–1926).

The increase in bank circulation credit lowers, and necessarily so, the market interest rate below the natural interest rate (which is determined by *societal time preference*). This, in turn, induces an artificial boom. The artificially lowered interest increases consumption at the expense of savings (out of current income), and, in addition, leads to a rise in investment. The economy starts living beyond its means. Once the injection of fiduciary media has run its course, market agents start readjusting their dispositions. As the societal time preference hasn't changed, there are insufficient savings and, therefore, insufficient real resources to complete all new investment projects. Investments, provoked by the artificial lowering of the market interest rate, become unprofitable. A liquidation process sets in, and the boom turns into a bust.

Central banking plays a crucial role for the boom-and-bust *cycle*. For under central banking the disciplinary checks on inflation, which prevail

---

41   Ibid., p. 219.

42   Taking recourse to the *progression theorem*, Rothbard identified a number of steps taken by government to replace commodity money by fiat money. In short, government monopolizes the minting of commodity money, then monopolizes the issuance of money substitutes (claims to money proper), allows for fractional reserve banking and central banking, and then—to avoid the collapse of banks issuing money substitutes in excess of money proper—suspends the redeemability of notes, thereby severing the link between paper tickets and book entries and money proper. The latter will be replaced by central bank money, resulting in a pure fiat money regime.

under free-market conditions, are removed. Commercial banks can embark upon a policy of issuing ever greater amounts of circulation credit and fiduciary media without having to fear adverse consequences. For the central bank stands ready to act as a "lender of last resort," bailing out ailing banks with newly issued (base) money. While central banking is a device for increasing inflation drastically, it cannot, of course, overcome economic laws. That a fiduciary media induced boom will, and inevitably so, ultimately result in a bust was unmistakably formulated in *TM&C*:

> Certainly, the banks would be able to postpone the collapse; but nevertheless, as has been shown, the moment must eventually come when no further extension of the circulation of fiduciary media is possible. Then the catastrophe occurs, and its consequences are the worse and the reaction against the bull tendency of the market the stronger, the longer the period during which the rate of interest on loans has been below the natural rate of interest and the greater the extent to which roundabout processes of production that are not justified by the state of the capital market have been adopted.[43]

Mises, after weighing the pros and cons of fiduciary media, came to the conclusion that the issue of fiduciary media should be suspended:

> It has gradually become recognized as a fundamental principle of monetary policy that intervention must be avoided as far as possible. Fiduciary media are scarcely different in nature from money; a supply of them affects the market in the same way as a supply of money proper; variations in their quantity influence the objective exchange-value of money in just the same way as do variations in the quantity of money proper. Hence, they should logically be subjected to the same principles that have been established with regard to money proper; the same attempts should be made in their case as well to eliminate as far as possible human influence on the exchange-ratio between money and other economic goods. The possibility of causing temporary fluctuations in the exchange-ratios between goods of higher and of lower orders by the issue of fiduciary media, and the pernicious consequences connected with a divergence between the natural and money rates of interest, are circumstances leading to the same conclusion. Now it is obvious that the only

---

43   Mises (1953), *TM&C*, pp. 365-66.

way of eliminating human influence on the credit system is to suppress all further issue of fiduciary media.[44]

In *TM&C* Mises identified central banking and *fractional reserve banking* as a source of economic and financial calamity, pointing out that central banking has not prevented but lent impetus to these unfavorable developments:

> Since the time of the Currency School, the policy adopted by the governments of Europe and America with regard to the issue of fiduciary media has been guided, on the whole, by the idea that it is necessary to impose some sort of restriction upon the banks in order to prevent them from extending the issue of fiduciary media in such a way as to cause a rise of prices that eventually culminates in an economic crisis. But the course of this policy has been continually broken by contrary aims. Endeavours have been made by means of credit policy to keep the rate of interest low; "cheap money" (i.e., low interest) and "reasonable" (i.e., high) prices have been aimed at. Since the beginning of the twentieth century these endeavours have noticeably gained in strength; during the War and for some time after it they were the prevailing aims.[45]

These words already echo Mises's later (and much more explicitly expressed) conclusion, namely that central banking not only destabilizes the economy but leads to a *recurrence* of boom-and-bust. Under central banking, per Mises, the boom-and-bust is thus not just a one-off affair, it becomes chronic. His political-economic explanation is as follows:

> The boom produces impoverishment. But still more disastrous are its moral ravages. It makes people despondent and dispirited. The more optimistic they were under the illusory prosperity of the boom, the greater is their despair and their feeling of frustration. The individual is always ready to ascribe his good luck to his own efficiency and to take it as a well-deserved reward for his talent, application, and probity. But reverses of fortune he always charges to other people, and most of all to the absurdity of social and political institutions. He does not blame the authorities for having fostered the boom. He reviles them for the inevitable collapse. In the opinion of the public, more inflation

---

44   Ibid., p. 407–08.

45   Ibid., p. 367.

and more credit expansion are the only remedy against the evils which inflation and credit expansion have brought about.[46]

VII. THE REGRESSION THEOREM: THE ETHICAL CASE AGAINST CENTRAL BANKING

In *Principles of Economics* (1871), Carl Menger (1840–1914) had put forward a theory of the origin of money. He argued that money emerged spontaneously in the free market, and out of a commodity. In his logic-historical account, Menger concluded:

> The origin of money (as distinct from coin, which is only one variety of money) is, as we have seen, entirely natural and thus displays legislative influence only in the rarest instances. Money is not an invention of the state. It is not the product of a legislative act. Even the sanction of political authority is not necessary for its existence. Certain commodities came to be money quite naturally, as the result of economic relationships that were independent of the power of the state.[47]

In *TM&C* Mises developed the *regression theorem*, which (1) gave Menger's theory of the origin of money effectively a praxeological fundament and (2) solved the alleged "Austrian circle," with the latter denoting the critique of not having succeeded in applying the marginal utility theory to money.[48] The "Austrian circle" denoted the following problem: The exchange value of money would be determined by the supply of and demand for money in the market. However, money is demanded because it has *pre-existing* purchasing power. Accordingly, one seems to get entangled in a *circular reasoning*: Money is demanded because it has purchasing power, but the latter is determined by the demand for and supply of money.

Mises, however, solved this problem, recognizing that money's exchange value has a *time dimension*: The exchange value of money in period *t* is determined by money's purchasing power in period *t*–1. Such a backward (regressive) reasoning ends precisely at the point in time when money

---

46   Mises (1996), *Human Action*, pp. 576–77.

47   Menger (2007), *Principles of Economics*, pp. 261–62.

48   See in this context Helfferich (1923), *Das Geld, 3. Kapitel, Einzelfunktionen des Geldes*, §5, pp. 297–311, esp. 302.

was useful only as a non-monetary commodity. The regression theorem thus yields two important insights, proving Menger's claims: namely that (1) money *must* have emerged from a market process, and (2) money can *only* emerge from a commodity (such as, for instance, precious metals). Money cannot be established by government decree or by a social contract —as argued most prominently by Georg F. Knapp (1842–1926) in his "state theory of money" in 1905.

The regression theorem explains why (intrinsically) worthless paper, or fiat, money cannot emerge out of the free market, but must have been launched by an act of expropriation, that is by having coercively severed the link between money proper (as established in the free market) and money substitutes, representing a claim on money proper. Hülsmann puts this insight succinctly: "Paper money has never been introduced through voluntary cooperation. In all known cases it has been introduced through coercion and compulsion, sometimes with the threat of the death penalty."[49]

VIII. Looking Ahead

Mises's theoretical insights developed in *TM&C* haven't found their way into the monetary theory of mainstream economics and, as a result, practical monetary policy making. In particular the institutional set-up of monetary affairs virtually all over the world has been following more or less Keynesian and Monetarist doctrines. This outcome, however, does by no means speak against the truth value of Mises's insights as laid out in *TM&C*. Quite to the contrary.

The current international financial and economic crisis, which started around the middle of 2007 in the United States and then developed into a truly global malaise, must be understood as a crisis of central banking—a monetary order in which money production is monopolized, where irredeemable fiat currencies, produced through bank circulation credit out of thin air, serve as money; and where boom-and-bust cycles and the accumulation of ever greater amounts of debt (relative to economic income) is the inevitable consequence.

---

49   Hülsmann (2008), *The Ethics of Money Production*, p. 172. In this context see also Hoppe (2006), "How is Fiat Money Possible?–or, The Devolution of Money and Credit."

In fact, the *demise of the international fiat money system*—which is actually what the current international financial and economic crisis stands for—is an empirical illustration of what Mises basically pointed out in his *TM&C* in 1912: A regime of central banking—that is government control over money production will result in an economic and political catastrophe on the grandest scale.

Mises formulated this insight as follows:

> [T]he [fiat money induced, *TP*] boom cannot continue indefinitely. There are two alternatives. Either the banks continue the credit expansion without restriction and thus cause constantly mounting price increases and an ever-growing orgy of speculation, which, as in all other cases of unlimited inflation, ends in a "crack-up boom" and in a collapse of the money and credit system. Or the banks stop before this point is reached, voluntarily renounce further credit expansion and thus bring about the crisis. The depression follows in both instances.[50]

In the 1953 edition of *TM&C* Mises recommended a return to sound money, formulating the *sound money principle*: "[T]he sound-money principle has two aspects. It is affirmative in approving the market's choice of a commonly-used medium of exchange. It is negative in obstructing the government's propensity to meddle with the currency system."[51] And further: "It is impossible to grasp the meaning of the idea of sound money if one does not realize that it was devised as an instrument for the protection of civil liberties against despotic inroads on the part of governments. Ideologically it belongs in the same class with political constitutions and bills of rights."[52]

To Mises, sound money is money determined by the demand for and supply of money in the free market place, and it is a defense line against government interference in individual freedom. It is against this backdrop that Mises put forward a plan for returning a fiat money system to a monetary order based on gold, effective gold coin circulation, and 100 percent reserve banking. The upshot of his proposal is the elimination of government interference in the fields of money production and the banking business

---

50   Mises (1998), *Interventionism: An Economic Critique*, p. 40.

51   Mises (1953), *TM&C*, p. 414. See in this context also the praxeological analysis of the sound money principle in Polleit (2001), "A Priori and Sound Money."

52   Ibid.

altogether. To Mises, *sound money effectively implies the privatization of money production, free banking with 100-percent reserve banking, and gold serving as money proper.*[53]

References

Alchian, A.A., and B. Klein. 1973. "On a Correct Measure of Inflation." *Journal of Money, Credit and Banking* 5, No. 1, Part 1 (February): 173–91.

Bank for International Settlement. 2009. *Issues in the Governance of Central Banks.* Bank for International Settlement (May): Chapter 2, pp. 17–55.

Barro, R., and D. Gordon. 1983. "A positive theory of monetary policy in a natural rate model." *Journal of Political Economy* 91: 589–610.

Belke, A., and T. Polleit. 2009. *Monetary Economics in Globalised Financial Markets.* Berlin, Heidelberg: Springer.

Cachanosky, N. 2009. "The Definition of Inflation According to Mises: Implications for the Debate on Free Banking." *Libertarian Papers* 1, No. 43.

Calvo, G. 1978. "On the time consistence of optimal policy in a monetary economy." *Econometrica* 46: 1411–28.

Cecchetti, S. G., H. Genberg, J. Lipsky, and S. Wadhwani. 2000. "Asset Prices and Central Bank Policy." *The Geneva Report on the World Economy* No. 2 (May 30). Published by ICMB and the CEPR.

Eijffinger, S. C. W., J. De Han. 1996. "The Political Economy of Central-Bank Independence." *Special Papers in International Economics* No. 19 (May). Department of Economics, Princeton University.

European Central Bank. 2005. *Asset Price Bubbles and Monetary Policy* (April): 47–60.

Fisher, I. [1911] 1963. *The Purchasing Power of Money: Its Determination and Relation to Credit, Interest, and Crises.* New York: Macmillan. Reprinted, New York: Augustus M. Kelley.

Goodhart, C. 2001. "What Weight Should be Given to Asset Prices in the Measurement of Inflation?" *The Economic Journal* 111, No. 472, Features (June): F335–56.

Helfferich, K. [1903] 1923. *Das Geld.* 6th ed. Leipzig: Verlag von C. L. Hirschfeld.

---

53   In this context see Salerno (2010), "White contra Mises on Fiduciary Media."

Hoppe, H.H. 2006. "How is Fiat Money Possible?–or, The Devolution of Money and Credit." *The Economics and Ethics of Private Property, Studies in Political Economy and Philosophy*. 2nd ed. Auburn, Ala.: Ludwig von Mises Institute.

———. 1995. *Economic Science and the Austrian Method*. Auburn, Ala.: Ludwig von Mises Institute.

Humphrey, T. M. 1997. "Fisher and Wicksell on the Quantity of Theory." Federal Reserve Bank of Richmond, *Economic Quarterly* 83, No. 4 (Fall): 71–90.

Hülsmann, J. G. 2008. "Mises on Monetary Reform: the Private Alternative." *Quarterly Journal of Austrian Economics* 11: 208–18.

———. 2008. *The Ethics of Money Production*. Auburn, Ala.: Ludwig von Mises Institute.

———. 2007. *The Last Knight of Liberalism*. Auburn, Ala.: Ludwig von Mises Institute.

———. [1960] 2003. *Epistemological Problems of Economics*. 3rd ed. Auburn, Ala.: Ludwig von Mises Institute.

Issing, O. 2009. "Asset Prices and Monetary Policy." *Cato Journal* 29, No. 1 (Winter): 45–51.

Knies, K. 1885. *Geld und Credit. Erste Abteilung, zweite verbesserte und vermehrte Auflage*. Berlin: Weidmannsche Buchhandlung.

Kohn, D. L. 2008. "Monetary Policy and Asset Prices Revisited." *Cato Journal* 29, No. 1 (Winter): 31–44.

Kydland, F., and E. Prescott. 1977. "Rules Rather than Discretion: The Inconsistency of Optimal Plans." *Journal of Political Economy* 85: 473–92.

Menger, C. [1871] 2007. *Principles of Economics*. Auburn, Ala.: Ludwig von Mises Institute.

Mises, L. v. 1996. *Human Action*. 4th ed. San Francisco: Fox & Wilkes.

———. [1940] 1998. *Interventionism: An Economic Analysis*. Irvington-on-Hudson, N.Y.: The Foundation for Economic Education.

———. 1953. *The Theory of Money and Credit*. New Haven, Conn.: Yale University Press.

Patinkin, D. 1993. "Irving Fisher and His Compensated Dollar Plan." Federal Reserve Bank of Richmond, *Economic Quarterly* 79, No. 3: 1–34.

Polleit, T. 2011. "A Priori and Sound Money." Daily Article (November 17). Ludwig von Mises Institute.

Polleit, T., and D. Gerdesmeier. 2005. "Measures of Excess Liquidity." Working paper series, No. 65, Frankfurt School of Finance and Management.

Rothbard, M. N. 2011. "The Austrian Theory of Money." *Economic Controversies.* Auburn, Ala.: Ludwig von Mises Institute. Pp. 685–707.

——. [1983] 2008. *The Mystery of Banking.* Auburn, Ala.: Ludwig von Mises Institute.

——. [1962] 2001. *Man, Economy and State.* Auburn, Ala.: Ludwig von Mises Institute.

——. 1999. "Ludwig von Mises: The Dean of the Austrian School." *15 Great Austrian Economists.* Auburn, Ala.: Ludwig von Mises Institute. Pp. 143–65.

Salerno, J. T. 2010. "Ludwig von Mises's Monetary Theory in Light of Modern Monetary Thought." *Money: Sound and Unsound.* Auburn, Ala.: Ludwig von Mises Institute. Pp. 61–114.

——. 2010. "White contra Mises on Fiduciary Media." Daily Article (May 14). Ludwig von Mises Institute.

Smith, V. C. [1936] 1990. *The Rationale of Central Banking and the Free Banking Alternative.* Reprint, Indianapolis: Liberty Press.

White, W. R. 2006. *Is Price Stability Enough?* BIS Working Paper, No. 205 (April).

Index